Without You

of related interest

Communicating with Children When a Parent is at the End of Life
Rachel Fearnley
ISBN 978 1 84905 234 4

Talking with Children and Young People about Death and Dying
Second Edition
Mary Turner
Illustrated by Bob Thomas
ISBN 978 1 84310 441 4

Supporting Traumatized Children and Teenagers
A Guide to Providing Understanding and Help
Atle Dyregrov
ISBN 978 1 84905 034 0

Still Here With Me
Teenagers and Children on Losing a Parent
Edited by Suzanne Sjöqvist
Translated by Margaret Myers
ISBN 978 1 84310 501 5

Grief in Children
A Handbook for Adults
Second Edition
Atle Dyregrov
ISBN 978 1 84310 612 8

Silent Grief
Living in the Wake of Suicide
Revised Edition
Christopher Lukas and Henry M. Seiden
ISBN 978 1 84310 847 4

Grandad's Ashes
Walter Smith
ISBN 978 1 84310 517 6

The Forgotten Mourners
Guidelines for Working with Bereaved Children
Second Edition
Susan C. Smith
ISBN 978 1 85302 758 1

When a Family Pet Dies
A Guide to Dealing with Children's Loss
JoAnn Tuzeo-Jarolmen
ISBN 978 1 85302 113 8

Without You

Children and Young People Growing Up with Loss and its Effects

Tamar Granot

Jessica Kingsley *Publishers*
London and Philadelphia

First published in Israel in 2000 by Ministry of Defence Publishing

This edition published in 2005
by Jessica Kingsley Publishers
116 Pentonville Road
London N1 9JB, UK
and
400 Market Street, Suite 400
Philadelphia, PA 19106, USA

www.jkp.com

Copyright © Tamar Granot 2005
Printed digitally since 2012

Library of Congress Cataloging in Publication Data
Granot, Tamar.
[Bil'adekha. English]
Without you : children and young people growing up with loss and its effects / Tamar Granot.— 1st American pbk. ed.
p. cm.
Includes bibliographical references and index.
ISBN 1-84310-297-8 (pbk.)
1. Loss (Psychology) in children. 2. Children and death. 3. Bereavement in children. 4. Grief in children. I. Title.
BF723.L68G7313 2005
155.9'3'0835—dc22

2004020571

British Library Cataloguing in Publication Data
A CIP catalogue record for this book is available from the British Library

ISBN 978 1 84310 297 7

Contents

Introduction   7
    What this book is about   7
    Why this book was written   15
    Being aware of your own experiences that you bring to the book as a reader   16

1   The Bereavement of Children   25
    Children's perception of loss   25
    Influence of the socio-cultural environment on children's understanding
       of death and loss   37
    Stages of grieving   38
    How children grieve   40

2   Reactions to Loss According to the Child's
    Developmental Stage   53
    Level of emotional and cognitive development   54
    Separation, attachment, and loss   57
    Responses to loss by age group   62
    Early childhood (birth to 3 years)   63
    The Oedipal stage (age 5 to 7)   69
    The latency period (age 7 to 11)   75
    Adolescence (age 12 to 18)   77
    Early adulthood (age 18 to 30)   97
    Summary: The intrapsychic experience of loss and its effects on personality
       development and pathology   103

3   Additional Variables Affecting the Child's
    Response   109
    Circumstances of loss   109
    Period of uncertainty   110
    Foreseeable death as compared to sudden death   116
    Suicide   118
    Murder   121
    Divorce   122
    Rejection and abandonment   127
    Previous and cumulative losses   133
    Loss of two parents   135
    Gender of the absent parent and the child   137
    The relationship prior to the loss   143
    Influence of cultural and socio-economic factors   145

4   The Remaining Parent and the Family System   149

How the parent copes with the loss   150
Personality of the parent and how it affects coping: implications for the child   157
Coping with loss within the family   162
Aspects of the family system that influence coping with loss   172
Bereaved siblings   180
New beginnings and other changes in life   193

5   A Few More Things That One Should Know   203

Dos   203
Don'ts   206
A few myths about children   208
How to respond: some practical suggestions   209
Good signs   214
Warning signs   215
Psychological treatment   216

GLOSSARY   225

RECOMMENDED READING   229

INDEX   231

Introduction

What this book is about

Why do we need a book about the effects of loss on children?

Loss, death, and children are concepts that seem to be at odds with one another. Such things simply should not happen to children. When children suffer, we adults want to wrap them in our arms and protect them. There is also something that makes us want to distance ourselves so we don't have to meet their eyes. And what about them? For the most part, they want to get on with their lives – and be no different than other children. Yet they also want us to feel their pain. They want us intuitively to know when they need a hug from us, without having to ask.

Over the past few decades, society has exhibited a heightened consciousness and comprehension of themes related to death and loss: the effects of loss, responses to it, and factors that influence these processes. This book focuses on children who have experienced loss. It seeks to deepen the understanding of the specific effects of loss on children.

Significant losses

The most significant loss of all for a child, and the one on which this book will concentrate, is the *loss of a parent*. Children can experience loss of a parent from a variety of circumstances: most traumatic of all is the *death* of a parent – from disease, car accident, military operation, act of terrorism, suicide, or murder. There are times that loss of a parent can result from the parents' *divorce* and the pulling away by one of the parents from the rest of the family. A child can experience loss of a parent when the parent ceases to function as such, as in the case of *addiction* to alcohol or drugs, an *emotionally debilitating condition*, emotional *rejection*, or *abandonment* – physical or mental – of the child for whatever reason. A child may also experience loss as a result of *long-term separation* from a parent who is far from home due to extended *travel, imprisonment,* or *hospitalization.* In certain cases, the loss of grandparents, aunts, or uncles who had filled a parental role may also constitute a traumatic experience of loss for a child.

In addition to the painful experience that results from the absence of a beloved and significant figure, such a loss also signifies a threat to the child's very being and to the continuity of his life and safety. Losing a parent means losing the figure who plays a critical role in the growing process, someone the child needs and relies upon. For the child, loss of a parent may adversely affect or undermine the basic support system he requires. It may trigger a loss of confidence – in life, in people, in the future, and in himself. It may also bring about dislocation of the bonds of love and human contact that the child needs for his continued growth and development.

There are other circumstances in which children may experience the trauma of loss. Death of a sibling constitutes a severe, traumatic loss, and I have devoted a special chapter to it. Other life experiences that may involve an acute sense of loss include *migration, disease,* and *disability.* Although the factors underlying the sense of loss in these instances are not the same as when a child loses a parent, the foundation of the child's existence is undermined nevertheless. These circumstances also disrupt the continuum of the child's life, adversely affecting his confidence in his very being, and have a powerful effect on his emotional state and the development of his personality. Their influences are deep, long term, and widespread into the child's life.

Effects of loss on children

For adults, the experience of loss draws its powerfulness from the past, because the adult is strongly aware of the significant role the missing person had in his life up to the time of the loss. For children, the focus is on the present and on the future. The child is very aware of what he misses now and very perturbed about how his life will continue without the missing person. Therefore, the loss experience affects the child along two planes. One has to do with the pain felt over an individual who had been a part of his life and who is no longer there; the other concerns the difficulties experienced in the present and the fears and anxieties of the future. These fears are exacerbated by a sense of dependency and detachment. The child senses that he has become different in some way, and is anxious about how he will survive "on his own" from now on.

Adults usually externalize their emotions and are able to express grief and other reactions to loss. They are cognizant of the range of intense effects that loss can have on all areas of their lives, and sometimes even "devote themselves" to these effects, especially during the initial years after the event. They sometimes make significant changes in their lifestyle and behavior in the wake of the loss.

Children are almost the exact opposite. They want to resume their normal life as soon as possible, and continue to be like all the other children. Their life instinct pushes them ahead, and more often than not they prefer to distance themselves from feelings associated with the loss; they try not to give in to these feelings, and do their utmost not to let them change their lives. Furthermore, in accordance with their specific age and stage of development, children may have a limited understanding of the loss and its implications. In many instances, their behavior can deceive people around them. Since they do not usually mourn the way adults do, and since they are usually able to quickly resume functioning as they did prior to the loss, adults gain the false impression that the child has either "forgotten," "gotten used," or "doesn't care." But the opposite is the case: although the child does not always externalize his mourning, he carries a heavy emotional burden throughout his childhood. His emotions are for the most part shrouded from the eyes of the world and even from the people closest to him. The child himself is often unaware of all his emotions and feelings, and does not know how to express them. At times, he lacks the sense of support that would facilitate the expression of these feelings.

Effects on the child's internal world and emotional development

Loss "colors" the child's internal world, his behavior, and even the development of his personality. The loss leaves a deep impression and will affect the way he sees and experiences the world from now on, as well as the choices and direction he will take in his life. A child who has experienced loss loses the naive trust that children have in a safe, cheerful world, in which happy dreams and fantasies come true. His world becomes more realistic, fraught with an abiding threat of separation and pain. The effects of loss on children are profound and long term, and the process of coping with the loss continues throughout their entire early life and development. The loss is "processed" by the child throughout his childhood. He returns to it on a recurrent basis, understanding it in accordance with his developing cognitive and emotional abilities, responding to it in accordance with his development and his changing needs. Loss takes on a new "face" in accordance with changes in the child's life. The diverse stages of his cognitive, emotional, and personality development will affect his response to the loss. Each new stage of development leads to a renewed encounter with the subject and a shift in how he processes it. The younger the child is at the time of the loss, the more vulnerable he is, as he lacks the emotional, cognitive, and mental tools to cope with such a difficult experience. As he matures, he will be able to cope with it differently, aided by the new tools at his disposal.

Effects of traumatic loss on normative developmental separation and loss

By definition, childhood is a period of growth and development. Numerous psychodynamic theories stress the importance that separation processes play in proper development and growth. Normative developmental separation and loss play an important role in formulating the child's personality as he moves toward independence and adulthood. Conversely, when the child undergoes a traumatic separation during his childhood, it constitutes a burden that is liable to hamper performance of normative separation tasks and separation processes. The harsh memories and emotions related to his traumatic loss will probably continue to be manifested whenever the child has to cope with separation situations, putting an extra burden on the normative developmental tasks.

This book describes the reciprocal, interrelated effects that implications of the loss can have on the child's development. The unique effects of loss at different age levels will be explained, the importance and influence of the age at which the loss occurred will be elucidated, and a differentiation will be made between short-term and long-term effects of the loss.

Adults who have experienced loss when they were children provide us with an opportunity to study the long-term effects of loss during child-

hood. Works of art, biographies, and other personal life stories and cre-
ations may shed light on the experiences of persons who suffered traumatic losses as children. They became accomplished individuals whose
experiences are reflected through their creative works or accomplishments. Throughout his life, the adult continues to carry the hurt child with
him. Sometimes he has a difficult time accepting the loss and living with it
in peace even in later years. Still, some of these adults claim that it was this
intense experience that imbued them with the added sensitivity and
unique qualities that shaped the course of their development and adult life.

The need to cope with the loss and its consequences gives the child an
opportunity to be strengthened and to mature early. It introduces him to
emotional worlds and life-and-death issues that require advanced coping
mechanisms. It develops within him a sensitivity for others. It teaches him
the complexities of life. To a certain extent, anyone who experienced loss
in his childhood feels "different." Because he was exposed to a complex
emotional world, he often becomes more vulnerable. He is also usually left
with increased sensitivity, understanding, and empathy for other people
and their emotional anguish.

Some individuals become conscious of the effects of the loss on them
only midway through adulthood. At times, this belated awareness is
sparked by a change in their lives, especially in the wake of a crisis during
adulthood. Seemingly "trivial" issues such as vacillation over career
choices, difficulties in maintaining relationships, and problems with their
own children may spark a sudden awareness of the connection between
present-day behavior and lifestyle and the trauma they underwent as
children.

Research studies have investigated the relationship between the loss of
a parent during childhood and the emotional problems and emotional
pathology that are manifested during later childhood and even adulthood.
While the results do not pinpoint a clear connection to pathologies, there
can be no doubt that losing a parent at an early age entails added difficulties during later stages of life. This is especially true when the remaining
parent raises the child in an unsatisfactory manner. The emotional damage
that relates to a traumatic loss in childhood may be expressed through
depression, overly rigid and inappropriate defense mechanisms, or other
personality disorders.

External factors

Without a doubt, the most important external influence on the emotional state of the child and on how he copes with his loss is the parent or adult who raises him. The physical and emotional support he provides to the child constitutes the most critical factor in the child's ability to cope with the loss and resume normal life and development. The loss of a parent leaves the child feeling alone and even abandoned. This sense is intensified if and when the remaining parent is wrapped up in his own mourning and is not entirely available to the child. A considerable portion of this book is devoted to understanding the behavior and influences of the remaining parent and of the family, which are critical to the child's coping and readjustment process.

Additional external factors that influence the child's response may include the specific circumstances in which the loss occurred – sudden death as opposed to an anticipated death that was prefaced by a waiting period, suicide, murder, parental abandonment, or certain instances of divorce.

The surrounding environment in which the child grows, the community with its social, cultural, and psychological characteristics, has significant influence on the coping process of the child and therefore must be taken into consideration.

Explaining the effects of loss is a challenging, difficult task, since each life story is different, and reflects a unique combination of factors related to the individual's life and personality. Explaining the effects of loss on children is a much more complicated task because of the enormous changes that take place in the child's life as he grows. The developmental route of the child combines with the effects of the loss, generating a singular, unique combination. As already noted, the parent who continues to raise the child has a dominant effect on the child's ability to cope and on his continued growth. Adding these factors makes it even more difficult to predict the effects of the loss on the child. Nevertheless, we will attempt to describe the vast number of factors that may influence the child, and the possible combinations that may result. By necessity, we will engage in generalizations, which must always be examined against the context of each child's individual reality. A proper understanding of each child must be based first and foremost on closely listening to his personal life story.

Normal, predictable reactions

This book is not about emotionally pathological or behaviorally aberrant children. It is about children who have lived through traumatic loss; it describes their normal, predictable reactions. For the most part, they do not behave significantly different from other "ordinary" children; they often conceal their inner experiences, to the extent that one cannot even tell they are affected by the loss. They are usually extremely "good" children, easy for the parent who raises them and the other adults in their environment. Often, they grow up to be adults who make sensitive positive contributions to their families, friends, and community. Yet it is the wish of this book to emphasize that children who have experienced traumatic loss are coping with a phenomenon that places very unique demands on them. This is the underlying theme of this book.

A significant number of research studies of children who were subjected to traumatic loss concentrated on children who were being treated for emotional problems. Much too little research and empirical documentation exists about the "silent majority," children who suffered a traumatic loss, but were not in the care of psychologists and psychiatrists. This book describes the world of these children.

Because most children who have experienced traumatic loss do not vent their emotions through abnormal behavior, many adults may fail to acknowledge their special needs, believing that they "don't understand," or that they "forget" or "don't care." Many adults think they can hide what happened from their children, or at least postpone telling them the full truth. They prefer to believe that "death and loss are not a matter for children." We will make it clear to what extent these matters are indeed on the child's mind, and the extent to which the adult must take an interest in what the child is going through, and help him through it.

Death and separation are hard on adults, and even harder for children. Some parents prefer to overlook warning signs that signal when the child is experiencing difficulties. The fear of discovering that the child "isn't okay" induces them to disregard the signs and even suppress them. Adults deny and ignore them, until the child "screams" out the signs by way of amplified, more noticeable symptoms. It is vital to understand what the child is going through and be sensitive to the child's experience, so as to offer the child appropriate aid when he needs it. At such times, adults can have significant and even critical influence. They can help a great deal, but if they are not sensitive and available to the child they can also cause damage and harm, and exacerbate the situation.

Role of the adult

The child has developmental "tasks" into which he will entwine the unique coping demands related to the loss. Adults have the "task" of assisting the child along this route. This book is meant to guide the adult on this "journey" alongside the child who has experienced loss. A glance at the attitudes of adults toward children who have experienced loss reveals how difficult the suffering of the children is for them. Many adults are afraid of the child's response. Many adults deny the fact that the child has a mourning process of his own, that he understands or is capable of understanding the real meaning of the loss. These attitudes stem from the fear of confronting the child's state of distress, and from the adults' own helplessness with these difficult situations, in which they too often lack the requisite strengths and solutions. The difficulties of adults are evident in many of the roles involving children – in the function of parents, in the behavior of teachers and the educational system, and even in the attitudes and functioning of therapeutic practitioners.

An adult who cannot "encounter" loss and deal with it in a mature, well-adjusted manner cannot encounter the child and his needs; he cannot and will not be "available" emotionally to the child. Emotional awareness and maturity of the adults is the key that allows them to be available to children in need. For this reason, I will begin this book with comments on the difficulties that we adults face in responding to the mourning of children and their reactions to loss. I believe that greater awareness of our own difficulties and defenses will pave the way to an "open" reading of the book; one that will later enhance the capacity to really be with the child, listen to him, and find the way to give him the support he needs.

Adults who experienced loss as children

The book also offers adults who experienced loss as children an opportunity to encounter their own experience and acknowledge the influence that the childhood loss had on their lives. Oftentimes, the effects of loss are buried deep in our psyches and personalities – so much so that we fail to recognize the connection between our feelings and behavior as adults and those childhood experiences. The encounter with them – and recognition of them – constitutes an additional opportunity for emotional processing. The better we are at identifying those experiences, the more we process them, and the better we control their effects on our lives.

Why this book was written

I have drawn most of my inspiration, and especially the motivation to write this book, from the personal and professional experience I acquired in the course of 25 years of work in the field, during which I became familiar with the life stories of numerous families – adults and children – who experienced loss, and shared thoughts and ideas with many other professionals working in this field.

This book was written for the sake of children. It is directed at adults – parents, teachers, advisers, and therapists, and anyone else who knows a child who requires understanding and a shoulder to lean on.

The book was also written for professionals in the therapeutic community, academic researchers, and instructors. Nevertheless, it avoids adopting an academic or theoretical approach, in the interest of making the subject matter accessible to all. The need to enhance the level of knowledge and understanding for the situation of the child who has experienced loss crosses all lines.

Theoretical backing

Theoretically speaking, the material presented relies on a paradigm compiled from fields of knowledge – theory and research – related to loss, separation, trauma, personality theories, psychodynamic theories, child development, and family-system theories. The amalgamation of all these sources of knowledge with experiences from the field has made it possible to illuminate this complex subject. Despite the complexity of the material,

I have made an effort to simplify things and portray them in a manner that does not require the reader to be familiar with the theories.

Appended to the book is a glossary of professional terms, for those readers who are unfamiliar with them. I have provided a list of recommended reading for those who wish to delve deeper into the subjects.

It is not an easy experience to read this book

It is sad to read about children living in a world filled with pain. It is upsetting to learn about the difficulties that stand in the way of their development, hardships they have to handle because of the loss they experienced. It is daunting to grasp the enormous responsibility placed on the shoulders of the adults who are called to help these children find their way. The "reward" will be in the better understanding the reader will gain of the child's world, enhanced insight and sensitivity for the child's difficulties, and the reinforced commitment to furnish the support and encouragement the child needs for a healthy upbringing, in spite of the loss that "ruined" his childhood.

Being aware of your own experiences that you bring to the book as a reader

Before we begin to understand the world of children and how they respond to loss, it would be worthwhile to explore a few aspects that may enhance the reader's awareness of his own thoughts, emotions, and conceptions about the subject. This encounter will, it is hoped, encourage contemplation and reflection on one's own experiences and reinforce the reader's ability to approach these subjects. Self-awareness will help the reader to be more emotionally open and accessible to the difficult subjects presented in this book.

Experience proves that it is very difficult for adults to encounter the sad, hurting, confused, or angry child. This encounter is difficult for all adults, including parents and professionals. When things are hard for us adults to bear, we protect ourselves – and not only the children, as we imagine to be the case. We do it by means of rationalization: "the child doesn't understand anyway"; or projection – "the child is afraid to hear about it" – even though it is really us who are afraid to hear about it or afraid to hear the child. Adults may employ many different "techniques" so as to avoid the hard confrontation with the child. These of course not only limit the amount of help they can offer the child, but also warp their perception of what is really happening to the child.

These behaviors allow us to modify our responses to conform with our own needs, needs that do not necessarily correlate with those of the child. It is better that we enter the discussion of the world of children and their responses to loss only once we ourselves are emotionally accessible. For that to happen, we must be aware of the root cause of our own difficulties. The encounter with the child who has experienced loss draws adults into several sensitive realms.

This child is me

The encounter with the child evokes memories and fears from our own childhood, arouses memories of pain and loneliness when we were children. We are reminded of our own vulnerability as children, our feelings of helplessness or anger when adults disappointed us, did not understand our troubles, or did not support us when we needed them.

Although these are not always conscious memories, they have left their mark on us, and are "aroused" when we encounter a child in a similar situation. Within each of us, even the most mature adult, there is a hidden child – the child we once were. This "child" is threatened by the encounter with the hurt child because it identifies with him. The "child" within us always remains sensitive and vulnerable.

Every child is afraid of his mother dying, that something bad would happen to his father, that he could be left alone and defenseless. These fears remain inscribed in everyone's emotional memory. Every adult remembers his need as a child for love, security, and care.

Defense mechanisms

Many adults, even if they have not lost a parent at a young age, have experienced "loss" through disappointment, separation, or emotional abandonment at the hands of their parents. These experiences have left painful emotional "scars" that are reopened by the suffering of the child. These scars are awakened when the adult encounters emotionally a child undergoing a similar experience. The sensitivities are liable to set various defense mechanisms into motion: the adult's strong identification with the child causes him to *project* his own sensitivities onto the child. Conversely, *denial* helps him "escape" his emotions and protect himself, but at the cost of disregarding the child's emotions.

It is likely that at such times the same defense mechanisms employed by the adult in the past will be reactivated. An adult who once coped by being strong will now try to cope in the same way, and will expect the child to be "strong." Someone who once escaped and denied his own pain will try to deny the pain suffered by the child. In these instances, the adult is incapable of fully relating to the child and helping him because he is too engrossed in himself. He translates the child's emotional needs to conform to his own world, and treats them through his own defense mechanisms. Therefore, when adults are preoccupied by their own sensitivities, it is hard for them to listen, and establish a real connection with the child, and the child is left alone, with a response that does not suit his needs.

It is therefore advisable, even before reading this book, that one should gain awareness of those childhood memories and experiences which pertain to loss and separation. Anyone who has experienced traumatic loss should recall the changes that occurred in his life as a result. Recognition of these memories – in spite of the emotional hardship – and recognition of the defenses deployed to deal with them, will help the adult to become more emotionally receptive to the child.

Do adults have to know everything?

Another burden is the belief that we adults have to know and understand everything; that we have to be able to explain the ways of the world. We feel that children expect us to guarantee a "righteous" world and we ourselves may feel that this is our job; that it is up to us to ensure a world in which children are not hurt.

It is often difficult for us to explain why a tragedy took place, why somebody left or abandoned his family, why doctors weren't able to save a patient, why somebody was run down by a car, or why there are wars. We adults have thoughts and reflections and questions, too. We also do not understand sometimes why painful things happen either and we surely want to "scream" against them. We too have a hard time coping with death, and with all the questions that arise in connection with death – the meaning of life, questions about an afterlife, and many other thoughts and reflections.

It is difficult for us adults to admit that we too are angry, that we do not have the answers, and that we too are at times defenseless. The child grapples with questions, ruminations, and feelings similar to our own, and comes to us in the expectation of receiving answers. We, the adults, feel a need to supply them. It is difficult for us to deal with a situation in which we lack the answers and explanations, as well as the means to protect the child.

We "solve" this quandary in various ways. Sometimes we simply opt to disregard the child's needs and questions, convincing ourselves that the child doesn't have any problems with what had happened. At other times we volunteer answers, albeit answers that lack credibility, made-up answers that are only meant to say something – anything. Nevertheless, children are very sensitive to truth, and can tell when adults are "faking it." That which we ourselves do not know and do not understand, we will not succeed at "explaining" in any persuasive manner. When we are not sure of ourselves, and pretend to have the situation under control, the child will almost always detect the fake.

Moreover, children can sense the feelings and fears of adults, especially those of their parents, and they act in accordance with those sensitivities, even catering to them. When the adult has a hard time accepting loss, the child will not confront him with questions or statements that will further challenge him. Therapists frequently hear children admit they would have liked to talk about a specific loss-related issue, but don't do so because they "know" the subject is taboo even though no one has explicitly told them so. A child may want to mention his dead father or make an attempt to find out more about how he died, but won't dare raise the subject because he "knows" his mother isn't ready to talk about it.

Should adults show or share their emotions?

Loss confronts adults with a host of difficult emotions – pain, grief, anger, helplessness. According to one popular myth, the adult should not show children his emotions, or share his emotions with them. Such a belief puts on the adult the demand to always be strong, always be in control. Believing that the adult must always be strong means that permitting a child see his pain and sadness, and even more so his sense of helplessness and confusion, is ostensibly not performing the duties of an adult. Those of us who accept this myth mask their true emotions in the presence of children, becoming actors in a "performance" that degrades the genuineness of our relationships with the child. The price of putting on this show is that we become emotionally sterile in our child's eyes, and emotionally inaccessible to him. We lack *emotional credibility*, and the child senses this. The child allows the adult to dictate the "performance" as it were. Both sides lose out, however, because the open line of communication, so necessary for providing support and help, is impaired.

Secrets

Frequently, loss has to do with issues that adults may consider inappropriate for children. They may believe that exposure ought to be avoided concerning the sort of secret subjects considered for adults only: "It's better that children do not know about divorce"; or "Children don't have to know about diseases"; or "Children don't have to be told the details of how someone died."

Secrets between adults and children constitute a very sensitive area. Great effort is invested in maintaining these secrets. Children are told all sorts of "stories" in the hope of diverting their attention. Due to the great lengths that go into keeping secrets, the adult is liable to seal himself off from the child's questions and queries, and – most importantly – from the child's need to know, understand, and be a partner in the reality of his life. We may be confident that the child doesn't know the "secrets." Perhaps he doesn't know the exact details, but he senses that something is going on. He picks up on various details, and responds to the sensitivities expressed by the adult in connection with the secret. The basic trust of the child in us as dependable truth-speaking adults is hampered. It might take years to rehabilitate this trust, and sometimes the child will grow up to be an ever-suspicious person.

It is important for us to remember that, in our generation, television and myriad other forms of entertainment expose children to "real-life issues," including death, murder, suicide, conspiracy, sex, adultery, and divorce. A great deal of the information is saturated with violence and sensationalism. This knowledge is gathered by the child, and will be referenced when he tries to understand what is happening in his private world. When something very serious happens in the child's life, it is preferable that he be furnished with accurate, balanced information, by an adult close to him. When the child lacks information and explanations, he is left to look for it on his own, and will rely on information that is often distorted and misconstrued. What is more, the information will "flow" to the child whether or not he wants it. Other children will tell him what they heard from their parents. He will overhear snippets of conversations from adults around him. In the absence of reliable, accurate information from people close to him, the child is incapable of filtering and classifying the distorted information that reaches him. If denied the opportunity to openly approach those closest to him for explanations and reinforcement, he is liable to be hurt by the random information. Painful as it may seem, the truth is preferable to lies, secrets, and distorted information. Factual information can strengthen the child. The bottom line is that adults must bravely provide the child with the truth.

Can adults always protect children?

Another belief is that adults are supposed to protect children. This is one of the primary roles of adults in every human society, and the primary role of every parent toward his children. When tragedy occurs, we may feel that we have failed in our duties. We are embarrassed by our *helplessness* and impotence, and feel a sense of *guilt* toward the child. Due to this helplessness and embarrassment, we sometimes prefer to disregard our own sense of "guilt" and persuade ourselves that the child does not feel or understand, and that he is unaware of the vulnerability of his situation.

We must remember that at the same time that the adult needs to attend to the child's needs he is also going through a hard time of his own, dealing with the issues of loss. He too fears death – his own death, and the death of his loved ones. He too seizes on various beliefs and nurtures them in order to stave off the threat of finality and irreversibility of death. Every adult knows that razor-sharp feeling of separation and loss, and does what he can to avoid it. Adults also employ various forms of suppression and denial to sidestep the encounter with pain. Our own hardships make it even more difficult for us to confront the hardships of our children. If we are engrossed in our own pain, it is very difficult to contain and bear the pain of our child.

By understanding why the encounter with the child is so difficult for us, we are better equipped to relate to the child, and more apt to find ways to help him. When adults are cognizant of the difficulties that threaten to overwhelm them, and successfully deal with those difficulties, they are ready to assume their duties to the child: providing support, offering appropriate explanations, and providing a sense of protection and guidance.

The adult has a great deal of responsibility toward the child who has experienced loss. He can and should offer the child tremendous support to help him cope with the loss. The child is largely dependent on the functioning of the adult. The proper contribution by the adult is the key to the child's healthy handling of the situation.

Readers who experienced loss

For those readers who experienced loss at a young age, who lost a parent or suffered some other traumatic loss, this book will rekindle painful and difficult memories. It is not easy to re-expose oneself to this anguish. Yet it may offer another opportunity to work through these memories, maybe resolve some, and in the process you may discover the "normality" of what you experienced, and the "legitimacy" of the hardships you endured. It is possible that this book will clarify the link between something that happened in the distant past and something that happened in the present: a connection you may not have recognized or did not consider important. The reference to deep-seated emotions, the opportunity for further clarification, and the fresh understanding of what happened in the past can combine to make a significant and beneficial contribution to your present and future well-being.

Parents raising a child after loss

It is not easy for a parent to raise a child following a traumatic loss, and this book will not ease that burden. Through this book, the parents will encounter many of the difficulties they experienced in the past, as well as those that continue to threaten and frighten them. The parent may be alarmed to read about the extent of the effects of loss on children, and the enormity of the responsibility placed on their shoulders. Yet it is my hope that this book will also persuade you how valuable and essential is your endeavor. It is daunting to think of how much the child depends on you, your actions and reactions. Yet your ability to help the child and contribute toward his continued healthy development is crucial.

The book sheds light on many common difficulties and potential setbacks, but also suggests means of coping with them. It is built upon the premise that traumatic loss leads to a series of responses that should be considered normal. Not only should they not be shunted aside or regarded as shameful or deviant, but the opposite is the case: they should be recognized as normal events in the life of a child who experienced traumatic loss. If we adults can be persuaded that these are normal and even necessary experiences, then we will be able to understand the significant role we play at the child's side, and the decisive importance of enabling him to embark on this journey – pitfalls and all.

Chapter 1

The Bereavement of Children

Children's perception of loss

It should be noted at the outset that the concepts of bereavement and mourning as we will employ them are not limited to the initial mourning period; nor are they restricted exclusively to situations of mourning following death. Rather, they apply to a range of responses to the loss of any significant, beloved person. Generally, when speaking of mourning, it is customary to solely consider those events that take place during the first years following the loss. Nevertheless, we will illustrate how and why these responses continue beyond the initial period into the ensuing years.

The commonly held assumption that reaction to loss ends with the initial mourning period is untrue. What is true is that during these initial years the individual is predominantly engaged in responding to the loss. These are the years during which the "stages" of mourning and "processing" of mourning take place. Nevertheless, it must be made clear that the loss and its implications will remain with the individual throughout his life. The loss will continue to affect many aspects of life, and most certainly the emotions. Recognition of the loss and the implications thereof will lead to recurring situations that require the "mourner" to re-confront the situation, and make the requisite readjustments and adaptations.

All of this is even more true for children. As he grows up, the child will confront his loss over and over again, understanding it at new levels of comprehension, adapting himself to the loss in accordance with his changing mental abilities, emotional state, and emotional needs. Life, after all, goes on, and the child will have to repeatedly adapt and readjust himself to the effects of the loss on the contemporary realities of his life.

His life is constantly changing because of his growth and development, and due to changing circumstances – some of which are related to the loss and some of which are related to changing life circumstances in general. Many of these changes stir up themes related to the loss, and in turn stir up emotions that are part of the "bereavement" process.

When we consider the diverse responses of the child to loss, it is useful to categorize them along chronological lines. First, the responses should be classified in accordance with the amount of time that has elapsed since the loss occurred – differentiating the initial mourning period from that of later years, when the mourning is no longer "fresh." The second division relates to the age of the child. The child's age reflects his stage of development, with all its implications. In addition, as time passes, other changes may occur, including internal changes within the family and those that are caused by external events.

The questions that are highly relevant to understanding experience of loss among children are:

- Is the child capable of mourning, and if so, from what age?

- Does the child understand the meaning of the loss – and primarily the meaning of death – and from what age?

- Does the child mourn differently from the adult?

Even the most conservative approaches agree that from a very young age, even during the first year of life, the child already senses and reacts to the loss of a parent. The parent is the object through which the young child lives and feels his existence. The younger the child, the more the absence of a parent wreaks an existential, narcissistic wound, depriving the child of emotional "oxygen." Lacking language and words, he can only express his response through alternate modes of expression: for the most part through bodily and sensory expression, such as fretfulness and crying, loss of appetite and failure to eat, and even moods such as sadness and even depression.

Theoreticians wonder if the response of the child could be considered "bereavement" or whether it is merely an instinctive response to perceived existential harm. There is no doubt that the child whose parent has "disappeared" from his life, whose parent no longer cares for him, nourishes him or protects him, and most of all no longer gives him love, feels the absence of all these and suffers greatly. The emotional responses to this – anger, sadness, longing – are evident from a very young age. Even if the child does not yet have the language to put them into words, the feelings exist nevertheless. These feelings are bereavement. The older the child, the more capable he is of understanding and expressing his feelings and his bereavement.

Children begin to understand the concept of "no more" at the most basic concrete levels: a mother who is suddenly not there, a bottle or breast taken away from them. Through the concrete experience, the more abstract perception of the concept develops. Between the first and the second year the child begins to become familiar with the concept of "no more."

Every baby "loses" or is temporarily separated from gratifying objects and situations. Feeling the presence of the parent, and "losing" him from time to time, is one of the most common yet important of these experiences. The objects of gratification constantly disappear and reappear: the breast of the mother, a toy. Through these experiences the baby learns about "there is" and "there is no more." Through these separations, he learns to cope. Since the object that went away usually comes back, it is not a never-ending traumatic experience. It may be frustrating and upsetting at times, but gratifying at others. The baby "learns" to endure the separation, and as it develops it grasps the situation, perceptively and cognitively. These experiences are very important in building his inner world and his mental–emotional ability. They also build up his ability to cope with absence, with "no more." When his parent is not there with him, the baby will respond to the situation. Although he may not be able to assess how long the condition lasted, or understand the cause of it, he senses and responds to the experience itself.

A young child who has the traumatic experience in which the parent is totally "no more" – in other words, when the parent does not just temporarily disappear – suffers a tremendous blow to the process he recently began of believing and trusting that good things do return. The total loss leaves the child in a void. He not only leaves the child alone and helpless, but also leaves him with the "lesson" that relationships with people are not a safe zone that merits trust. His perception of "no more" is tainted.

By the age of four or five, children can grasp the idea of "no more" with their intellect. They understand a situation in which "Father isn't here," and they also understand that he can return later on. They are already familiar with the concrete aspects of death. They have come across death among animals, they've heard of someone in their social or familial environment – a grandparent, perhaps – that died. They are exposed to the concept of death through stories, movies, and television. They are also exposed to news in the media, where they hear about death resulting from wars and terrorist attacks, traffic accidents, murders, and natural disasters. Comprehension of the significance of "no more" and death continues to develop until they reach perception–comprehension maturity at adolescence.

Death

Death is a difficult concept to grasp because it requires understanding of concrete and abstract dimensions, as well as spiritual aspects relating to the essence of life. Along with his intellectual and emotional development, the child develops an ability to conceptualize at the abstract level. The comprehension and conceptualization of death has to include four primary elements: its irreversibility, its finality, its universality, and its causality.

IRREVERSIBILITY OF DEATH

Understanding that the dead person will not come back, that death is irreversible, that even if the child asks very nicely and promises to be good, he won't be able to restore his dead mother to life. The child who does not understand this concept continues to search and does what he can to restore the situation to its previous state – through prayers, promises, or various ceremonies and rituals.

Even when children understand the concept of irreversibility at the intellectual level, there remains the issue of its acceptance at the emotional level. This, we must emphasize, is a problem for adults as well. Acceptance of the idea of irreversibility is a constituent element of bereavement work. Factual understanding is the foundation on which emotional acceptance will be built. The understanding of irreversibility includes the understanding and acceptance of our own limitations.

Adults frequently leave children in a "fog," and avoid having to explain that the loss is irreversible. They too have a hard time accepting it. If it has not been made clear to the child that the situation cannot be rectified one should not be surprised when the child will search for ways to "correct" the loss or expect the dead to come back.

FINALITY OF DEATH

The concept of finality emphasizes that the nonexistence is absolute: the dead person no longer has human characteristics; no parts of the dead person remain alive; he doesn't feel anything, doesn't feel cold, can't see or hear. A child who believes that his dead father still feels the cold cannot sleep on rainy nights because "Father is wet and cold in his grave." A child who is told "Mother is looking down on you from heaven" may feel her sheltering as well as scrutinizing eyes following him wherever he goes. Sensations and thoughts of this sort are emotionally burdensome, as they prevent the child from internalizing the finality of the situation and, as such, prevent emotional adjustment to the finality of the loss.

UNIVERSALITY OF DEATH

Every living thing is destined to die. Death is not a punishment imposed on anybody, but a trait that is common to all living things. Death is the unavoidable end, sooner or later, of every living thing and of every human being. In order to develop a mature understanding of death, children must understand these three concepts.

CAUSALITY OF DEATH

In addition, it is critically important to help the child understand the causality of the death and explain the circumstances of the death and why it could not be prevented. Young children tend to classify events as bad or good, as punishment or prize. In the child's perception, death is a punishment. In order that the child not fear that he might be punished in the same manner, the causes of the death must be made clear.

If the mother's death was the result of a disease, the death should not be described with superficial descriptions that seem less painful, such as "Mother was sleeping, and then she died." The child is liable to be afraid to go to sleep lest he too die while asleep. If the person died in a car accident, it is best to describe the circumstances of the accident so that the child can differentiate between driving on a road and safely reaching one's destination, and the specific conditions in which a fatal accident is liable to occur.

When the circumstances of death are especially violent, such as suicide or murder, there is a tendency to conceal the facts from the children and invent a "cover story." The negative effects of concealing the truth from the child will be discussed at a later stage. At this point, however, we will suffice by stressing the importance of presenting the true facts – difficult as they may be to bear – since they serve the child as a basis for understanding the death.

It is not easy for adults to conceptualize the meaning of death, and explaining this to a child is harder yet. For adults, this difficulty does not stem from an inability to understand, but from the emotional hardship that hinders the ability to accept.

The use of language

The use of language – the choice of words and concepts – reflects the manner in which society copes with the subject. The words and concepts that are used to describe the condition of death often reflect the difficulty we have in accepting the irreversibility and finality of death. They contribute to an atmosphere of obscurity and ambiguity, and nurture illusions as well. The dead person "passed away," "is no longer with us," "went to another world," "left us," or is "somewhere up there," "in paradise," "with the angels," "has gone to a better place," or is "looking down on us from above." All of these terms serve the purpose of blunting the painful encounter with death. By using these terms, adults prevent the child from gaining full exposure to the facts, and thereby prevent him or her from fully coping with this difficult experience.

The child's cultural background should be taken into account vis-à-vis language use. Certain concepts take on specific meanings in the particular subculture in which the child grew up, and he learns to recognize the hidden meanings behind the words. Concepts like "rests in peace" or "the deceased" serve as familiar codes in certain cultures for denoting the dead person. Children learn to recognize these codes.

Even when the child already understands the concepts of nonexistence and death and their constituent elements, he is still likely to react in irrational, "childish" ways at times, creating the impression that he does not understand. Children may resort to magical thinking in the hope of fixing the situation: "If I'll be a good boy, Mother will come back to life." Small children anthropomorphize death, transmuting it into a figure they can fight or run away from. They fantasize that they are superheroes who fight death, which is represented by another "bad" figure. Their victory over the figure that represents death will correct the bad that happened to them.

Although they may seem to be irrational and "childish," these responses actually indicate that the child senses and realizes what happened. He summons up defense mechanisms from his world of concepts, in the hope of rectifying the damage. Magical thoughts, unrealistic imaginary powers, denial – all of these are mechanisms suited to the way children think, and are invoked as defense mechanisms at times of distress. When a child employs such mechanisms, it should be viewed as a warning sign, an indicator that the child needs assistance and support to cope with the threatening reality.

The child's readiness to understand the loss is conditional upon his age – his emotional and intellectual development. In order to boost his level of comprehension, the child needs clarifications and explanations from adults. The adult should offer these explanations at the child's level of understanding, and use concepts and examples drawn from the world of the child. By borrowing from a world with which the child is most familiar, the adult will be more successful at getting across these difficult concepts.

It is important to repeatedly describe the facts of what took place, and talk about every facet of the event, its circumstances and its causes, while at the same time emphasizing the irreversibility, finality, and universality. Repeated discussion alongside with explanations should take place not only during the initial period after the event but years later, as well. As the years pass and the child grows up, his ability to comprehend will continue to develop. The adult should allow the child to ask questions at all times, and make sure he receives the information that will help him understand and internalize what happened. The child will repeat this exercise on a recurrent basis, in accordance with his changing levels of development and maturity and his changing needs.

The requisite conditions for acceptance of death as described here are in many cases equally applicable to the child's comprehension of other losses. Every loss has elements of irreversibility and finality, and only when these are clearly understood can one begin the process of emotional acceptance. This is equally true for divorce of parents, or illnesses that lead to disability, abandonment, and other traumatic losses. The child needs to understand that the situation is irreversible, and cannot be restored to its previous state. On the basis of this realization, he will have to accept the loss and the new situation and adapt.

A child must know that his parents are divorced, as opposed to separated or angry with one another after a fight, and understand the concrete meaning of divorce. It is natural for him to have a hard time accepting the situation as irreversible, and he will therefore search for ways to "repair" the break-up of the family. Precisely because of this difficulty, he has to fully understand and recognize the fact that his parents are divorced, that they are no longer the family they were before, that they will no longer live together. Only when the child understands the irreversibility of the situation can he be helped to stop trying to rectify the circumstances, and stop seizing on hopes of reuniting the family.

Cultural and religious frameworks

Every religion and every culture deals with the theme of death, with the question of life after death. Religions try to explain why good and bad things happen in people's lives, and offer answers to questions about the meaning of life. The child absorbs the beliefs of the culture in which he is raised, and usually accepts the answers it provides. This cultural and religious framework of beliefs helps adults offer answers to the difficult questions with which children, as well as adults, grapple in the aftermath of a loss. Just as the beliefs can comfort the adults, they can also provide comfort to the child.

Numerous faiths speak of an afterlife, of reincarnation, of a continuation of life after this world. On the face of it, these beliefs are incompatible with the concepts of irreversibility and finality. But in actuality, there need not be contradiction between them. They can even be complementary provided that the child fully understands the distinction between reality and faith.

At the concrete, factual level, the child should have a clear understanding of irreversibility and finality. The dead person will not come back to live with us here, in our lives, and he is not a partner in our lives: he does not see, hear, or know what is happening to us. On the other hand, these beliefs can be presented as a means of understanding death at the abstract level; as a spiritual answer to questions about the meaning of life.

It is important to stress to the child that the dead person lives on in our hearts; his enduring image gives us comfort and strength. When the concept of the deceased person's continued "existence" is presented in tandem with a no-nonsense explanation about finality and irreversibility, the explanations can soothe the child and give him something to cling to.

It is vital to make the child clearly aware of the difference between beliefs and reality. If this is not made clear, especially to children who are too young to differentiate between reality and imagination, the children are liable to take things out of context and mix between the realities of their life and their wishful thinking and imagination – now fed by fears and hopes relating to the loss.

When the child is presented with the idea of a world to come, the difference between this world and the next has to be made clear. It must be emphasized that the other world cannot suddenly penetrate into his life, nor will he suddenly "roll out" into that world. Alongside the idea of the "soul" which "lives" beyond this world must come a clear explanation that the soul has no human characteristics: the soul does not feel pain or cold, nor can it interfere in his life on this world.

In this regard, the age of the child is extremely important. As mentioned before, the younger the child, and the more limited his ability to comprehend abstract concepts, the more important it is to explain the spiritual concepts in such a way that they should not blur his perception of the irreversibility, finality, and causality of the death. Adults often prefer to use obscure spiritual concepts so as to avoid giving the child straightforward explanations. They too sometimes prefer to escape to these beliefs rather than accepting the loss and all its harsh implications. Adults should avoid employing terminology drawn from the world of beliefs, which can obscure these concepts, sow confusion, and hinder the process of understanding and acceptance of the loss.

The child depends on the adult to help him understand the facts of life. Based on his age, he may lack the appropriate cognitive capacity, know-how, and information to understand what happened. Anything that is not explained or clarified will leave a void which the child will fill with the help of his imagination, and with the help of information to which he is randomly exposed. If the child is not offered explanations, he will invent them. The younger the child, the greater the chance that he will invoke his imagination as a defense mechanism. Even when explanations are offered, the child is still liable to escape to an imaginary world, one that offers comfort and a less painful reality. This is all the more true when explanations and information are not provided.

Regression

A temporary emotional regression is a normal response to loss, and may be part of the mourning reaction. This is the case for adults as well as children. Regression is a healthy defense mechanism that is employed by the ego to protect and maintain the vulnerable and hurt psyche. Among children, regression is usually reflected by reverting to a more childish state. Small children will revert to bedwetting, thumb sucking, and crying, and will want to spend a great deal of time with the remaining parent. Older children will revert to stronger emotional dependence on the remaining parent, childish moods, outbursts and fits of anger, and childish demands.

Because children are emotionally spontaneous, they are very susceptible to being overcome by sadness, and feel the loneliness and helplessness immediately. They must protect themselves from these distressing sensations, so they "escape" into denial and avoidance. They soon begin to search for "soothing" alternatives. Young children will quickly begin to look for an alternative parent figure. They feel comforted when offered ice cream or a favorite candy. Gifts give the child a feeling of receiving love, thereby dulling the sense of abandonment.

Difficult questions

As the child matures, more thoughts and questions form in his mind regarding the loss. He develops the capacity for philosophical thought, and attempts to comprehend the essence of life, raising some hard questions along the way. Why do things turn out the way they do? What is the meaning of life? Why did it happen to me? These questions sound as if they belong to the adult world, but the child who has experienced a traumatic loss that significantly affects his life is already grappling with these questions at a young age.

All children are preoccupied by existential questions – questions about the essence and nature of life. But for a child who has experienced loss, these issues are more threatening and emotionally charged, and more personal. Will I die, too? Do tragedies have "laws," and can they be anticipated? These questions undermine the child's existential confidence. He is liable to feel that all sorts of dangers constantly hover above and threaten him: the unexpected becomes expected. He worries about the death of another person who is dear to him, dreads the loss of the remaining parent, is afraid of harm coming to his siblings or close friends. He fears that hardships will continue to befall him. He often lives in fear and anxiety over situations he feels incapable of anticipating or controlling.

In order to help the child cope with these feelings, he has to be provided with soothing and ensuring messages along with facts and information to understand what is happening in his life. The adult must make an effort to mitigate and allay what might seem like an all-encompassing threat over which the child has no control. By gaining an understanding of the issues, the child will be able to set up "boundaries" that will stave off the threat of future dangers, and develop the cognitive insight to compartmentalize the trauma and create an unthreatening safe zone.

Securing trust in adults

Responses of adults to the anxieties of children often have two components: denial of what is worrying the child; a desire to protect him by offering promises and assurances that cannot be backed up. The guarantee that "No one else is going to die," or that "Mother will never leave you," may buy peace and quiet in the short term, but cannot withstand the test of reality. When the child encounters a reality different than that which he has been promised, his anxieties will only increase. Worse yet, his faith in adults will be undermined. Trust in adults is one of the child's most important sources of support; through it he derives his sense of existential confidence. For a child who has experienced traumatic loss, this is critical. Therefore, answers that embellish reality not only might end up proven untrustworthy and therefore trust destroying, but might also prevent the child from being able to express his doubts and anxieties. The net result is that he feels very much alone, and the threatening thoughts and fantasies are left to fester.

It is important to understand that all children are occupied by the subject of death and loss. They are exposed to deaths and losses that occur in their immediate environment: a grandfather who dies; a neighborhood dog run over by a car; a friend's parents who divorced. Children hear about things happening around them, even if adults think they are successful at shielding some of it from them. The subject of death is of great concern to children because it is part and parcel of the process of development and the encounter with life. It preoccupies children from a very young age. Their preoccupation with death varies in accordance with each child's emotional and cognitive development, and developmental needs. While young, it interests them at the concrete level: how people die; what happens to the body after death; and other aspects that drive home the reality of the event. As they get older, it occupies them at the philosophical, abstract, and spiritual levels as well.

The child's preoccupation with death, loss, and other traumatic and existence-threatening losses will increase in relation to the frequency that such events occur in his environment. The frequency of car accidents, wars, and acts of violence in society, the incidence of divorce and separation in families – all of these will result in the child being concerned even if he has not been personally affected. These issues are even more emotionally threatening to the child who has already experienced loss, because he relates to them in terms of his own personal experiences. For him, they are not only potential threats, but also emotional stimuli that remind him of his personal experiences. When a child who has experienced traumatic loss hears of a tragedy, even if it happened to someone else, he is bewildered and flooded with emotions, since the event not only reminds him of his experience, but it once again underscores the fact that there is no security, and that something bad can happen to him again.

It is customary to use the terms of "loss" and "separation," but it is important that it be made clear that for everyone, children included, the person that is no longer here has not "been lost." Neither are we "separating" from that person in the sense that he will no longer have internal meaning for us, or play a role in our life. Separation does not mean forgetting or expunging the memory of the person who is no longer here. We do not "leave" or end the "connection" with the person. Someone who played an important role in the child's life, especially a parent, will continue to be a significant figure; a figure that continues to live within the inner entity of the child. That person will continue to be there with him and, it is hoped, for him throughout his childhood, and for the rest of his life.

Influence of the socio-cultural environment on children's understanding of death and loss

The child's attitude to the subject of death is related, inter alia, to the cultural and socioeconomic environment in which he is raised. Twentieth-century western culture has largely removed death from the context of home and family. Children are not exposed to many of the life passages, primarily those that pertain to sickness, old age, and death. The elderly no longer live with their families, and usually die in old-age homes or hospitals. Terminally ill patients are often not cared for at home, and the child does not have a chance to witness the approach of death. Funerals, which at one time set out from the home of the deceased, are now held at funeral homes and cemeteries, far from the child's eyes.

In stories, movies, and video games, death is represented as the end that lies in store for the "bad guys." The good, powerful hero always wins, never dies. In science fiction, whenever a hero dies, he comes back to life after some sleight of hand. As such, works of science fiction and virtual reality serve to blur the boundaries between reality and imagination, genuine and simulated. No matter how dire the situation, invariably it can be controlled and "won." In popular lore, reality can be controlled by man, through science, computers, or advanced technology.

On the other hand, television presents family life, and especially the more painful family issues, in an extreme, distorted manner that is replete with violence, backhanded scheming and conspiracy, separation, and divorce. Soap operas depict distressful personal and family situations. The media expose and bring into every home disasters, wars, violence, traffic accidents, and other dramatic events that result in loss. These subjects constitute topics of everyday conversation. The young child is exposed to all this information and stimuli from a very early age, yet the exposure does not necessarily prepare him for better coping, or make him any more insightful. The child receives a dual message: on the one hand, he learns that the world is full of violence and danger; on the other, he is led to believe that modern man has nearly absolute control over his life and world.

Conversely, in regions beset by natural disasters, epidemics, wars, and terrorism, or in societies in which violence and drug use is rife, loss and death are part of the ordinary lives of children, from early childhood onward. There are many societies where violence, hunger and disease, wars and terrorism, natural disasters, domestic violence, and domestic separations cause much suffering and loss. In these circumstances children have an intimate knowledge of "loss realities" from a very young age. They "prepare" themselves for them long before they understand them. To children who live in these societies, loss and death are burdens they shoulder from early childhood.

In modern western societies, children are not given a chance to take active part in the natural cycle of death and loss, as is the case in traditional and "primitive" societies. On the other hand, wars, acts of terrorism, car accidents, and violence are part of daily life, the subjects of everyday life, and children are therefore aware of them. In such social circumstances, for example in the case of Israeli and Palestinian children, the children are very much aware of death and loss, and are worried that they or someone close to them could be affected. One might say that the child is cognizant of the danger, and "prepares" for it through the fear that he too will be a victim.

Stages of grieving

The grieving process is often described through "stages." We shall describe the major three stages, and then address the question of whether children go through the same stages as adults.

First stage: Shock

The predominant feature of this initial stage is numbness. After the loss occurs, and especially if it happened in a sudden way, there is no real assimilation or internalization of what happened. All of the responses, even when sharply pronounced, are "external." They range from unresponsiveness to emotional turmoil, from an inability to function to overreacting. In most instances, the person's behavior corresponds with what has happened, and it may therefore seem as if he "understands" and has internalized what happened. Nevertheless, this generally reflects a very "external" understanding, and the response is not the product of insight or emotional awareness. At this stage, strong defense mechanisms are activated, protecting the individual from the full impact of the bleak reality.

Strange phenomena may occur at this stage, such as "forgetting" that the dead person is no longer there, and thinking of him as if nothing has happened. The person may hear his voice or footsteps, or even see him. These hallucinations do not stem from an emotional disorder; they are evidence of the mental difficulty to grasp what has happened. This stage is frequently accompanied by physiological symptoms, such as loss of appetite or obsessive eating, respiratory distress, digestive problems, a strong need to sleep, or an inability to sleep.

Second stage: Intensified response and internalization

During this stage, the individual begins to comprehend the emotional reality of the loss, and to respond to it by grieving and mourning. The response becomes more and more intense and is expressed through a wide range of emotions: anger, accusation, guilt feelings, depression, intense sorrow and sadness, pain, fits of crying and longing, nightmares. The responses increase in intensity as the individual continues to take in what has happened.

Concurrent with the more intense emotions, cognitive comprehension becomes more distinct, and the individual gains a more profound understanding of the significance and implications of the loss. In combination with the stronger emotional "grip" on the new reality, a process of internalization is initiated. The mourner experiences periodic "encounters" with the loss; with the fact that there is a void, that there is "no more." These encounters add new layers of emotions, insight, and response. This stage is very important in terms of the "grief work." Articulation and processing of emotions is at the heart of this process. The loss is taking its place in one's being. Its painful significance is fully expressed and clarified. This painful process enables the individual to move on to the third stage.

Third stage: Acceptance and readjustment

In this stage, the person understands that the loss is part of the reality of his or her life, and begins the process of adaptation to this new and painful reality. This readjustment reflects acceptance of the loss – accepting its emotional significance and understanding its implications. "Acceptance" should not be interpreted as acquiescence or forgetting what happened. Nor does it mean that the mourner no longer feels sorrow, pain, or other emotions that are related to the loss. Acceptance refers to adaptation to the changed reality: adjustment to the new situation, resumption of a life that is not engulfed and overwhelmed by the loss and its repercussions, but leaves room for other areas of interest and activity. This readjustment is expressed through large as well as small events, as the individual searches for the right way to integrate the new reality into his or her life.

Although it is convenient to describe the grieving process as this three-stage progression, in fact we are speaking of three different types of response, which weave in and out of one another, at times succeeding one another, at times intertwined. There may be some realms in which the mourner is still in shock, while he may have already readjusted in other realms. In other words, we are not speaking of one-dimensional or one-directional behavior, but a combination of behavioral and emotional responses. The general "direction" is transition from the state of shock and emotional upheaval during the initial period – which may last several months or even a year – to a state of readjustment that is characterized by greater control of one's emotions and actions that reflect internalization of the changed reality and acceptance of the loss.

How children grieve

The process of grieving is more complex for children. Their responses and stages of grieving are closely linked to age and stage of development. The ability of teenage boys and girls to grieve and the stages they go through are similar to those of adults, but the younger the children, the more their behavior differs from that of adults. We will now describe the unique characteristics of the grieving process of children, especially the younger ones.

Shock

In the first stage – the shock stage – some children barely respond to what has happened. Their state of "non-response" is not the same as the state of "shock" we find among adults. These children are either not reacting or reacting in minimalist fashion because they are not yet fully aware of what happened and surely do not fully understand. Especially at the initial period, the first days, when the adults themselves are still confused, overwhelmed, and do not fully grasp what happened, they prefer to keep the kids in the dark. The kids usually receive minimal information and explanation from the adults, who are "pleased" that the child does not understand. The children sense that this is a difficult time for the adults and therefore usually don't ask too many questions. Some children sense that the news is hurtful and prefer not to know. Whatever the reason, the child sometimes seems not to understand and not to care; a response that suits the adults who do not have the needed extra energy to handle the child's response to the loss.

Expression of emotions

When the painful facts do begin to emerge, children sometimes activate "childish" *denial mechanisms*: "It's not true, he's not dead, you're just saying that to scare me." They refuse to hear what is being said to them, countering that the grown-ups "are lying." Occasionally, children ignore the facts that were presented to them, and act as if nothing happened. "I'm waiting up for Dad, and when he comes home I'll go to bed." During the shock stage, adults also have moments in which their contact with reality is distorted and they "forget" what happened. This scenario is even more common for the child for whom imagination is part of his world, and who frequently "decides" that reality is whatever he wants it to be. Children use a much less rigid test of reality. Denial of bitter news is an intuitive mechanism through which the child protects himself. At times, the denial is more of an external act, like an experiment or ritual in which the child imagines carrying out some sort of magic trick. The child hopes or even fantasizes that if he refuses to accept the bitter news, it may simply disappear. Precisely because he understands that the news is so bleak and bitter, he wishes to strike it out of his life. Children use *magical thinking* in an attempt to negotiate with fate, conducting a give and take that goes something like this: If I am a good boy, then maybe he'll come back, maybe the loss will be undone.

Children see and sense the gloomy response of the adults around them, and are *frightened*. They prefer to escape into their own worlds rather than join in with the adults in this horrifying reality.

Like the adults, children can develop *physiological responses* such as stomach aches, diarrhea, vomiting, loss of appetite, insomnia, headaches, breathing difficulties, and skin rashes. These responses are an indication of the children's discomfiture with the loss. They may also be an unconscious way to draw the attention of adults back to themselves. It may be the child's way of "demanding" the parental investment he so greatly needs, especially after the loss when the child senses the threat to his well-being. Adults who are mired in the initial stage of bereavement are very much pre-occupied with themselves and their grieving. The child must sometimes send out strong distress signals to make it clear that he needs their attention and support.

The child's capacity to grieve is qualified by his level of awareness and understanding of what happened. It also depends on the "permission" he is given to openly express his feelings and whether he feels there will be somebody to support him when he does. Children's feelings are similar to those of adults: sadness and pain, helplessness, anger, accusation, and guilt.

A typical response is being *angry and accusatory* toward the parents – the one lost and the remaining one – and other adults the child holds responsible: Why didn't they notice and do something to prevent it? Why didn't the doctor give proper treatment? How could God do such a thing?! This accusatory position expresses the child's disappointment in adults. He trusted in them, believed that they would protect him, and they didn't. He is afraid of what will happen next. What will happen to him?

Many children experience feelings of *guilt*, fearing that they brought on the loss. These thoughts are profoundly upsetting and frightening to them. The younger the child, the less he knows and understands the facts that caused the loss, and the more he is prone to mix in his imaginary world and think that he had the power to cause the loss or at least to prevent it. In general, children are spontaneous, venting their emotions, unless they are made to feel that the expression of these emotions is "forbidden."

At this stage, children are beset by fears and anxiety regarding the future. They sense that the loss has disrupted the order of their world, and they are uncertain who will look after them and how their world will be secured from now on. This is usually a period during which adults are unavailable for soothing conversations that may allay their worries, and the child finds himself very much alone with his fears.

Mourning

When children realize that there is no way to change what happened, when they understand the implications of the loss and feel its effects in their everyday lives – Dad will not be coming home; Mom is no longer around, and won't be reading any more bedtime stories – they enter a period of intense *mourning*. During this period, some children respond like adults, with strong, turbulent responses. They stop eating, cry a great deal, have a hard time falling asleep, and even display signs of depression. Some children refrain from ordinary activities, such as playing with friends.

As the child repeatedly "encounters" the absence of his loved one, the full significance of the loss begins to seep in, and the emotional responses of sadness, longing, and pain flood over him. Adults have a hard time finding the words to express the depth of the pain and the essence of their emotions. Children have an even harder time, because they still lack the words and the concepts, and are inexperienced at expressing emotions and thoughts through words. They express them through everyday behavior and in games. The adult has to know how to "read" these expressions and help the child find the words for them.

As compared to adults, children can shift from one emotional state to another in a very brief period of time. They can quickly swing from a low mood to a cheerful one, shifting from the issue of loss to other matters of interest. The *detachment* they are capable of making does not mean they have forgotten or finished their grieving. They will repeatedly come back to the emotions of grieving at other times. But for children, unlike adults, it is easier to detach from a harsh emotion and move on to another. It is difficult for children to sustain harsh, threatening emotions over an extended period.

Since children have an instinctive need to continue their normal life, it is not rare to see a child express very strong emotions of sadness or anger and then go back to watching television or go outside to play with friends. The younger the child, the more one can expect these sort of *sharp transitions*. Because of these rapid transitions, adults often think that the child "has already forgotten," "doesn't care," or "doesn't even understand what happened." Children do not forget, and do not stop hurting from the loss any easier than adults, but they resume life faster than adults, and do not generally allow these emotions to break up their routine.

Integrating the loss

Children also have to pass through the "third stage," in which they accept the loss and the ensuing readjustment. They must integrate the loss and the new realities of their life – with all that entails – into their lives. Their lives change immensely after the loss. For children, readjustment is not simply a stage. It is a process that the child will continue to work on, again and again, for years. The child grows up and matures, his perspective and understanding of the world changes, and the loss takes on new meanings, wears a different "face." Many changes will occur during the child's lifetime, and each of these will necessitate further readjustment, whereby he will assimilate the meaning and influences of the loss.

For some adults, the transition to the readjustment stage is exacerbated by an inhibition. They are apt to feel that by readjusting successfully they accept the loss. They are not prepared to admit that they accept this reality. Children readjust and resume their lives more spontaneously than do adults, and exhibit less opposition to this stage. Young children do not usually exhibit emotional inhibitions. They do not generally worry about social conventions. They do not consider the resumption of one's routine as having betrayed the memory of their loved one. In those instances that young children exhibit a sense of guilt regarding the resumption of everyday activities, they are apparently reacting to messages transmitted by parents and other adults.

The reticence of children to resume regular life may result from other factors. They may feel ashamed and "different." A child of kindergarten age may think that his father's death means that something is intrinsically wrong with him. He feels and understands that he is different from other children and may be ashamed of it. He is also afraid of the reactions of his kindergarten friends. He remembers how they reacted on previous occasions – how they rejected a child who was different from them and laughed at him. He is afraid of being given the same reception when he returns to kindergarten.

The older the child, the more hesitant he will be to resume life because, like the adults, he becomes aware and sensitive to "what will people say." Older children are sensitive to stigmatizing and confusing social messages. Although they may not want to be different, they sense that society expects them to behave "differently." They are unsure how to behave in their new situation and how to fill their new role. They may also respond to their parents' latent expectations and messages, which hint that they should suspend their ordinary life and devote themselves to grieving, as their parent is doing. These messages make it difficult for children to consciously choose to resume normal life. No matter what their ages, children must confront the difficulty of assimilating their new status into their everyday lives:

- How is a girl supposed to act when the teacher asks the class which mother can bake a cake for the class party?

- Should a boy attend a soccer game shortly after his brother's death?

- Should he tell the new Scout leader he can't go on the outing because he has to visit his father, who now lives in a different city?

- Do they want to join their friends and go to a party?

- When asked on a questionnaire for the name of his father, should the boy mention the fact that his father is dead?

- After the divorce, which home address should a girl give at school – that of her mother or of her father?

After the loss, reality confronts children with many unfamiliar, difficult, and confusing situations. They face difficulties for which they have no familiar response, complex situations with which they are not accustomed. They don't know what is expected of them, and most of all they are very confused regarding their expectations of themselves in the new situation. They may want to be like everyone else, but want special treatment, as well. They don't want to be pitied, but feel vulnerable, and want special consideration. They want to be invited to parties, but are afraid of what everyone will say if they come, and how they themselves will feel. These are emotionally wrenching situations, and the solutions to them are complicated. The child needs an older partner with whom he can share his quandaries and questions, and explore possible solutions. He very much needs a guiding hand to encourage and bolster him.

The child's readjustment is highly influenced by how the parent copes and readjusts. It is difficult for the child to readjust and resume normal life if his parent is not yet at that level of readjustment, and especially if his parent has not given the child his unspoken "permission" to do so. The child may be ready to accept his father's leaving home, and is prepared to accept the new arrangement through which he can continue to see his father. However, if his mother is still beset by anger, accusation, and non-acceptance of the separation, it will be much more difficult for the child to accept and readjust to the new terms of the relationship with his father.

In spite of all the difficulties, children generally readjust faster than adults. They make a rather rapid transition, and soon focus their attentions and energies back to the present and the future.

Dissociation and separation

Despite what is often presented in theoretical literature, "dissociation and separation" from the absent person is not a welcome result of a person's readjustment and resumption of life after the loss. Separation does not mean absolute emotional dissociation from that which is no longer there. The image of the missing person continues to be part of the inner world of the mourner. He thinks about what would have happened if that person were here; he draws energy and strength from his memories and from the spiritual image. It is an *internal object*, a figure that becomes part of the inner self.

It is therefore important to know that children do not disengage, do not separate, and do not end their "connection" with the person who is no longer here, nor are they supposed to do so. The image of the dead or missing parent is very important to the child and will constitute an important source of psychological and spiritual energy in the child's growth process. The child's memories of the parent are vital for the parent's continued presence as an internal object. In the child's perception, the image of the missing person evolves – "growing" apace with his own development and changing needs.

It is important to point out that the younger the child at the time of the loss, the more inclined he will be to postpone some of the "tasks" from the second and third stages of grieving. The child will take up these tasks at a later time, when he is intellectually and mentally ready to carry them out. This means that tasks from the second stage – expression of emotions – and the third stage – readjustment – will gradually be completed in the course of childhood and adulthood.

Dysfunction

Adults who have a hard time making the transition to the third stage, who are still mired in their grieving process, usually exhibit a depressive state that might signal the beginning of pathological grieving, which is characterized by a failure to resume full functioning. When children have a hard time working their way through the acceptance and readjustment stage, it usually stems from different reasons. Depression and non-resumption of normative functioning usually result from the child's difficulty in reestablishing a *behavioral norm* that is appropriate to the new situation; the new reality exposes the child to unfamiliar, embarrassing, complicated situations, and he may lack the tools and resources to handle them. The child may feel he is in a "no way out" situation that leads him into a state of depression and/or dysfunction. If this is the case, it means that the child needs someone with whom he can share his difficulties and from whom he can seek advice and support.

If a child whose father died exhibits reluctance to go to school, it may be because he is unsure how to handle his new status with his peers. When a youngster is reluctant to go to kindergarten, it may be because he feels that he is being excluded by his friends. Older kids may feel they are having a hard time concentrating on their studies, and may be afraid that the teachers will not understand or be considerate of their situation.

Sometimes the child is deterred from certain situations, preferring to stay away from people or situations that remind him of the new, difficult reality. He may avoid the basketball court where he used to play with his father, or may refuse to meet with his aunt because she looks like his late mother.

It is harder for children to find the words to describe and explain their difficulties. Their behavior may seem strange and inappropriate. An adult may not necessarily understand the connotation a certain situation may have for the child. Asking the child to logically explain himself and behave rationally is usually of no help, and he will remain in this state of limbo until he can achieve some emotional relief. The adult's role is to help the child identify his emotions and difficulties, help him define and isolate the problem, and work together to find an appropriate solution. As a rule, one should bear in mind that a child generally wants to return to a normal level of function, and if he does not, there must be a good reason for it.

Children often communicate their distress through *acting out, regressive behavior*, or other *extreme behavior* that reflects their state of turmoil. With young children, it is not rare to find regression to childish or babyish behavior: incessant crying, recurrence of bedwetting, fears of sleeping alone, and a desire to sleep in the parent's bed. The distress of older children is expressed through inappropriate behavior at home or at school, such as failure to do homework, obnoxious or provocative behavior, withdrawal, or an aggressive and impatient temperament. When these forms of behavior occur during the period immediately after the loss, they should be considered normal expressions of grief and should be handled within this context.

As opposed to those children who express their grieving in extreme, regressive ways, there are also the "good kids." They sense that it is a difficult time for the adults, and adjust their behavior so as not to disturb or be a burden. They try to be quiet, they do their homework, they do their best to be "good," they don't make excessive demands and don't seek attention. The older and more mature children may even care for the remaining parent and for their younger siblings, offering concrete help and emotional support. They willingly place themselves at their family's disposal. It is these children we must be especially concerned about, since they forego their own emotional needs in favor of helping the parent. This represents a reversal of roles, and the child is left emotionally neglected. Not only do the adults not look after him and help him through his mourning, but the child ignores himself and his own needs, relinquishing the right to express his own grief and distress.

Children often respond in this way when they sense that the adult world around them is heading toward collapse. They are alarmed by the acute grieving response of adults. They observe the breakdown and dysfunction, and feel they have to marshal their forces in an effort to preserve the remaining parent, and their family, and ensure stability and continued functioning. These children not only conceal their grieving, but also their need for the continued support of their parent. They feel very much alone, yet they may feel guilty for having needs of their own while the parent is going through such a hard time.

Processing of the grief

Processing of the grief is the backbone of the bereavement process. Among children, this is a dynamic process that extends over a period of years. They must continually revisit their loss, processing it over and over again. They will experience their loss in new and evolving contexts, with new understanding. The expressions of emotion that accompany each "revisit" are part of the bereavement process; the lack of an opportunity to process them causes an emotional "abscess" that will complicate and delay important progress.

The child depends on adults, primarily the remaining parent, who must give him the opportunity to undergo this process. Adults must enable the child to repeat the cycle of loss processing and bereavement, and should even facilitate this undertaking. It is up to the adults to provide a personal example and support him in this effort. Since most children quickly resume normal life, adults tend to "exploit" what is for them a comfortable situation, and are generally in no rush to encourage their children to "revisit" their grief or the processing of their encounter with the loss.

A child who lost his father when he was an infant will "encounter" the absence of the father over and over as he grows up, each time understanding and experiencing the absence differently. Each such encounter will be accompanied by expressions of grief over the father's absence. It is important that the child is able to express anger, sadness, or any other feelings he may have. In kindergarten, he will be aware of his father's absence because "other children have a father to go with them on the class trip, and I don't." When he gets older and wants to go to a soccer game, he'll have to find a substitute for the father who should be taking him. There will be many other situations in which he will feel the absence of his father; each situation brings about an encounter that rekindles the sensations of grief, and each encounter requires the child to face his reality and work through it – emotionally as well as cognitively. If the child is not left alone during such times, and can share them, even be encouraged to do so, his processing is more likely to bring to a true "working through" and even relief.

Some grieving responses of adults may have a frightening effect on children. During the initial grieving period, some adults express their emotions in a strong, turbulent manner: fits of incessant crying, screaming out, and in certain cultures pulling out of hair and self-flagellation. It is hard for children to see their parents in this state. Some parents exhibit a diminished ability to carry out everyday duties: mothers stop cooking and baking, fathers stop going to work on a regular basis. When children see their parents in a state of dysfunction or loss of control, they are concerned that the parent will "fall apart," and that the family will follow suit. Frightened, they may choose to behave in a very adult and constrained manner in order to save their parent and family. Older children are sometimes embarrassed to have their friends witness the "different" behavior of their parents and the gloomy atmosphere at home, and therefore prefer that their friends not come to visit them at home.

At the other end of the spectrum are parents who pretend that "life goes on," "business as usual." They refrain from expressing emotions in the child's presence, fearing the child's response. They wish to protect the child, but this emotional reserve and suppression creates a barrier of emotional alienation between them and the child. The child understands that he is not "invited" to express his emotions or share them, especially not when they are strong and turbulent.

Information and explanations

Another difficulty relates to giving information and explanations. It is very common, especially during the initial period, for adults to prevent children from receiving clear, factual, and up-to-date information regarding the essence of the loss, its circumstances and causes. This lack of information makes it more difficult for the child to mourn and cope with the loss. As described above, the absence of information leaves the child to use his own imagination, or relate to "outside" and random information that reaches him, so as to explain to himself what the adults have not explained. These self-derived explanations may cause the child to understand the new reality from a highly distorted and anxiety-ridden perspective. The lack of information and explanations prevents the child from using his cognitive capacities to understand what has happened. Cognitive comprehension aids in the process of bereavement; through it, fears, anxiety, guilt and anger can be mitigated. The lack of information and understanding prevents the child from getting the most out of this opportunity.

Emotional isolation

Many adults who experienced loss during their childhood report that one of the factors that made the loss all the more difficult was the failure of their parents and other adults to facilitate their own participation in the mourning, especially during the initial period. The adults did not truthfully share with them what was happening, avoided expressing their own grief in the child's presence, and denied their participation in situations in which the issue was addressed. Children were sent away from home during the initial mourning period. They were not taken to the hospital to visit the sick and dying, and did not receive even minimal information about what was happening. All of this left them emotionally isolated and confused.

By isolating the child, adults prevent him from understanding or participating in what has a direct bearing on his life. He is robbed of the opportunity to express emotion or receive support at a time when he needs it most. Not only has he lost one parent, but the other parent and other adults are disappointing him too because they fail to stay close and sensitive to his needs. He feels helpless or angry, but dares not express these emotions. The state of hazy ambiguity gives rise to a great deal of anger and "unfinished business." He has been denied an appropriate response to his needs at the time that his needs are most grave. Often he carries these angers and disappointment way into adulthood.

Aside from the damage caused to the child by his emotional isolation during the initial period, these actions can have long-term detrimental implications as well. The child learns that he should not express harsh emotions. He is not provided with any "modeling" of how to express himself and handle emotional problems. He does not learn how to share his world with others, and therefore does not experience the strengthening that one can draw from such collaboration. He "learns" that emotional suppression is the behavior of choice, and like the adults is forced to call on defense mechanisms as a substitute for expressing emotions and directly coping with the problem. As a result troubles or difficulties will be expressed in an indirect, distorted manner.

If a child who feels anger at his parents because they divorced is not given an opportunity to express that anger directly, he will take it out by hitting his brother, fighting with friends, or breaking toys. The child who was not allowed to express anxiety and pain after his mother died will adopt *emotional suppression* or *denial* as a solution to emotionally distressful situations in the future. The pattern of suppression that he learned at the beginning of the grieving will repeat itself in subsequent situations of emotional distress. Since he did not learn how to handle difficult emotions, they will paralyze him in the future. Subconsciously, he will avoid situations that pose any risk of separation and loss, for he has not learned how to cope with the difficult emotions they entail. As an adult, he will have to invest much self-awareness and hard work to correct the patterns he internalized during the initial grieving period.

We should bear in mind that even when adults conceal their emotions from children, children can sense them. Unconsciously, adults communicate their emotions. Children intuitively know which subjects are taboo, and adjust themselves to the messages and distress signals transmitted by adults. Children know much more about their parents than their parents imagine, much more than they want their children to know. What's more, children know how to hide what they know. Children grieve in response and adaptation to the expressed as well as hidden and disguised agenda of their parents.

Chapter 2

Reactions to Loss According to the Child's Developmental Stage

The experience of loss affects the child's emergent personality and behavior. In order to learn and understand these effects, adults must "keep tabs" on him not only during the period directly following the event but also during the years to come, until he reaches adulthood. Depending on the child's age, he will have different developmental abilities and needs and those will influence his response to the loss, and how he copes and understands its meaning. At the same time, the child's developmental needs and the manner in which he copes with the developmental tasks at hand will in turn be affected by the "imprints" of the loss.

Consequently, this complex process is manifested during each stage of childhood:

- early childhood (birth to age 3)
- the Oedipal stage (age 5 to 7)
- latency stage (age 8 to 12)
- adolescence (age 12 to 18)
- early adulthood (age 18 to 30).

In order to give the full picture of these complex processes, each stage will be examined from two perspectives:

1. characteristic responses and displays of loss when it occurs at this age

2.   present-tense repercussions of a past loss that occurred when
      the child was younger.

This chapter will consider events involving the loss of a parent as a result of death, divorce, separation and displacement, mental neglect, or other causes. The loss of a parent is a uniquely powerful event that affects the child's emotional development and personality, including such aspects as formation of the ego, gender identity, and self-image. Yet, one may infer from this discussion to other losses, such as loss of a sibling, a physical handicap, or immigration and resettlement. Any loss that causes a rupture in the flow of the child's life, that takes from the child those people and things that are part of his daily existence, has a traumatic impact. Many of the responses to such losses work along the same lines as after the loss of a parent.

This chapter focuses on the effects of loss on the child and how the child copes within the context of his or her cognitive, emotional, and personality development. In Chapters 3 and 4, we examine the other important factors that influence the child's way of coping: circumstances in which the loss occurred, socio-cultural influences, and the influence of the remaining parent and the family system.

Level of emotional and cognitive development

The most significant factor determining the child's response to loss is his or her stage of development. This is first and foremost a function of the child's age, and is indicated by two main parameters: the emotional-personality state of development and the cognitive-understanding state of development. Personality theories describe the development of emotional capacities in the child and, along with other dimensions, consider the child's ability to deal with separation issues. The ability of the child to cope with separation is one of the primary indicators that help us assess his ability to cope with the loss.

As the child develops emotionally, he is also honing his *cognitive skills*. He understands issues on a more sophisticated and multidimensional level. An experience of loss requires not only emotional adjustment, but also an ability to understand the loss itself and the new reality in the wake of the loss. The more advanced the child's level of cognition and perception, the more cognitive tools will be at his disposal for understanding the meaning and significance of the loss. In those instances where the cause of the loss was death, the child's cognitive development is a critical factor that determines his ability to understand this complex and abstract concept.

Each age, every developmental stage, is characterized by specific cognition and perception skills and by a characteristic state of emotional–personality development. The juxtaposition of the various elements provides a glimpse of the "tools" that are available to the child at that particular developmental stage. Knowing the skills and capabilities of each specific age group, it is possible to gauge which tasks the child is able to handle and which will be deferred to a more advanced developmental stage. As he grows older, the child will periodically repeat the processing of the loss, and relate to the experience in accordance with his evolving capabilities and needs. In addition, each stage of childhood has its specific *developmental tasks* through which the child grows and advances. These tasks put "demands" on the child; the loss will affect how the child carries out these tasks and his ability to handle age-appropriate demands.

The *developmental needs* of each stage re-confront the child, in various contexts, with the experience of the loss and its meaning for him, thereby triggering a reprocessing of the loss. Each developmental stage has its particular sensitive areas and themes, some of which may be exacerbated by the fact that the child has experienced loss. It is important to pay close attention to how the loss affects the child's ability to perform those tasks, particularly those that skirt along the margins of these sensitive issues. All of these encounters may prove difficult for the child, but they also provide an opportunity to cope with the loss at a more advanced level, thereby helping him to work through hitherto unprocessed parts of the mourning.

In conclusion, we should note that the protracted process of coping with the loss is strongly affected by the child's condition and state of development when the loss occurred: what internal resources – personality and cognitive development – did he have at his disposal at that time, and what external resources were available to him:

- Did the loss occur when he was very young?
- Who cared for him during the initial phase?
- Who supported him, and how?

- What was explained to him, and how did those around him help him cope?

- What was he capable of understanding?

- In which areas of the child's life did the loss cause immediate damage?

Based on this initial data, one may assess how the child coped with the event at the start and, based upon this start, one may extrapolate what "burdens" the child will subsequently have to grapple with.

Various studies and reports describe the short-term as well as long-term effects of loss on children. In the short term, following the loss, the studies report that young children respond with behavioral regression, sadness, and even withdrawal. Older children exhibit anxieties, and behavior difficulties in school, with other children, and at home. In extreme cases, especially with teenagers, there are reports of drug and alcohol abuse, and criminal behavior. Children of all ages might exhibit acute somatic symptoms and depression. Studies found that in some instances the long-term effects of loss that occurred at a very young age included emotional pathologies that appear during adolescence or adulthood. Other phenomena observed were difficulties sustaining intimate relationships, delinquent behavior, depression, and suicide attempts.

Some of the most common phenomena associated with an experience of loss in childhood are low self-esteem, low self-image, and difficulties in interpersonal areas. It should be stressed that many of the studies surveyed only those individuals with extreme, atypical responses, who were already in psychotherapy. It is therefore hard to draw any sweeping conclusions regarding normative responses of children to loss. According to various other studies and reports, there are no indications that a child who experienced loss will necessarily have pathological emotional problems or abnormal behavior. Nevertheless, there is ample evidence that this event has oppressive repercussions on the emotional world of the child, and will continue to affect him for years to come.

Understanding the normal and normative effects of loss is important, and even necessary. This will help us determine what help the child requires. Without a doubt, this knowledge can prevent or at least alleviate a sizable portion of the harsh effects, and improve the child's chances of continuing to grow, and realize his full potential.

Separation, attachment, and loss

From the moment a child is born, he experiences separation and learns to cope with it. The baby separates from his mother's warm and sustaining womb; he separates from his mother whenever he is placed in his crib; he separates from the toy he wanted to keep on holding; when the time comes for him to go to nursery school, he will separate from the safety of his home and from the loving, familiar members of his family. The older the child, the more separations there will be. These separations facilitate development of the child's personality, individuality, and independence. They are therefore necessary and healthy separations.

Separations that are part of the normal and normative childhood experience constitute an important part of the developmental tasks the child undergoes as he matures emotionally. Usually, they are controlled, safe separations that end with the return of the object — be it the mother, the father, a bottle, or favorite blanket. Sometimes the beloved object does not return, but the child profits from the "substitute": kindergarten pleasures instead of mommy; freedom in exchange for closeness and safety. Separations during infancy expose the child to new and challenging experiences and worlds. During adolescence, they offer the adolescent freedom, independence, and adult privileges. Positive and controlled experiences of separation initiate the formation of inner strengths, self-containing, and the ability to be alone.

Separation is a central and sensitive theme for the child who has experienced a traumatic loss. It assumes a special meaning for the child, and accompanies the child throughout the various stages of childhood and adulthood. When related to a traumatic loss, separation has very harsh repercussions. The loss leaves the child with a narcissistic–existential wound, with an experience of intense pain, and other complex emotions and difficulties. The loss of a parent is often perceived as abandonment. All in all it leaves a deep emotional imprint. From now on, every separation — even those that are considered developmentally normative — will stir up consciously or unconsciously the memories and fears related to the traumatic loss. The terrible pain that comes with separation will from now on color every situation in which separation of any sort is experienced.

The younger the child when the loss occurs, the deeper the scar left by the separation experience, and the more veiled its imprint. When the child is older at the time of the loss, he or she will have a more detailed emotional memory of what happened. This can help to relieve some of the pain of the experience. A baby that loses his mother cannot make any distinction or understand whom he has lost and who still remains. When the baby senses the loss of the safe, physical care he had enjoyed and the embracing love he needs, he is assaulted by a wave of threat and pain that floods his senses. Conversely, if the child is older when his mother dies, he understands that his father is there, and is caring for him; he understands that someone is looking after him. This understanding does not dull the terrible pain, but it does "make some order out of the world," slightly reducing the sense of all-pervading threat. The more differentiated the initial threat, the less intense and overwhelming will be the imprint of the loss on the child's psyche.

An important part of the bereavement work that the child will have to carry out in the years to come concerns his or her ability to cope with separation. The child will learn to handle his emotions and memories with greater awareness and control, and will be better able to respond to threats of separation. He will learn to differentiate between threatening separations and separations that are part of the growing process.

Capacity to form relationships

The ability of children to form relationships constitutes an important part of the process of emotional crystallization, and is related to their capacity to cope with developmental separations. The capacity to form a relationship in which the child feels loved and secure constitutes a basis on which additional personality and emotional developments are built. A close, intimate relationship in which the child can feel safe will lead to a sense of security, belonging, acceptance, and love. Such relationships are a source of energy for continued development. Children need to experience close and safe relationships because they learn from them; through them they find the courage to open themselves up to other relationships.

The first and most important relationship of the child is with his parents. When this relationship is cut off due to a loss, a "scar" forms, and every subsequent relationship will be affected. The disappointment and pain from the loss of a relationship that was so important and nurturing may deter the child from establishing relationships in the future. If relationships and the conferring of trust are destined to be prematurely cut off, and end up causing so much pain, it may be better not to form relationships at all. This is not a rational, calculated thought, but an instinctive and for the most part unconscious mechanism that protects the child from being hurt again. The imprint of the pain of the experience will require special processing and coping effort as the child gets older, and has to build and expand relationships based on trust, intimacy, and love.

Alongside the tangible sense of loss and the process of accepting and adjusting to it, there is also an emotional–spiritual process in which the child's "relationship" with the missing person, and that person's image, are preserved. As the child gets older, he or she is able to maintain the "relationship" through the *internal representation* of the missing person. Thus, the person who is no longer there continues to be a part of the child's life, by becoming an internal object.

Linking objects help children to maintain their relationship with the image of the missing person, and make it tangible – father's sweater, a picture of mother, a song that father used to sing to the child, mother's perfume. An object that belonged to the missing person or is associated with him or her evokes memories, and even triggers other senses that may make the memories more real. The senses of touching, smelling, sight, and sound can all give the child a sense of closeness to the person they miss. The linking objects alleviate the feeling that the loved one is no longer here, imparting the feeling that something still remains, that the relationship and the memories can be preserved. The linking objects can have a soothing effect. Through them, the child can prolong a nurturing "relationship" with the figure, imparting a sense of security.

Some children search for and find *substitutes* – substitutes for the love they miss, substitutes for what has been taken from them. They may grow attached to animals, or find an alternate parental figure, perhaps in a grandfather or a youth movement counselor. They may take up pursuits that bring meaning to their lives, such as volunteering or helping the needy.

There are also less healthy substitutes, such as overeating, excessive spending, drug and alcohol abuse, and kleptomania. All of these are means of compensating the self for the loss, ways to fill the void, and especially the lack of love.

Although we have emphasized that separation is an essential element in the process of mourning, the intent is not separation that requires disso-ciation from the image of the absent person. In contradistinction to previous views on this subject, it is now clear that this sort of complete detachment is undesirable. The image, and the child's internal relationship with it, will continue to be part of the life of the child, even upon reaching adulthood. The image is part of the child's memories, and an inseparable part of the child's inner entity. There is no separation, nor need there be any separation from the image of a parent who is no longer there. This image can and should continue to nurture the growing child, representing a source of support and security, and a figure for identification that con-tributes to the development of the identity of the child. The use of the term "separation" is meant to emphasize that there should be a boundary between that which belongs to memories and inner existence and that which belongs to the here and now. The function of separation is to make it clear that life goes on, even in the absence of a loved one.

As the child gets older, he will have to "separate" from the image of the parent, in the developmental sense. The child will have to reinforce his individuality, breaking free and declaring his emotional and functional independence. As they grow older, all children separate from their parents, both symbolically and substantively. The child whose parent is not present in the substantive sense can and should carry out the tasks of separation at the emotional level. Only if the figure "exists" internally will the child and, especially later, the adolescent take his or her distance and achieve inde-pendence. The onset of developmental independence does not mean the end of the child's relationship with the figure. It represents only a shift in the "space" and "location" it occupies in the child's mental life.

Changes

When loss occurs, it is often accompanied by other changes in the child's life into which the feelings of separation and loss are intertwined. There are liable to be substantive changes: decline in the economic status of the family; moving to a different home; the child's mother having to go to work; or even moving in with a foster family. Every such change, especially if it happens soon after the loss, is experienced as an additional threat, another blow, one more loss. The child has not yet learned to cope with the previous trauma, has not yet regrouped and readjusted, and already has to confront another difficult experience. The change may seem "merely" technical to adults, who may be insensitive to the emotional implications of the change on the child. Adults may be too busy in their daily lives or making technical arrangements related to the change, and do not always pay enough attention to the child's immense need for reinforcement and emotional hand-holding in the wake of the new trauma he or she is experiencing.

Other changes may take place at the symbolic and emotional levels. The remaining parent is not functioning as he did before the loss, is paying less attention to the child and investing less energy in him, especially emotionally. The child often loses the special relationship he used to have with the parent. The family atmosphere has been altered, and the home is not as happy as it once was. The sense of security is impaired. There is a feeling that the status of the family has been compromised, that the intimacy and boundaries of family life are in danger. The parent may start to date and the threat of a "new replacement mother/father" is on the horizon. All these are significant losses, and exacerbate the sense of overall loss experienced by the child, who feels as if the entire world is slipping through his or her hands, that nothing is safe, that everything is labile. The child feels vulnerable and exposed.

There are also positive changes in the aftermath of a loss that can lead to subsequent rehabilitation. These changes symbolize the hope for a better and safer tomorrow, a new restorative opportunity, renewed happiness, and the child's resumption of normal life. A new spouse whom the child likes may join the family. The family may move to a nicer home. Yet even when the change is positive, the child's response may be tempered by sadness, tension, or fear because any change, even the most positive, still bears elements of separation from the previous situation. For a child who has experienced traumatic loss, change dredges up painful memories, recalling fears of the unfamiliar and the unsafe.

As life continues, life events might present other changes, some of which may bear the painful taste of separation and loss: the death of a grandparent; illness of the remaining parent; enlistment of a brother in the army. All of these are normal and even predictable events, but for a child who has experienced traumatic loss they generate oppressive feelings. When the loss-related emotions have not been processed or the child is still young and not yet able to process them, these changes are liable to be experienced as traumas, even if they are essentially normative life events.

Sometimes all it takes to evoke an extreme reaction from the child is a minor, marginal event. In some cases, the current event is the straw that breaks the camel's back, as the child is simply unable to bear any more loss. This sort of response reveals a great deal about the painful and unresolved memories of the traumatic loss. Still, since the child is now older, he has a more thorough understanding and is better able to express himself. Therefore, it is hoped, such an event can serve as a chance to handle the threat or loss with more mature "tools." In spite of the painful reaction, any event that raises associations of separation and loss can provide an opportunity for a *corrective experience*, in which issues left untreated in the past can be addressed.

Responses to loss by age group

Any discussion of the effects of loss on children becomes more focused when we localize it to the specific age of the child. The responses of children in each of the age groups described below refer to two points along the chronological scale:

1. We describe the responses that may be expected for each age group immediately after the loss occurs.

2. We assess the long-term effects and repercussions of the loss as the child passes through subsequent age groups and developmental crossroads.

This differentiation between the immediate reactions and subsequent reactions is important.

As described in the previous chapter, children also experience initial grieving responses that are at times expressed through eccentric and non-normative behavior, which should be considered legitimate and normative immediately after the loss. We will describe how the child's age and developmental stage may affect his or her response during the initial period following the loss.

The long-term effects of the loss, as already noted, are affected by the cognitive and emotional state of development the child reaches at each stage of his growth. We will be better able to understand the long-term effects of the loss after having outlined the main developmental tasks for each age group, and after having pinpointed the specific places of intersection between the effects of loss and the tasks of each age. We will try to assess how the loss may leave its imprint on the execution of these tasks.

Early childhood (birth to 3 years)

During the first years of his life the child develops the basic physical and mental faculties required for existence as an individual. The baby receives the basic existential needs from his parents – food and drink, physical protection, love and warmth – all of which facilitate his development. Satisfaction of these needs allows the child to develop a sense of security and trust in his caregivers.

The death or other loss of a parent and the subsequent deterioration in the quality of parental care provided by the remaining parent while he or she are still suffering from the loss are liable to lead to a situation in which the child's basic needs are not fully met, and he suffers from a decline in the quality of care he receives. The disappearance of the person who had cared for him will harm the baby's sense of basic security and trust in his caregivers, thereby wounding the basic infrastructure for the child's mental and physical development.

The response of the baby is liable to be expressed first and foremost through physical symptoms – eating and sleeping problems, and a decline in general health. It may also be reflected in the baby's inability to respond positively to soothing and beneficial contact with his caregivers. He will not calm down even when attended to; he will lack vitality and happiness when in physical contact with his caregivers. Subsequently, there is the chance of a slowdown or even regression of the child's development: primarily motor development and motor independence, including crawling, walking, talking, and feeding himself. The baby may exhibit signs of depression by smiling less, withdrawing into himself, failing to react to physical stimuli, crying more often, and exhibiting restlessness. In extreme cases, the child's physiognomic development may be arrested.

The negative effects of the loss of the parent can be tempered by the presence of an unwavering parental figure that will continue to care for the child. It is critical that this be a stable presence in the child's life who provides not only physical care but also warmth, love, and attention. The baby's confidence that the parent will always be there for him gives him a sense of *security* and allows the development of *trust*, which are prerequisites for the development of a sound *ego* and *self*, and the ability to separate from the parent. During his first years of life, *object consistency* develops, and the parent becomes an *internalized object*. This is a crucial part of the child's developing personality. The child will continue to draw the strength for his continued personality development from this foundation.

When the baby loses a parent, these processes are adversely affected. The loss of a parent is a devastating experience that shatters the primary process by which the child learns to feel secure in its relationships and confident that separation can be safe. It interrupts the process by which the parent's image is internalized as part of the baby's. This experience will bring about insecurity, fear, emptiness, and detachment.

There are diverse professional opinions regarding the question of how much a baby understands the loss in its common connotation. There is no doubt that a baby is incapable of fully understanding it. Babies do not yet have language – words through which feelings can be conceptualized – and their experience is still limited to the existential senses. At this age, the baby is wholly occupied by its own existence, and all of its experiences are processed through this limited perspective. The baby will undoubtedly sense and experience the loss, since the satisfaction of his needs and his sense of existential security have been damaged. He perceives these frightening changes as threats to his very existence. The baby does not possess the cognitive tools available to adults which would enable him to understand what happened; nor has he developed the mental faculties to help him cope with the experience at the emotional level. Yet, clearly, the loss of a parent leaves the baby in a highly vulnerable emotional state.

John Bowlby was one of the first theoreticians to study the responses of babies to separation from their mothers, from which he developed the theory of attachment. He noticed that babies respond to the loss of the mother in three grieving "stages":

- protest – in which the child expresses his anger and sorrow

- despair – in which the child "understands" and responds to the fact that she will not return, despite its "protests" and cries of pain

- detachment – in which the child disengages from contact with those around him.

The baby's basic trust in the protective relationship has been impaired; his withdrawal and detachment "protect" him from future disappointments, and in so doing he also expresses his response to being abandoned.

The terms with which Bowlby describes the baby's emotional response leave no room for doubt as to the serious impact made by the loss of a parent on the baby, or the long-term mental health implications of loss at such a young age. Clearly, the fact that a child at this age has lost a parent must not be disregarded, and it should never be assumed that the baby is "too little to understand." On the contrary, the caregivers must pay a great deal of attention to the child's emotional state, and make an optimal effort to meet his needs.

Since young children lack the vocabulary to express their emotions, especially anxiety, sorrow, and anger, they show their feelings in other ways. Their behavior serves as the outlet of these unverbalized emotions. They may burst into tears over minor things, cling to the remaining parent, be unwilling to be left alone, and often regress to bedwetting or thumb sucking. These responses may occur not only during the period immediately following the loss but afterward as well. The trauma will leave a deep imprint on the child, and it may take a long time before the child is able to regain a sense of equanimity and security.

It should be emphasized that the remaining parent who has recently lost his or her spouse is often unavailable emotionally to invest the fullest efforts in the baby, which is in dire need of parental contact and interaction. The parent under the influence of the fresh loss has probably lost his sense of security and will therefore have a hard time giving the child the sense that "life is safe." All these circumstances will only exacerbate further the child's sense of defenselessness, insecurity, and abandonment. While an older child is capable of understanding that the remaining parent is there, even if he or she is not physically accessible and caring, a baby is unable to comprehend this. If the parent does not spend time with the baby, care for him or bestow love, warmth, and security, the baby experiences this as yet another loss.

Reconstruction and completion of the child's understanding and memory

Since at the time of the loss the baby lacked the cognitive ability to understand what happened, it is vitally important that as part of his future upbringing the child be provided information and explanations about the loss. As the child develops emotionally and cognitively, he should be continually exposed to facts and details about the circumstances of the loss. Each time the subject is raised, an added layer of description and explanation should be provided, corresponding with the child's evolving capacity to understand and his or her needs. There is absolutely no reason to assume that the child "already knows," "has already figured it out for himself," "has already gotten used to it," or is "not perturbed by" or "not interested" in the subject.

Another important task is reconstruction and completion of the child's memory of the absent figure. One must bear in mind that the baby's memory of the missing person is dim at best, and at times does not even consciously exist. Others must therefore reconstruct the memory and image of the absent person, providing the child with details, telling him or her about the looks, character, and behavior of the person. The image should be further illustrated and concretized with the help of photographs and objects that belonged to the person. This is critically important since by rounding out the details about the figure the child can continue to build its inner representation. This is vital in terms of permitting the child to move ahead in his or her own development of the self. A full, accurate image constitutes a source for identification from which the child needs to draw strength. Only from a full clear image will he be able to separate when the time comes to realize his independent self.

It should be stressed how undesirable it is to portray an ideal, perfect image for the child. If the figure is portrayed as flawless and perfect, this will only make things harder on the child. If father was perfect, the child has no chance of being like him, and will feel worthless and mediocre. It is hard to reject undesired traits from the image of a perfect parent; it is impossible to argue with perfection. The image of a parent must be human, full of different "colors," traits, and stories: how he was as a child, as a teenager, as a husband, and as a parent.

Formation of a stable intact ego and later that of the "self" is exceedingly more difficult for those who lost a parent during their infancy, since they sustained the damage during the formative stage of object constancy. Under such circumstances it may be assumed that the child was adversely affected to some extent, in terms of the formation of his internal object. This internal object is the source of inner strengths that will nurture and reinforce the ego, enabling it to cope and withstand difficulties. It is probable that the internal resources of a child who lost a parent at a very young age are weaker. A child with weakened inner strengths will require a great deal of reinforcement, nurturing, and containing for many years.

Ego strength

Ego strength is the foundation with which the child sets out to realize other developmental tasks. Any damage incurred at this level will obviously impair the development process. At adolescence, ego strength will be put to the test, and will have to contend with the demanding tasks of that age. This is one of the periods in which ego strength is subjected to much stress, because the adolescent must now redefine his self. At adolescence, children undergo a process of readjustment of their inner identity, in order to build their adult individuality and establish their own niche in the world. The adolescent with inadequate internal ego strengths will have a harder time executing these tasks, and will require emotional support and external reinforcement to brace him during the process. At the same time, these tasks present an opportunity to reinforce, fix, or fill the gaps left from childhood. These "corrections" will enable the adolescent to strengthen his ego and construct a balanced, adult personality.

Separation–Individuation

When a baby undergoes loss, it complicates the separation–individuation process that takes place during this stage of development. Although "nearing–distancing" experiences frighten all babies, they also provide good, enriching experiences through which babies begin to exert their individuality and their newly acquired abilities. However, the loss of a parent constitutes a "distancing" experience on an altogether different scale – one of severe *existential pain*. In subsequent experiences in which the baby and later on the growing child is required to undergo a process of separation and distancing, the aroused "memory" of the original trauma will interfere, making it difficult to perform the task. Every task of developmental separation and distancing will have to contend with the harsh, painful memories of separation and loss. *Defense mechanisms* will be called into play, and these will often be the same defense mechanisms that were first invoked by the child at the time of the loss.

At adolescence, there is a repeated process of separation–individuation, in which the adolescent is required to carry out the task once more, and repeat the experience of separation and distancing. The painful trauma of separation may once again interfere with the child's full execution of the separation tasks. Since the task of separation during early childhood was carried out in the "shadow" of existential pain of loss, it was not fully realized, or conceived as a constructive, beneficial process. The fear is that the same shadow will again get in the way of proper completion of the task, as required during adolescence. At the same time, adolescence provides a new opportunity to correct the experience and strengthen the separation–individuation capabilities. By this time, the child has, it is hoped, developed insightful, well-developed ego strengths, which can be a powerful resource for the successful execution of the restorative separation–individuation process.

The experience of loss at a young age "scars" the child's sense of trust in a relationship, damaging his belief in safe and protective relationships. This in turn damages his ability to rely on and trust future relationship as a source of love, strength, and security. If relationships and trust end in pain of separation and loss – as happened to him as a baby – he may "conclude" that it is best to avoid such closeness altogether. The painful potential of disconnection and loss is liable to make relationships and trust seem like a daunting threat instead of a source of tranquility and security.

One of the tasks of adolescents is to learn to build intimate relationships with members of the other sex. The painful experiences of the distant past are liable to present an obstacle, preventing the young man or woman from entering into relationships, or motivating them to "ruin" them and end the relationships prematurely, so as to avoid the experience of painful loss and separation in situations they cannot control. The "scars" of the early childhood pain – associated with an emotional relationship of dependence that led to painful disconnection and disappointment – will nurture ambivalent attitudes toward close, intimate relationships and bonds of trust with others. Fear of abandonment, disappointment, and additional loss will dictate the actions of those who experienced these same sensations as primary early childhood experiences.

Several studies have identified children who have experienced loss in their early childhood as being at high risk of suffering personality disorders related to basic ego function. However, it should be made clear that most of the studies identified this risk when the remaining parent failed to fulfill his or her parental duties toward the baby, did not provide the child with a sense of security, and did not continue to invest the requisite parental effort in the child. It is clear that loss at a very young age may have significant effects on the continued development of the child. The question is, which other factors will alleviate or hinder the baby's and later the child's ability to heal the wounds.

The Oedipal stage (age 5 to 7)

When loss occurs to a child in the 5 to 7 age group, the child is at a much more mature stage in terms of his personality, and has more developed cognitive skills. He thinks in a concrete fashion, and this is his primary way of understanding the nature of the world around him. He has an active imagination, and the definitive boundaries of reality are not yet set in stone, and do not "hinder" him. He is very preoccupied with himself, and his orientation toward life and his immediate environment is distinctly egocentric.

At this age, the child understands the concept of "no more," understands that things that are not seen can exist and may come back, and even understands the concrete aspects of death. He is interested in what happens to the body after it is buried, and knows that people die for all sorts of reasons. However, the abstract meaning of death is still unclear, and difficult to grasp. Death is conceived in terms like those of living, somewhat similar to sleeping and dreaming. It is yet another phenomenon that is related to the circle of life – it is something that happens. At this age, children still have a difficult time understanding and accepting the concept of irreversibility, since their imagination tends to compensate for the "limiting aspects" of death. On the other hand, the child is capable of understanding the concrete part of the experience he has undergone. He understands that the dead person no longer exists in the factual sense. He can understand the reality of what it means when a parent leaves home for good.

Imagination

This is an age at which children make much use of their imaginations, and there is still some blurring between reality and fantasy. Imagination helps the child to cope with reality, smoothing his or her emotional adjustment to unpleasant situations. The child can call upon omnipotent "charms" and scenarios that surpass the limitations of reality, and help him. He may imagine that the dead person is about to come back, appearing in a variety of forms. He may concoct a futuristic "screenplay" – and believe in it – in which his divorced parents once again live together, take vacations together, and everyone is happy again.

Death can be personified and given tangible form, wearing the concrete appearance of a living creature – human, animal, or another figure from the child's fantasy. The child might believe that in this form he or the adults can fight with that figure and win the battle. Nevertheless, imagination can also serve as fertile ground for terrifying and threatening thoughts, such as the feeling that he, the child, caused the death because of something he did or thought. He might imagine that the dead person can see and hear him from "out of the wall" or out of all sorts of other unusual places. The child is liable to feel persecuted and defenseless.

When the facts of the loss are explained and elucidated to a child of this age group in a clear, concrete manner, he or she is capable of understanding them. This comprehension reduces the need to resort to fantasy. Conversely, when explanations are provided in an evasive and non-factual way, and when abstract, conceptual evasive terms are used to describe what happened, the child is left to interpret them on his own and understand them for himself. Somewhere within the fluctuating boundaries between the child's worlds of reality and fantasy he will find a place to look for the solutions he needs. Yet it is also a place where his anxieties and fears can develop.

Instead of telling the child that his father is dead and making sure he understands what that entails, if the child is told that "Father went for a long trip" he is liable to do what he can to help father return from the trip, or even try to join him on the trip. If a dead mother is described as "sleeping," the child is liable to be afraid of going to sleep, lest he too be unable to wake up. When explanations are borrowed from the world of faith and religion, they must be "concretized." An explanation such as "God loved mother so He took her" leaves open the possibility that if God loves him – the child – he might decide to take him too. The child may want God to love him as well, so that he too should be taken to heaven, where he will meet his mother.

The young child does not fully understand the realistic boundaries of his powers. The sense of omnipotence that relies on the imagination is liable to make him believe he caused his mother's death, maybe because he got angry at her and said he wanted her to die. He feels tremendous guilt, and conceals this "truth" which only he "knows." It is therefore important to ascertain whether the child understands what happened, to make sure the causality of the loss is clear to him. It is extremely important that the child should fully understand that his thoughts or actions played no part in causing the loss.

Children of this age like to express themselves through games. It is therefore possible and desirable to communicate with them through games, using them as a medium for exploring the child's inner world and sending messages to the child. Through games, adults can help children to express their fear and pain about the loss.

Verbal expression

By this age children have a relatively enriched vocabulary. They are capable of verbally expressing themselves, and do so with greater freedom and spontaneity than adults. Children will express their grief through words so long as adults help them to do so. The child is inquisitive, wants to understand, and will ask many questions. It is important that the child have someone to talk to, someone who enables him freely to express himself. There is nothing wrong with expressing thoughts through imagery and imagination. On the contrary, it is a productive way of venting fears and emotions. This is how children of this age express their thoughts and feelings. Nevertheless, it is important to make sure that the child is aware of the boundaries between his thoughts and imaginings and reality.

If the loss of the parent occurred when the child was much younger, upon reaching this age he will be ready to express himself verbally, and transform the feelings that were until now only experienced, but not voiced, into words and sentences. This is the time to once again discuss what happened, clarifying and explaining the loss, giving the child an opportunity to express whatever questions, thoughts, or emotions he or she has. The child is curious, and wants to understand the fundamental nature of the world. He needs to adapt this newfound understanding of the loss that occurred in the past to his present life. At this stage, it is vitally important for adults to intervene in the process by which the child comprehends and processes the loss, because the child's newly acquired ability to understand allows adults to explain that which was previously impossible to explain. This intervention prevents the child from having to fabricate explanations.

Development of autonomy

One developmental task that is characteristic of this age group is the development of autonomy. The child wants to do things by himself, and tests his ability to be self-supporting, but he is still afraid to be alone, and needs an adult to provide a place of support, a safe haven. When the child loses a parent at this age, he is extremely anxious about his security and even his existence. He fears that no one can protect him. This adversely affects the process of separation and the development of autonomy that begins at this age, and a cessation or even regression of these processes may be expected. The child fears the loss of the remaining parent, which in turn prevents him from pulling away, being bold and daring, staking out his new autonomy. He will become more dependent on adults as a means of guaranteeing that he will never be left alone again, making sure he "keeps" them. It is therefore important to help the child regain a sense of existential security. The remaining parent and other adults should offer the child their encouragement and reinforcement, and "promise" to stay and continue to watch over him. They must encourage him to embark on his little autonomy "excursions," all the while guaranteeing that he will always have a place to return to.

Development of sexual identity

One of the primary developmental tasks at this age, which is also known as the *Oedipal period*, is the development of *sexual identity*. Evolution of the child's sexual identity takes place through the Oedipal conflict; gender functions are learned concurrently. Development takes place along two parallel axes: the first involves study and imitation of the gender roles from the parent who is the same sex as the child – the son learns from his father, the daughter from her mother; the second revolves along the lines of the *Oedipal triangle* – the son's wooing of his mother, the daughter's wooing of her father, and the competition with the same-sex parent. The juxtaposition of these two processes allows the child to develop his or her sexual identity and learn the gender functions, simultaneously letting go of the Oedipal fantasy.

Following the loss, one of the parents is no longer there to fulfill his or her part, thereby creating a void that adversely affects the process. A child who loses its same-sex parent – the boy his father, the girl her mother – loses his or her object for imitation and study, as well as his or her competitor. On the face of it, the Oedipal fantasy has been realized, and the remaining parent, of the other sex, is now "available" as the child's mate. The son can now be his mother's suitor, the daughter can be her father's princess. This constitutes victory in the Oedipal conflict, but it is a pyrrhic victory, because the process of the conflict was not completed and resolved. At least for the time being, the third side of the Oedipal triangle is missing. This harms the process and leaves unresolved issues, which will have to be resolved at a later stage.

If the loss occurred at a younger age and the child has now reached the Oedipal phase, evolution of the child's sexual identity is more complicated if the "third side" of its family triangle is still missing. The child's subject for imitation, which also serves as his object of competition, is missing. The lack of competition causes a blurring of reality and fantasy, and seemingly creates the opportunity for intimate union of child and parent. In fact, it is the tangibility of this possibility that threatens the child. Subconsciously, the child is afraid of being "swallowed up" by this intimacy, losing his ability to maintain distance and preserve individuality.

The child often seeks an alternative figure to fill the void. The daughter seeks a "suitor" among the men in the family, such as uncles or cousins, and flirts with her mother's suitors and friends. The son seeks a maternal figure among his aunts and family friends, and tries to "adopt" his father's girlfriends as mothers. The son adopts masculine figures for identification and contact; the daughter will seek the mother she misses among her sisters.

The Oedipal fantasy stems from the developmental needs of the child, but at times it also fills the needs of the remaining parent, who is in need of support and a mate. In such cases things get even more complicated. Discussion of this subject will be expanded in subsequent chapters, where we will describe the dangers when the parent does not place clear boundaries and restrictions on the "mating" relationships between parent and child, or when the parent even encourages this sort of relationship. This condition will adversely affect the normal development of the child's sexual identity. The child is lured into accepting inappropriate gender roles, and lives out his or her fantasy of "mating" with the parent. These experiences interfere with the development of independent age-appropriate sexual identity.

If the loss of the parent occurred when the child was younger, this is an appropriate time to fill in the child's "picture" of the image of the missing parent. The parent's gender traits should be emphasized. A daughter can be told what her mother looked like and what she liked to wear; a son can be told what sports his father engaged in and what he did in the army. The children are attentive to "stories," and the more detailed, the better. They are in need of this information, which they learn, identify with, emulate, and internalize.

We reiterate how important it is that the figure of the missing parent be described truthfully and not one-dimensionally. The child will only be able to identify with a realistic image. A "perfect" image cannot be imitated, for the child will always feel inferior to it. A mother who was "the most beautiful" woman and "the best" cook constitutes an image to which a daughter cannot compare herself. A father who was the "biggest hero" and the "best soccer player in the neighborhood" constitutes a challenge with which the son might have a hard time competing. Although children at this age want their heroes to be "the best," in the long run a perfect image will present an intimidating challenge that is too hard to emulate or identify with.

The reverse situation, in which the image of the missing parent is "blackened," is equally dangerous. In instances where the remaining parent is angry and still has "unfinished business" with the missing parent, such as in cases of divorce and abandonment, that parent's image can at times be described in altogether negative terms. The child is unable to identify with an image of this sort, and is thereby denied a critical resource in the formation of his or her own identity. In the same way that the "idealized" parent surely had some flaws and weaknesses, the "negative" parent certainly had some positive traits with which the child can identify, and would perhaps want to emulate.

The latency period (age 7 to 11)

At this age, children are occupied by a desire to understand how the world works, especially the technical aspects. When the subject is death and loss, they want to understand what happened and how it happened. When the loss occurs at this age, children will immerse themselves in the details, for the most part technical. The child is cognitively ready to understand what happened. He or she is in need of information and explanations from adults, and should be allowed to inquire and investigate. The child can cognitively process the information in a concrete form, and by representing the facts in as descriptive and detailed a manner as possible, the child is able to understand situations such as disease, accidents, or even complex human relations issues, such as pertain to divorce. At this age, children are able to comprehend complex concepts such as irreversibility and finality, but only if they are offered adequate descriptions and concrete explanations that drive home the point. Comprehension of these facts constitutes the first requisite layer of understanding on which the process of emotional readjustment can be built.

Emotionally speaking, this is a relatively "dormant" age. Children are more occupied by concrete deeds than abstract thoughts or emotions. They are busy with their expanding social lives, friends, hobbies, extracurricular activities, and studies, which are on a more advanced level. They are busy with coed relationships on a group level, setting the ground for the one-on-one boy–girl issues that will be addressed during adolescence.

Loss floods the child with "adult" emotions: sadness, anger, guilt, and longing. Typically, the child will swing sharply between the painful, chaotic emotional world that results from the loss, and his "ordinary" world where he resumes his activities and pursuits. Adults will have to "invite" the child to express and share his or her emotions. If left to their own devices, children will almost certainly prefer to remain in their routine world. At this age, children still have a limited ability to verbalize their emotions. They have not yet mustered insight and abstract understanding through which emotions and thoughts can be worked. They are confused and bewildered by the powerful emotional currents flowing within them. Children require help and "modeling," which facilitates learning by personal example, showing them how to express themselves and handle their emotions.

When the loss occurred when the child was younger and he reaches this age, we can assume that he or she has reached the level of autonomy that is typical of this age. The child can be expected to conduct his life in an independent fashion, busying himself with the normal pursuits of this age – friends, hobbies, sports – most of which take place outside the home. If this is not the case and we find the boy or girl still very attached to the parent – preferring to stay home, avoiding outside activities, socially very shy – then we may suspect that themes which pertain to the loss and its aftermath have not yet been resolved. These patterns of behavior might point at anxieties from separation, unresolved separateness from the parent, and other issues that were touched by the loss and hindered normative developmental achievements. These signs should alert the parent and other adults who are involved in the child's growth. This is a very good time to "tie up" these loose ends and help the child work through the loss experience and other issues affected by it.

Emotionally these are low intensity times for the child. The casual observer might even be tempted into thinking that the child has forgotten the loss. Yet this is by no means the case, and there can be no doubt that deep down inside the child is preoccupied by the loss. However, this is an age at which the developmental tasks are "insensitive" to the implications or repercussions of loss. Loss-related developmental issues are not particularly sensitive at this age and therefore the child usually seems calm and remote from the subject.

This is a good time to deal with some of the as yet untreated experiences of the loss. Now is the time to ascertain whether the child knows and understands all of the facts pertaining to the loss, including its causes and circumstances. The child is cognitively ready to understand concepts and details that were previously difficult to understand. Due to the inquisitiveness that is characteristic of this age group, the child is interested in hearing as many details as possible, and will try to understand them. This is the time to encourage the child to ask questions, and through them become acquainted with his or her inner world and how the loss is perceived. Since this is a relatively calm period in terms of emotions, he or she will be able to "listen" emotionally as well, and adjust his or her perspective on what happened. By encouraging the child to come to terms with this subject, adults will help the child undergo another round of processing, matching the child's more developed emotional and cognitive faculties.

Since this age makes relatively low emotional demands on the child – especially as compared to adolescence – it should be "used" for the child's advancement in these important issues. Adolescence is at his "doorstep," and as we shall be demonstrating in the next chapter, it will place high demands on the child, particularly because of issues that are intertwined with the loss. He will need all the mental strength he can muster. Latency years are a good opportunity to make up and prepare for the forthcoming difficult adolescence period.

Adolescence (age 12 to 18)

By the time they reach adolescence, children have a relatively well-formed personality nucleus and ego strength. Cognitively, they are more or less at an adult level of comprehension. But emotionally, this is a time of turmoil with upheavals deriving from biological–hormonal changes as well as from the developmental, mental, and social tasks. Loss, which in itself is a very emotionally loaded experience, imposes added hardship during this already turbulent period. Once again, we examine two different situations:

- when loss occurs during this age period
- when loss occurred in the distant past, in an earlier stage of childhood.

We describe how the loss and its repercussions affect the way the adolescent copes with his age tasks, and, conversely, how the attributes of this age may affect loss-related tasks.

When the loss occurs during adolescence, the young person's cognitive maturity enables him or her to fully understand what happened. Conversely, the adolescents' chaotic emotional world will shape their view of the new reality and the loss itself. At this age, young people are preoccupied by attempts to understand the meaning of the world at philosophical, spiritual, moral, and social levels. A resoundingly harsh event such as loss causes the adolescent to invest a great deal of energy into understanding what happened and why it happened, and how the event will influence his or her outlook on life.

Adolescents may pose their questions with a generalized, philosophical diffidence, but the questions emanate from a very personal contemplation that is nurtured by their pain and bewilderment:

- What is the meaning of life?
- Is life worth living if such painful events are entailed?
- How can one accept what happened, and "consent" to it?
- Where is the justice in a world in which terrible things happen?

Questions about the essence of life take on penetrating personal connotations, and profoundly influence the mental attitude of the adolescent.

To other adolescents, who have not been touched by loss, these momentous issues are hypothetical subjects and even as such they preoccupy them a great deal. However, here we are speaking of young men and women for whom these issues have become part of their personal reality. These are issues with which even adults have a hard time coping. Indeed, is life worth living? And for what? Why is there suffering? The questions with which adolescents must grapple may lead them to reach harsh, even pessimistic conclusions.

Moral and ethical opinions develop at this age. The experience of loss adds a sharp, jagged angle to these issues:

- Who is to blame?
- Who should bear the responsibility for what happened?
- And what should the punishment be?

At this age the world is seen in stark, black-and-white terms. Everything is classified into good or bad, correct and just, or unfair and unethical. To the adolescent, the loss is framed in a "blackened" light; it is wrong that people have to die prematurely, it is unjust that innocent people are made to suffer.

The mechanism known as *intellectualization* develops significantly at this age. Adolescents begin to view the world through intellectual "glasses," judging it by newly acquired philosophical and ethical criteria. The world is observed from a distance, from without. Adolescents are extremely judgmental, comparing what does exist with what should exist. Intellectualization serves, inter alia, as a *defense mechanism* to sublimate and regulate the emotional outpouring and strong sexual impulses that are typical of this age. It enables the young person to distance himself from the powerful emotions flooding him. Intellectualization may deflect full emotional coping with the loss; providing an escape from emotional experience to intellectual statement. Indeed, adolescents who have been affected by loss often resort to this means of escape, distancing themselves from their feelings through the mechanism of intellectualization.

During adolescence, the youngster develops his *social consciousness* and his expectations about the mutual relationship between the individual and society. The loss poses questions regarding his or her relationship with other people, people who have not been hurt and are not suffering. At times, the adolescent feels different and even estranged from the others. He may want others to be more sensitive to his needs, but does not want to be pitied or made to feel different. Sometimes even his closest friends, lacking sufficient tact and sensitivity, disappoint him.

Some adolescents seem not to relate to their loss at all. It is as if they have moved on to their normal agenda, and are once again consumed by the minutiae of everyday life – what to wear, who to get together with that night. Nevertheless, this behavior should never be misconstrued. The adolescent usually operates on two parallel levels: the overt level, in which he or she pursues a normal lifestyle, complete with all the characteristic "vanities" of adolescence; the hidden level, where the adolescent is preoccupied by intensely bleak thoughts and feelings that result from the loss. There is no doubt that deep down inside the adolescent is consumed with thoughts about the world that has just been shattered, trying to understand and conceive how to go on living with what happened.

Adolescents do not want to seem weak because it is important for them to be perceived as mature enough to take care of themselves. They may think that any exhibition of spiritual and emotional confusion will be seen as weakness; that the need for emotional support will be viewed as a regression to childish behavior. Given this choice, they may prefer to conceal this inner world, and pretend that they do not need to lean on anyone. Adults who judge these young people by their external behavior may reach the conclusion that "they only care about what is important to them." This erroneous conclusion causes adults to get angry with the adolescent and put pressure on him or her to participate in the mourning practices, especially during the initial grieving period. This pressure does not usually lead to the desired change, and only adds another layer of misunderstanding, anger, isolation, and alienation to an already complicated relationship. It is very hard to co-opt the adolescent into the family's grieving process. Adolescents have a different way of expressing their grief than do adults. As with other important issues, they require more free rein in order to express themselves in the manner, style, and time period that suits them. The mourning style of adults may be disagreeable to them, in the same way that anything adults do may be derisively rejected.

The grieving style of adults is at times excessive and externalized, and may be frightening to the adolescent, leaving him bewildered. The adolescent has a need to see his "enemy," the adult, as strong and self-possessed. Yet suddenly he sees the parent weak, confused, lacking self-control, and in pain. In response, the adolescent restrains his own emotions and behavior.

Some adolescents quickly resume their regular lifestyle and adolescent pursuits, thereby avoiding the grief and harsh realities of the fresh loss. In these instances the adolescent represses his grieving and the encounter with the loss and its repercussions. In most such cases he is alarmed at the sheer volume of emotion, and is afraid to reveal that he is upset and needs support. Perhaps he has not found anyone with whom to share these feelings.

In other instances he is afraid to be different from his peers and prefers to suppress his emotions for the sake of keeping up with his friends. Meanwhile, to the outside world, he seems to have adjusted to the loss, "forgotten," or not have been moved by it. All these are essentially forms of *delayed mourning.* The adolescent will have to return at a later time to process his or her grieving. For the meantime, it is likely that the ramifications of loss and separation will surface through various forms of behavior: crude and destructive conduct, discipline problems, non-functioning in school, and, above all, emotional outbursts and forceful expressions of antagonism, grievance, disappointment, and accusation. The adolescent will unconsciously vent his distress through "peripheral" issues. The delayed mourning disrupts emotional development because it takes a lot of energy to suppress reactions to the loss. It diverts needed energy from the handling of various age-related issues. Delayed mourning may even lead to emotional withdrawal and the manifestation of symptoms associated with depression.

The residual effects of delayed mourning may be apparent for several years following the loss. In many instances, problems that are ostensibly unrelated to the loss are rooted in the repressed emotions and conflicts of that experience. It is more difficult to treat delayed mourning than fresh mourning proximate to the time of the loss, since as time passes the mourning assumes a more complex character. Considering the stormy behavior that characterizes this age, the grieving responses of adolescents – even of those who do not delay and suppress – tend to be relatively restrained. This restraint stems from the unconscious fear of having a flood of emotions inundate an already turbulent inner world. The adolescent fears loss of control.

At times, this restraint is imposed due to family-related roles that the young person takes upon himself during the initial mourning period. Adolescents are often "enlisted" during this period to serve as their parent's main helper. They may be called upon to help their younger siblings, or take on roles that will assure continuity of home and family. These roles require the young person to demonstrate grown-up behavior and emotional self-restraint.

When the young person does not repress the new, painful reality, the demands of the initial mourning period will require much emotional investment, leaving little energy for age-related tasks. During the initial mourning period, he or she may lose interest in subjects that were previously deemed important. Things that had been exciting, and occupied the young person's attentions, may suddenly seem silly. As is the case for adults, the adolescent is absorbed in his grief, and needs time. He has to pass through at least some of the stages of grieving before he can once again express interest in the ordinary aspects of life.

Developmental tasks

The loss experience affects all of the important developmental tasks assigned to this age: renewed separation from parents, concurrent with the establishment of an independent and well-defined self; formation of sexual identity and self-image; initiation of intimate relations with members of the other sex. The loss will affect the way the young person meets these challenges. It also works in the other direction. The way the adolescent copes with his mourning will be influenced by the tasks and context of adolescence.

During the initial mourning stage, some adolescents demonstrate a slowdown or suspension of the process of separation and rebellion against their parents. The adolescent "regresses" to a closer, less rebellious, less argumentative relationship, and seeks emotional intimacy with them. This behavior is a response to the exigencies of the fresh mourning, a time during which everybody – adolescents included – strives for closeness, warmth, support, and security. Adolescents seek to have these needs met by the people closest to them, parents and family. They require a sensation of family unity in order to feel less threatened and exposed. These needs override the developmental need for distance and defiance.

This closer, post-loss relationship will at times contend with an intense conflict. While the adolescent seeks the support and "embrace" of adults, he is also rebuffing the offers of emotional closeness and partnership. The "embrace" threatens to undermine the separation distancing accomplishments he has already made, and he fears losing the independence he has already attained. His behavior is volatile, confused, and confusing. It reflects the conflict he is experiencing between the desire for closeness and the need for independence; the wish to pursue the normal age tasks and the need to devote himself to his grief. He feels a great deal of ambivalence. He is sad, and misses the person who is no longer there, but is also angry about the disruption to his life, angry at being "different" from his friends, at not being able to be a "normal" teenager. "Why did this have to happen to me?!" "Of all times, why now?!" After the anger come the feelings of guilt that he is even entertaining such thoughts and feelings in spite of the more important, tragic experience of loss.

Emotions

The ability of adolescents to share what they are going through and accept emotional support from their parents is a complex matter for them as well as for their parents. Parents of adolescents normally have to call upon prodigious mental acrobatic skills in order to weather the frequent and powerful mood swings of their children. This struggle is further exacerbated by the loss, since the parent is also going through a difficult, mentally stressful period. Into this equation enters the emotionally overwrought, confused adolescent, who has a hard time making his or her emotional needs clear to the parent, transmitting simultaneously divergent messages: requests for closeness and help and demands for distance.

We therefore find that the adolescent sometimes refuses to let the parent draw closer and extend support. He is unwilling to share his emotions. He sends messages of "I don't need" or "I don't want" to other mourners around him, and refuses to participate in the family support process. Although there is no doubt that he needs emotional support and partnership, he is deterred by the fear of losing his identity and independence, of once again seeming "childlishly" weak and needing the support of his parents. Given these parameters, it is difficult to achieve a meaningful emotional encounter between the grieving adolescent and the grieving parent.

Adults are baffled by the confused needs and messages of the adolescent, and are unsure how to act. They are occupied by their own feelings of grief, which explains why they sometimes "hurry" to accept the message of dissociation and rejection, and decline to make the effort at connecting with the adolescent.

In the process of accepting the loss, the mourner must acquiesce, and come to terms with the relationship he once had with the absent person. During adolescence, children are often on bad terms with their parents, and have a strained and tense relationship with them. If relations with the parent were on a poor footing prior to the parent's loss, this will exacerbate the child's acceptance of the loss. The adolescent will be consumed by guilt – "If I hadn't behaved like that… If I had done things differently…"

He is perturbed by thoughts and feelings about the missed opportunity; he longs to turn back the clock and mend the relationship. At other times he is preoccupied by unexpressed and unprocessed anger about the things he needed to say but didn't. The adolescent is troubled by these feelings, and may have a difficult time progressing in the grieving process and the acceptance of the loss.

Needs of remaining parent

The responses and behavior of the adolescent are affected by the needs of the remaining parent and the immediate family. In some instances, the remaining parent requires the support of the adolescent, who answers the call for help. If there are younger siblings, they sometimes seek out a supportive parental figure among their older brothers or sisters. There is a sense of emotional fragility and vulnerability within the family, as well as the fear of breakdown. The adolescent devotes himself to supporting the family, thereby postponing the distancing that is natural to this age. This desire to reinforce the family structure emanates not only from his concern for others, but also from his need for a family with a firm base. The adolescent needs a strong family structure from which he can allow himself to grow distant. The adolescent who lacks a strong family to which he can return to receive support will be afraid of separating and distancing himself.

The parent's intense emotional needs at the initial period after the loss may induce him to consider his adolescent children as equals and therefore partners in his duties, in his troubles, and in his emotions. This invitation to partnership and "mating" is likely to prove tempting to the adolescent. The elevated adult status is flattering to him, and the duties of filling the role will alleviate his sense of loneliness. If the remaining parent is of the opposite sex, this closeness also responds to his unconscious fantasies relating to sexual identity issues.

Nevertheless, these closer relations with the parent during the initial mourning period are liable to spill over the intergenerational boundaries that are required for the continued crystallization of the adolescent's separate individuality. The familial intimacy that takes place during the mourning period may lead to suspension or even regression in the age-related tasks. The adult should ensure that this regression, should it occur, is not too pronounced or prolonged, and does not impede the age-needed processes.

Sometimes, during the initial mourning period, the parents or surviving parent are preoccupied with their grief, and the adolescent may find that he has essentially been left to raise himself. The adults assume that he is old enough to take care of himself. The parent, consumed by his own grief, prefers to believe that his son or daughter no longer needs him. This makes it easy for the parent to forfeit his duty to help him or her deal with the loss as well as with the tasks of adolescence. In the absence of parental support, the adolescent may not be able to fully realize his age tasks.

The loss "jostles" adolescents into an early encounter with adulthood. The problems they face are real and difficult. They may pertain to economic or existential adversity, or the well-being of other loved ones. These concerns will overshadow the issues that normally preoccupy at this age. The adolescent feels the opening of a breach and a loss of common language with his age peers, at least during the initial mourning period. Grieving for one's father or mother eclipses the general gamut of anxieties that preoccupy the adolescent's friends, such as unrequited infatuations or parties that did not go well.

Sense of continuity and security

A sense of continuity is an important basis for the development of self-identity. The young person is in transition from his past as a child to his future as an adult. He requires a sense of security and continuity, which will facilitate his need to "add" or "remove" parts of his sense of belonging. The loss throws this continuity into tumult, damaging his confidence in the safety of this foundation and in the ability to rely on it.

Image of the self

Even among adults, loss can damage self-image and self-confidence. For the adolescent, this damage is sustained during an especially sensitive period. The young person is in the throes of the process of formation of his own self-image and identity, and is occupied by the question of who he is and what he wants to be. His perception of self is still fragile, placing him in an especially vulnerable position. The loss of the parent may be attended by a sense of abandonment or rejection, and at such a sensitive age, the effect of these feelings on the self-image and self-worth may have serious and even harmful repercussions as regards the optimal continuation of these processes.

In order to further crystallize and reinforce self-image, the adolescent must be able to call upon internal and external forces that are difficult to marshal during the initial period after a loss, since all the individual's efforts are directed toward mental survival and self-maintenance. The adolescent is weakened by the expenditure of these energies. Moreover, his external sources of support, primarily his parents, have also been damaged.

The loss creates a double-edged deficiency for the adolescent. Besides the difficult experience of loss, he loses the person who was supposed to help him build and reinforce his self-image, the individual who was meant to provide backing. Nor is the surviving parent sufficiently accessible and available, and cannot be a sufficient source of support or strength. Under these circumstances it is no surprise that the tasks are often delayed.

As part of the process whereby identity is established, the parent constitutes a subject for emulation as well as an object of defiance. The adolescent builds his self-image and self-confidence with the support of an ongoing dialogue he has with the parent. However, when the parent is gone this dialogue is disrupted. The mourning and pain are fresh, and the child longs for the parent; it is impossible to fight with him, separate, or grow distant from him. How can the child argue or challenge someone whose very absence is so painful to him? Nor is it the right time for arguing or challenging the surviving parent, who is grieving and hurting, and unavailable for the give and take of parent–adolescent relations.

Acting out

Acting out is common behavior during adolescence. Grieving adolescents may behave in extreme, unusual ways that have no logical connection to the loss. Reckless driving, going out with friends every night, insolence, and blatant disregard of what is happening at home are some of the more common displays of what is sometimes interpreted as the adolescent's indifference to the loss: "He only thinks of himself, his friends, and having a good time." One gets the impression that the adolescent has moved on, and resumed his normal routine. The turbulent behavior seems to be unrelated to the anguish of the loss. But in fact this behavior is often only a camouflage for the distress and difficulties caused by the suspension of adolescent processes in the wake of the loss. Acting out is misinterpreted as defiant disobedience of the rules, obnoxious behavior that is the "common language" of adolescents. Instead, it needs to be understood within the context of the recent loss.

The function of adults is to locate and identify the distress that underlies this behavior, bring it to the adolescent's attention, and elicit his verbal expression of the real issues at hand. The adult must help him to directly and verbally take care of the problem, rather than resort to acting out as a way of expressing this distress.

Peer group

Age peers are very important to the adolescent. It is important for him to belong and be accepted by his age group, and to be like everyone else. Following the loss, he becomes "different," both in his own and his friends' perspective. He is afraid of frightening his friends away and being ostracized. Due to the atmosphere at home, he is likely to avoid bringing friends home, and will spend more time away from home. Among his peers, he is free to behave as he wishes; with his friends, he can continue his normal life, outwardly at least. He does not want to be labeled a "poor wretch." When he is with his age peers he will probably prefer to conceal his grief and suffering, pretending that he has moved on and is in control of the situation. Nevertheless, the escape and masquerade, and the inability to share his genuine thoughts and feelings, imposes a high mental cost, eventually leaving the young man or woman alienated and isolated among his or her friends.

Sexual identity

Development of sexual identity is one of the primary tasks of adolescence. This is a period of sharp transitions – hormonal, mental, and social – during which sexual identity fully develops. Boys and girls become young men and women. Although this task does not have any obvious connection to loss, it is liable to take on a unique hue during the fresh grieving phase, which disrupts and may even suspend the delicate and complex process.

Both parents play important roles in the development of the adolescent's sexual identity. The influence of the loss is different when the parent missing is of the same gender as the child or the parent is of the opposite gender. When a daughter loses her mother, she loses her role model for identification and learning feminine roles and traits, her partner in her vacillation vis-à-vis her feminine identity. A daughter who loses her father loses the "suitor" who reinforces her confidence as a woman; the person who must "release" her to find an intimate partner among her age peers. A son who loses his father loses his role model for identification with masculine behavior traits. A son who loses his mother loses the soft, warm, supportive feminine contact from which he is supposed to learn about relationships with members of the opposite sex, and from whom he is supposed to break away in favor of relationships with his female age peers.

When a daughter loses her father or a son loses his mother, the process of separation from the intimate relationship with the "suitor" parent is truncated. The normal Oedipal triangle (father–mother–child) is disrupted, and the main staging ground for sexual conflict and identification is eliminated in the midst of the process. Roles are liable to be confused. What "intimate" role will the surviving parent assign to the adolescent? What role will the adolescent take upon himself? What about the competition between the same-sex parent and child?

What's more, the new family situation is fluid, and sex-related issues may crop up. How long will the other parent remain without a spouse? What sort of spouse will he or she choose? Will the new spouse assume roles within the family? All of these aspects influence the continued development of the young person's sexual identity. In a family that is still reeling from fresh loss, these are indistinct, wide-open issues that leave the adolescent confused.

All these issues put unique pressures and at times accelerate and distort processes that relate to the developing sexual identity behavior. This may be reflected in premature initiation of sexual behavior and relations. In such cases, the young person is liable to leapfrog over the requisite emotional development that needs to be an integral part of the establishment of sexual identity. Sometimes the collision of adolescence and fresh loss can have the opposite effect. Establishment of sexual identity may be slowed or even suspended. This can be expressed in the adolescent's avoidance of bonding with members of the opposite sex or denial of sexuality through the way he or she dresses.

Sexuality is linked to pleasure and the will to live. Agonizing over the question of whether one is allowed to enjoy life after the loss can have a deterrent effect on sexuality. In the same way that some adults are deterred from sexual pleasure, feeling that it is inappropriate or even "forbidden" during the initial period of loss, it is no wonder that the adolescent may also feel that he does not deserve pleasure, and is uncertain whether he even wants it. Yet, at the other extreme, he might be drawn to premature sexual relations which might be the outburst of the need to "get something out of life," to compensate for the suffering, and a way to get attention when so needy for warmth and belonging.

Whatever the case, the initial period of mourning – the first year or two – is a period of contemplation, hardship, and readjustment. The adolescent has developmental tasks that become more complicated and complex in the wake of the loss. We have seen that when a traumatic loss occurs during adolescence, it finds the young man or woman at an emotionally confusing, troubling age and can easily overflow the adolescent's emotional capacity. He requires a great deal of attention and support, even as he may demand that others stop interfering in his life and leave him alone. It is critical to monitor the adolescent and keep close track of his emotional state, so as to identify the distress signals when intervention is required.

Earlier loss and adolescence

We will now move on to describing the situation when the loss occurs at a younger age and the child has reached the age of adolescence. The juxtaposition of the age tasks of adolescence and the deep imprint of the loss that occurred previously pose a complex challenge. Many of the tasks of coping with loss recur at subsequent stages of development, especially during adolescence. Central themes in the experience of loss, such as separation, also happen to be primary features of adolescence. Due to the unique sensitivity of the young person who experienced loss earlier in childhood, these processes will take on a special character.

The well-developed cognitive level of the adolescent enables him to fully understand the facts related to the loss that occurred in the past, and the consequences thereof. As a young person, he or she presumably received partial information about the circumstances of the loss, and understood what took place within the narrow limits of a young child's comprehension. Now is the time to round out the information and address any and all aspects of the loss that have been left untreated. Adults commonly assume, or would like to believe, that the adolescent "already knows," or that "it's no longer important to him." Yet when one speaks with adolescents, it is astounding to find that they still don't know exactly what happened. Most of them explain that they are hesitant to raise the issue again, as they know how hard it is for the adults, especially their parents, to deal with it.

By opening up discussion of the issue and making it accessible to the adolescent, the adult facilitates and establishes a grown-up dialogue, sending the message that the adolescent has the right to find out, ask questions, pore over the facts. He has the right to expect his parent to be a serious partner in this process. It is important that the adolescent be given an opportunity to relate to the loss and its implications from a grown-up perspective, from which he will be able to understand its full significance. Generally, he will have to ask – several times over – about various details and aspects of the loss, in order to understand the event through the new tools available to him, and in order to find answers that are suited to his more grown-up perspective on life. Now that he understands more about life and relationships, and is more aware of his own personality, he will be able to have insights vis-à-vis the effect of the loss on his growth. He needs to be acquainted with the facts in order to work through these insights.

The essence of life

Adolescents are consumed by questions about the essence of life. The young person is occupied by issues that affect how he understands the ways of the world at the universal level. He is trying to shape his own outlook to incorporate those concerns into his personal world. Young men and women who in their childhood experienced events as profound and traumatic as loss have already "learned" very significant lessons about life. The immersion of these adolescents in questions about the meaning of life is not only an intellectual exercise related to the process of adolescence, but a need to understand what personally happened to them.

These adolescents are usually more mature in how they view the world. The world seems less "rosy" and promising to them; they are more suspicious and cynical, and may also have a more pessimistic view of life than their age peers. They are in no rush to share these thoughts with their peers, so as not to call added attention to the differences between them, as well as out of a concern that they will not be understood. Nor are they in a rush to share their thoughts with adults, due to the natural distancing from adults that is characteristic of this age. The adolescent may therefore find himself alone with his hard, complex thoughts and questions. Some young people will search for answers in literature that considers the meaning of life, be it philosophy, poetry, or fiction. Others channel their energies into activities through which they seek answers to questions that preoccupy them, hoping to find meaning through political or social involvement, leadership roles in school or youth movements, or volunteering. Such activities help them translate their questions into action, through which they can wield influence and make the world a better place. Other young people who have both the inclination and the talent will seek meaning and express their inner feelings through creative endeavor, be it writing, music, art, or dance.

Some adolescents are attracted by solutions held out by *sects and faiths.* Religions may offer cogent answers to the troubles of humanity, including answers to questions on the meaning of life, issues of life and death. They usually offer a framework of belonging as well. Religions and sects have the attraction of being able to help defuse emotionally painful issues. Since the experience of a traumatic loss and its repercussions may lead to a sense of emptiness, lack of love, and lack of belonging, these young people may be easy prey for those who want to force their beliefs and solutions on them. Adolescents can easily develop emotional dependence on anyone who offers them "answers," and may be lured by those who give them a sense of belonging and "love." In exchange for an answer to their troubles, these young people relinquish their emotional independence as well as their freedom of thought.

Acting out

Acting out, which is in any case characteristic at this age, may become even more intense as the adolescent confronts the troubles and questions he or she is unable to solve. By resorting to "solutions" such as alcohol consumption, drug abuse, reckless driving, and violent criminal behavior, the adolescent finds a means of venting the pressures of coping with difficult issues.

Separation

Loss, and issues related to loss, is part and parcel of the emotional processes that any adolescent undergoes. The juxtaposition of normative adolescent "loss" experiences with the traumatic loss that the youngster experienced in the past will require intense coping efforts. The primary issue is separation. Separation from parents and becoming independent and mature is one of the main tasks of adolescence. It involves a process of emotional separation. For the adolescent who has experienced loss as a young child, separation is not simply a developmental task; it is a painful experience and memory. Any separation at the age of adolescence consciously or unconsciously reawakens memories of the loss and separation that were experienced as a child. The adolescent is emotionally transplanted to the initial experience, and before he can go about coping with the present-day separation, he will have to tackle the still unresolved issues of the past separation. Every encounter with the experience of separation will necessitate a reprocessing of the pain of separation and loss that occurred in the past. The encounter will bring the adolescent into contact with sensations of longing, pain, worry, fear, anger, and helplessness.

The repeated encounter with issues of separation that is brought on by the age tasks of adolescence will provide the adolescent with another opportunity to process the loss, enabling him to treat the difficulties of separation in a more mature fashion. He now has more developed cognitive capacity and ego strength at his disposal, and the encounter constitutes an opportunity to reinforce his capacity to cope with the loss and with separation in general, and buttress the mechanisms that will serve him in similar situations.

Old defense mechanisms may be activated, since the issues are often unresolved and threatening. The effort of coping with these burdensome, long-smoldering issues provides an important opportunity for developing more effective defense mechanisms and readjustment techniques than those that served the adolescent when he was a younger child. For example, if the child was 3 years old when he lost his parent, it is possible that he related the parent's "disappearance" to something bad that he himself did. As a young child, it may have been appropriate to use a primitive defense mechanism such as splitting, in which the world is split into good and bad. This may have helped the child to accept the disappearance of his parent. However, by adolescence, the child has evolved ego strength, personality, and defense mechanisms, as well as more developed cognitive faculties, and can reprocess the understanding of the loss without having to resort to an early childhood defense mechanism such as splitting. He is able to use more developed and mature coping tools.

The emotional memory of the experience of separation and loss during childhood leaves the child feeling vulnerable, with its existential confidence compromised. The memories are liable to be a source of additional anxiety. Nevertheless, this period also offers an opportunity for corrective experience. When adolescents feel that they are strong enough to cope and separation is no longer experienced as an existential threat, they are empowered by the discovery that they can rely on themselves.

Separation–individuation

During adolescence, a repeat process of separation–individuation occurs, in which the ability of the child, now the adolescent, to take a meaningful step forward toward *self-definition*, separate from his or her parents, is tested. There is a danger that loss of a parent at a young age will adversely affect this basic process, because it left the child with limited ego strength. Now, as the child reaches adolescence and is again required to carry out the task of separation, he or she is liable to experience difficulties in separating, as is likely to occur when ego strength is not available. The difficulties are usually experienced unconsciously, and explained away by rational excuses. An adolescent who is afraid to leave home for a few days will claim to have no interest in the class trip; a young person who has a hard time establishing relationships with age peers may claim that "they're not on my level." The adolescent has anxieties, and lacks the internal ego strength to cope with them. In such situations, the adolescent's ability to take part in peer-group activities may be harmed, as are the normative processes of growth and separation.

Conversely, if during childhood the child had positive experiences of relationships and trust, and had separation experiences from which he developed a stronger ego, and if he was given positive reinforcement to bolster his self-image, then when he reaches adolescence he will be better equipped to go through developmental separation in a healthy and growth conducive manner.

Parents can make a critical contribution toward the development of the child's ability to separate during early childhood, as well as adolescence. Every adolescent needs a parent at his side to enable him to separate. The adolescent who has experienced loss as a child needs even more parental support and requires more help in the process. His relationship with the parent raising him is more complex and convoluted, so it is especially important that the parent does his or her part and makes it possible for the child to "cut loose."

If the child grows up feeling that the parent needs him and depends on him emotionally, when he reaches adolescence he will have a much greater need for the parent's "permission" for separation and distancing. The parent who sends messages that make it even harder for the adolescent to pull away may adversely affect these processes. These parental influences will be discussed in greater detail in the chapters to follow. The adolescent must define for himself who he is, which he does in relation to his parental figures. He emulates and espouses some of their characteristics, while rejecting others. This process is more complicated for someone who lost a parent at a young age, because the parent is not there, and the adolescent must carry out the process relative to the parent's image, rather than relative to a real person. Is the adolescent familiar enough with the parent's image to carry out this process in optimal fashion? Is he or she familiar with all the pertinent personality and character traits of the parent? In order for the adolescent to select which traits he wants to identify with and which traits to reject, he has to be thoroughly familiar with all aspects, which does not always happen. If the image is portrayed as being ideal, it is hard for the adolescent to "step into his shoes." If he feels that the adults expect him to carry on in the same fashion, he is denied the freedom to define his own identity. If the image of the parent is depicted negatively, this adversely affects the young person's ability to internalize, emulate, or identify with his traits. It hinders the child's ability to make the parent part of his internal object and a source of strength and support. This could harm the child's own self-image as well.

- How does one separate from a parent who is no longer there?

- How can one "disconnect" from a parent who has not been there for the child all along the way?

- How can you distance yourself from the very same parent whom you long for, to whom you wholeheartedly want to return?

- How do you "argue" and define your individuality vis-à-vis a parent who does not really exist, a parent whom you don't know very well?

Gender and sexual identity

One of the primary tasks of adolescence is the development of sexual identity which takes place along two axes – identification with the parent of the same sex, and attraction to and distancing from the parent of the opposite sex. Development of sexual identity is strongly influenced by what the child has gone through between the time of the loss and the age of adolescence. Has the remaining parent formed a new long-term intimate relationship? Does the new partner serve as an alternate parental figure to the child, and does he or she constitute a figure for identification? There are numerous possibilities, but it is clear that when the child is raised in a family that includes spousal relationships and intimacy, and normative parenting models and gender roles, the child has a greater chance of reaching adolescence with the appropriate perspective and experience to see him through the developmental tasks of adolescence.

Conversely, in some families, events that followed the loss distorted gender roles, thereby possibly harming the healthy development of sexual identity. Some parents allocate "spousal" roles to their child; other parents compete sexually with their children. Such experiences constitute a burden that is liable to hamper and harm the adolescent's ability to form a healthy, sound sexual identity. If the remaining parent does not have a permanent spouse and the adolescent does not have any alternate parental image, it is more difficult to achieve the desired processes at this stage.

A son growing up with his mother and who serves as her "partner" lacks "competition" for this role. Even when the mother has temporary spousal relationships, or even a permanent spouse, she may at times maintain a special relationship with her son, thereby making it more difficult for him to separate, distance himself, and form adequate relationships with age peers of the opposite sex. Similarly, let us consider the situation of a daughter being raised by her father. If her relationship with her father is close and intimate, she may feel the need to be faithful to him, and in so doing her ability to develop close relationships with boys her own age is adversely affected. When a daughter loses her father, she has her mother with whom she can identify in a feminine way, but the "courting" father who provides the initial reinforcement of her femininity and self-confidence is missing. It is not uncommon for daughters without fathers to flirt for the attention of adult males, including their mother's friends, other men in the family, counselors, teachers, or other masculine figures. There may be open or veiled competition with their mothers for the affections of men. In extreme cases, the need for a relationship with a masculine, fatherly figure continues into adulthood, at which point the daughter will form romantic liaisons with men so old that "they could have been her father."

A son whose mother is not there for him will grow up without maternal warmth and emotional contact and might lack the capacity to establish intimate connections, and build emotionally open and warm relationships with members of the opposite sex. He might be looking for "motherly" relationships with his girlfriends rather than romantic yet "equal" relationships.

The difficulties of coping with developmental tasks that pertain to sexual identity are reflected in several other ways too. Some adolescents adopt extreme forms of sexual behavior and accentuate their sexuality through provocative dress, spending a great deal of time and energy in contact with members of the opposite sex, or even multiple sexual relationships. Under the mask of ostentatious sexuality, we often find a lack of self-confidence and/or immature sexual identity, and a strong need for compensation for emotional deprivation. Extreme behavior can also be directed in the opposite direction – suppressed sexual expression, minimization of external sexual indicators, or avoidance of contact with members of the opposite sex. Excessive responses – in either direction – reflect the dilemmas and the challenges that young men and women face in shaping their sexual identity and forming intimate relationships with members of the opposite sex.

Table 2.1 outlines the major themes of developmental tasks of adolescence and themes related to sensitivities after loss. The juxtaposition makes it clear how close these themes are.

Early adulthood (age 18 to 30)

Early adulthood is not generally included among the classic stages of childhood development. Nevertheless, as part of the overall discussion of the subject at hand it is a critical stage of development, since many indications of childhood loss are still surfacing at this time of life. These phenomena are related to age tasks, and arise as a result of the issues young people must confront during post-adolescence.

Early adulthood is characterized by decisions to pursue higher education and/or professional studies, initial experience in the working world, career development, moving out of the family home, taking occasional extended trips and far-off journeys, romantic relationships and choice of partners with whom one can develop a mature, long-term, intimate commitment and begin a family.

Young adults who have experienced loss during childhood may at times exhibit behavior that extends beyond the common norms: difficulty leaving home and adopting a more independent lifestyle or, alternatively, an acute level of estrangement from parent and family; trouble choosing a field of studies or profession; difficulty adjusting to a place of work, especially due to poor relationships with superiors; difficulty and aversion to making commitments in employment and study situations; difficulty forming romantic liaisons, difficulty creating and maintaining intimate relationships, and making "wrong" choices of spouses.

For some young people, this is the first time they experience any difficulties, or act in any way differently from their age peers. So long as they were in the care of their parent, within the family framework, they did not exhibit any special difficulty, and everything seemed to proceed apace.

Table 2.1 Developmental tasks as compared to responses and needs related to loss sustained during adolescence

Developmental tasks	Loss-related situations
Cognitive–spiritual development: questions about the ways of the world and the meaning of life	The post-loss reality raises questions regarding the meaning of life, justice, guilt, punishment, and suffering.
Period of emotional turmoil	During the initial period after the loss, there is a great deal of emotional turmoil, making it hard to handle any additional turmoil. Recurrent "encounters" with loss-related emotions require great emotional investment.
Separation as a developmental task	Separation is and remains a sensitive issue that sets into motion painful memories and defense mechanisms.
Separation and distancing from parents, and formation of self	During the grieving period, there is a need for greater closeness with the remaining parent. Difficulty "separating" from the absent parent. Children do not want to create "distance" from the remaining parent for whom they now have a greater need. Difficulty identifying with or differentiating from an unfamiliar figure. Absence of parent from whom the child should be receiving energies for forming his individuality and self.
Formation of the self	The loss adversely affects self-image.
Formation of sexual identity	Absence of a key figure in the process of formation of sexual identity: a figure for identification as well as competition; or a figure for "intimacy" from which the child must disconnect. Absence of a role model of intimate couple relationship.
Reinforcement of self-confidence	The loss and its repercussions adversely affect self-confidence and existential confidence.
Need for a safe family base from which separation can be experienced	The loss endangers the continuity of family and weakens confidence in it.
Greater connection and closeness with age peers	There is a sense of aloofness and even alienation from age peers who have not experienced loss and who do not understand its meaning.
Defiance and rejection of the adult world	In fresh grieving, there is a need for closeness and cooperation with adults, and support from them.

Now, for what may be the first time, their adult individuality is being put to the test. They need to be independent and responsible for themselves and this encounter raises hitherto hidden difficulties.

It would be incorrect to claim that every hardship and problem encountered in early adulthood is necessarily related to or influenced by the loss experienced as a child. The reasons and circumstances can be different and varied, rooted in personality and family issues, or in other matters. Furthermore, the various ways in which loss may affect the individual are usually not the sole reason, but form part of a larger picture.

Building independence

In early adulthood, young men and women embark on their independent journeys of the world. They complete their separation from family and home, with the purpose of living an adult and independent life. During this transition, separation problems that have not yet been processed or treated are liable to surface. This is no longer about symbolic, brief, or experimental separations that may have been the case during previous stages of development. Now the theme is concrete, long-term separation, in many areas of life, with the object of creating an independent living framework.

During this stage, emotional "omissions" of the past may surface. Individuals who have not undergone full developmental separation will be required to make up what they have missed. Those who have not processed the trauma of separation and loss may be beset by emotional issues related to the trauma. In certain cases, this period may be the first opportunity in which the young person can fully realize the actual work of separation. When the remaining parent has difficulty coping with separation and permitting his children to distance themselves from him – physical separation as well as symbolic and emotional separation – these tasks will not have been fully completed as yet, and will become the major challenge of this period. Chapter 4 considers how the remaining parent influences the process through which his child copes with the loss and what implications this will have on the child's ability to cope with separation in general.

When the young person leaves home and removes himself from the parent's sphere of protection and influence, or when it becomes obvious that the time has come for the young person to leave home and strike out on his or her own, he or she must confront separation issues. This is not an easy task for the young adult who suffered loss at a younger age and who has had a hard time completing separation tasks ever since. In many instances the youngster also has a lower level of ego strengths that can be called upon to help realize these tasks. In such cases, the young person usually exhibits strong emotional dependence on the parent. Similarly, it is not unreasonable to assume that the parent who previously placed obstacles in the path of his child towards independence will continue to do so at this stage as well.

Young people in this category may excuse their hardships by offering so-called "reasons" for their lack of independence. A young man who finds it difficult to move away from home may claim that he could not find the right apartment; a young woman who finds it hard to leave her mother might say she has not traveled abroad because she cannot find a suitable companion; a young man who lacks the confidence to live far away from home may rule out studying at a distant university, arguing that the school's academic standards are not to his liking. *Denial and unawareness* of the problem are often characteristic of such situations.

Some people cope with their difficulties by adopting radical courses of action that 'force' separation: travel abroad for long periods of time; recurrent confrontation with the parent, constant defiance of the parent and his expectations, to the extent of cutting all ties. By these actions, the young person tries to generate a process through which he will overcome his own inhibitions and difficulties as well as the obstacles that the parent continues to put in his path. This sort of coerced separation may be of partial help, but the genuine separation will result from an inner process within himself, in tandem with a process that involves him and his parent.

Some young people may outwardly seem to have separated, but emotionally they continue to be dependent on the parent. They still call their parents frequently, share with them the most mundane details of their daily lives, continue to seek much advice and support, and fail to take responsibility over their own lives. They may form relationships with a spouse, yet remain in an "intimate" relationship with their parent. Awareness of the difficulty of separation arises when the problems recur, and the young person realizes he is "stuck" in a pattern of life that prevents him from realizing dreams and plans, forming complete, intimate relationships or feeling genuinely independent. Over time, those individuals who live in denial of their recurring hardships and who make no attempt to change may feel stranded, and may even experience symptoms of depression.

Intimate relationships

The issues pertaining to formation and maintaining of intimate relationships exhibit themselves in problems finding a spouse, building a long-term intimate relationship, creating bonds of trust, commitment, and love. Unresolved Oedipal issues – the lack of any separation whether emotional or symbolic – from the opposite-sex parent may lead to the constant search for a substitute parent in the spouse. Those who are still bound to the remaining parent by a strong "intimate" commitment will not be open to another close relationship with an age peer. A young man who is very close to his mother will resist setting up clear boundaries between the new intimate relationship with his spouse and the relationship with his mother; his loyalty to his mother will come at the expense of a strong, trusting relationship with his new partner. Some examples of unresolved emotional needs from childhood that are transferred onto spousal relationship include:

- daughters who form relationships with older men, who are looking for a protective and paternal figure in a spouse

- young women who form dependent relationships with their spouses

- sons who seek a maternal woman to look after them, a strong woman to manage their lives.

The relationship with the spouse is not based on equality between two adults; rather, it reflects the unresolved childhood needs one unconsciously hopes to fulfill. The choice of a homosexual lifestyle can also be the result of circumstances involving loss of a parent and what happened thereafter.

Another common phenomenon is for relationships to be cut off before they have been given a chance to mature. Some individuals do not let intimate relationships begin; others cut them off in their prime. The young person may destroy the budding relationship, holding it back so as to avoid the development of intimate, emotional bonds. In his experience it is preferable to control and put an end to a relationship because the love and dependency that may subsequently be lost will cause pain and suffering. The object is to maintain a safe emotional distance that steers clear of potential disappointment, separation, or loss.

Some young people feel that the emotional burden they carry inside them from their childhood experience will constitute a threat to their potential partners. They cannot believe that anyone would be willing to accept them, complete with the heavy burden they bear, or be capable of shouldering the burden together with them over the course of a lifetime. They feel that no one will want them because they are emotionally "defective."

During this stage of life, young people build the foundations of their adult lives. Fear of a recurrent fate, and the apprehension that what happened to their parent will also happen to them, constitutes a black cloud that hovers overhead. This may unconsciously prevent investment in the distant future, and is liable to adversely affect the process of building a full adult life.

Study and employment

Difficulty choosing a study major or profession may reflect difficulties in formation of the self. Employment instability can reflect trouble in acceptance of authority, having never experienced a healthy parental authority. We have discussed how these growth areas are influenced by the experience of loss at a young age. Strong identification with the absent parent, or overdominant influence by the remaining parent, can affect the individual's independent and mature choice of profession. Fear of failure and lack of self-confidence in one's abilities and skills can contribute to the young person's difficulties in these areas.

All in all, the first years of adult life not only bring into focus the unresolved and uncompleted issues and problems that are the aftermath of the loss, but also serve as an important opportunity to become more aware of these issues, and attend to them. The external and internal resources now at his disposal give the young person a better chance of handling these difficult issues. This is the "last chance" before they begin to come at a higher price – a price that not only weighs on a person's own adult life, but also that of his spouse and his children.

Summary: The intrapsychic experience of loss and its effects on personality development and pathology

We have described the effects of loss according to age groups. In this chapter, we comprehensively summarize the primary aspects of the intrapsychic experience as related to loss, and its connection with personality development and the possible development of aberrant emotional responses and pathologies.

Internal void

Experiencing loss, the individual feels "crushed," temporarily losing part of himself, part of his wholeness, part of his self. He is consumed by an acute sense of internal void. Processing of grief is a means by which the self readjusts, restoring the sensation of full inner existence.

Since the self of the child is not yet complete and strong, the loss leaves him feeling helpless, that he has lost part of his self – part of himself. In order to alleviate this sense of impending threat, the child needs holding and containing, reinforcement and nurturing from without, from adults, and most especially from the remaining parent. He is dependent on the support and reinforcement the parent can provide, needing him to assuage his anxieties and dispel the sense of void.

The loss of a parent deprives the child of one of his primary sources of nourishment. During the initial mourning period, the other parent is usually unable to carry out the full parental duties, and the child feels he is left "alone." To the child, it is as if he was lost, as if his parents have lost him. He feels abandoned, cut adrift. In the child's experience, the parent is part of himself, and the loss of parent generates a sense of partial loss of himself. The child feels incapable of maintaining the objects of the self.

The child suffers from a *loss complex* – the feeling that he is at perpetual risk of losing some of his internal objects. There is a feeling of inner fragility and emptiness that is difficult to dispel; a feeling of incompleteness of self, of inferiority, void, and overriding vulnerability.

Following the loss, something is missing within. There is a hollow void, and a perpetual need to fill it. Frequently, there is a sensation that it is impossible to fill this void from within, by himself, from internalized objects. This sensation drives the individual to look for "filling" from the outside. He hopes to get it from love that has no constraints, from career achievements or an endless race after new challenges, from accumulation of power, control, or money. Others find relief by escaping to drugs and alcohol, which may assuage and obscure the sense of void.

Children who have experienced loss also lose the sense of naive omnipotence that typifies children. At times, their sense of energy and vitality may be wounded.

The process of *grief work* prevents this sense of emptiness from becoming a permanent state of mind. It sets up an encounter with harsh, threatening emotions such as pain, loneliness, anger, and sorrow, the processing and verbalization of which blunts their intensity, making them accessible and conscious. They are given a specific name and an identity. In so doing the pervasive sense of void, fragility, and collapse is reduced.

The experience of loss leaves a threatening emotional memory where separation issues are concerned. It imprints a strong emotional memory, that "separation is a threat to the self." Individuals who have experienced such a trauma will develop various ways to avoid having to revisit this experience. Some of these solutions negatively affect full development and proper function, and may even prove destructive, such as the development of *dependent relationships*, and an obsessive clinging to people and relationships that leaves no room for distance or leave taking. The individual may beg for attention and love, and is willing to pay almost any price in exchange – including humiliation and abuse. Sexual relations may become a substitute for attention and love. At times, immense, even desperate efforts are invested – to be "good" and accommodating at all times and at all cost, when the real object is to prevent at any price the additional experience of separation or loss. Interpersonal relationships are constantly put to the test, and impossible tests are set up. There is an insatiable demand for assurances and guarantees concerning the relationship. There is no limit to how many proofs of love must be provided, nor any sense of satisfaction when love is received. Each separation, every distancing of the other party, may be perceived as an act of abandonment, and a failure of the self to hold on to what is dear and important.

According to research studies, traumatic loss during childhood may adversely affect development of the personality, sense of self-worth, and the ability to form significant and long-term adult relationships. Loss at a young age may lead toward pathological responses. Mechanisms such as denial, repression, splitting, and intellectualization may become pathological defense mechanisms. Depression, suicidal tendencies, and rigid defense mechanisms are some of the pathological responses that may develop.

Table 2.2 differentiates between expressions of normal grief and indications of clinical depression in children as a result of loss.

Table 2.2 Expressions of normal grief and indications of clinical depression in children as a result of loss	
Indications of normal grieving in children	*Indications of clinical depression that may appear following loss*
Child responds to attempts to offer him support and increased contact	Rejects offers of support and contact, isolates himself in his room, does not share his feelings
Openly articulates anger	Complains and demonstrates a sense of unease, but fails to articulate his status in an open, focused manner
Shows his sadness	Radiates hopelessness, emptiness and melancholy
Feels "depressed" and attributes it to the loss	Does not attribute his sense of despondency to any particular event
Expresses focused feelings and thoughts of guilt about the loss	Expresses generalized and non-focused thoughts and feelings of guilt
Complains of changing ailments	Complains of chronic physical ailments that have no physiological basis
Demonstrates and expresses periodic sensations of diminished self-esteem	Lives with constant and intense feelings of low self-esteem
Reassumes feelings and behavior of happiness and satisfaction while engaging in enjoyable activities	Feels and displays sense of nothingness and ceases to pursue ordinary activities of a child his age

Detachment is employed by children as a defense mechanism, so as to enable the child to avoid an inundation of emotions related to the loss and the harsh new realities of life. During the first period after the loss – up to one year – it is a healthy mechanism that works in the service of the ego. However, if this defense mechanism becomes permanent, in other words if the child employs it whenever he faces any emotional future hardship, then it harms healthy emotional functions. Children who employ detachment as a regular defense mechanism have difficulty placing trust in people. Their fear of being hurt harms their ability to trust relationships as a source of security and love. This will damage the child's ability to form intimate relationships, invest emotional efforts in others, and accept love from others. The following list enumerates some of the more frequently appearing symptoms that may characterize the individual who employs detachment as a defense mechanism:

- difficulty giving and/or accepting affection
- self-destructive behavior
- failure to maintain childhood friendships and long-term friendships
- establishment of artificial friendships with strangers
- inauthentic behavior with people and artificiality in reactions and expressions
- difficulty making eye contact with other people
- speech difficulties
- difficulty exercising self-restraint and self-control
- short-tempered behavior when performing parental duties
- cruelty to animals and at times also to people
- lying and stealing
- over-occupation with "violent" materials such as fire and blood.

Attenuating factors

There is a broad consensus regarding several factors that greatly attenuate the harsh effect of loss during childhood and stave off the formation of pathological responses:

1. The remaining parent fulfills his parental duties and continues to nurture the child emotionally, bestowing attention, love, support, and reinforcement.

2. The parent continues to fill his duties, maintaining continuity and proper function of the family; sustaining the family at an adequate level and handling the unique tasks that result from the loss.

3. The family has familial and communal resources available to it, to provide aid and support, helping it during the initial stage after the loss as well as during subsequent periods of crisis.

4. The family had a healthy structure and level of function previous to the loss.

5. The family has the capacity to facilitate normative developmental separations ("separation tolerance").

It goes without saying that anyone who experiences a harsh loss during childhood sustains damage to his psyche, and that this damage will leave its mark on his personality. But nor is there any doubt that most individuals who experienced loss as children grow up to become functioning adults who progress positively with their own lives, as well as being a contributing member of their families and society. Many become sensitive, "personality-rich" individuals thanks to the special sensitivities they developed in the aftermath of their own intense experience: an experience that may have exacted a high cost, but also contributed a great deal toward their own perspective on life.

Chapter 3

Additional Variables Affecting the Child's Response

Thus far we have engaged in explaining the responses of the child to loss, taking into account various factors related to the child's age and level of development. In this chapter we consider the "external" variables that affect the process the child is undergoing.

Circumstances of loss

The specific circumstances in which the loss occurred confer unique significance to the event. There is a difference in the impact made by a sudden loss and that which is made by a foreseeable loss, for which one can prepare. A long period of uncertainty prior to the loss will have implications on certain responses to the loss, when and if it occurred.

When abandonment or rejection accompanies the circumstances of loss, this poses an additional difficulty. The same holds true for deaths that result from violence, suicide, or murder, in which the child is left with a labyrinth of emotions that make it more difficult for him to cope with the loss itself. When parents divorce, the child experiences a sense of loss because his relationship with the parent who is leaving the home changes, and because his family is no longer the same as before.

In cases of "cumulative loss," when the child is subjected to a second or third traumatic loss, he must contend with hardships that are several times more intense. The gender of the parent and the nature of the relationship with the parent prior to the loss may substantially influence how well the child copes with the loss. Social and cultural variables also greatly affect the child's response. All of the above-mentioned variables will be elaborated in this chapter.

Period of uncertainty

When the separation and loss were prefaced by a period of uncertainty, this period with its special characteristics will become part of the overall experience of loss. This period is of importance to us for two reasons:

1. In itself it is an extremely difficult period of time for children.

2. What happens during this period will determine how the child "enters" the subsequent mourning period, when the loss has become a certainty, and how the child copes with what happens later on.

During the period of uncertainty, children may go through negative, disturbing experiences that can make their subsequent readjustment more difficult.

There are two possible uncertainty scenarios: one, when it is already certain that there will be a loss, but it is yet unknown when it will occur; two, when there is uncertainty as to whether the loss will even come to pass.

When the loss involves an ill person about to die, or a married couple that has agreed to divorce, but not yet finalized the actual date of divorce or specific day when one parent is moving out, the loss is foreseeable even though the precise timing is still unknown. Since the upcoming loss is a certainty, there is much tension in the air. There is also much anxiety and often also anger. Conversely, when there is a possibility, but no certainty, of loss, the period of uncertainty is not only a time of great fear and worry, but also of hope and prayer. This is the case when someone is seriously injured and it is not known if he will survive or die; when someone is suffering from a serious illness, and it is not known if it will become terminal or recovery is possible; when a couple has a serious fight, one walks out and the threat of divorce looms, but the spouses and even more so the children are unsure if the crisis will end in separation and divorce or reconciliation. In all these cases, the waiting period is filled with a great deal of strong emotion. This period will leave its after effects on the child, if and when the loss comes to pass.

Similar to the post-loss period, responses during the waiting period transpire along two planes: the intrapsychic plane of every individual within him or herself; the "outside" plane, with family members, and mainly the parents. When there is a waiting situation, there is an additional plane of interaction: the relationship with the person who may soon be gone. This particular relationship is difficult and complex for adults and children alike.

- Should one address the subject, or ignore it?

- What is permissible, or possible, to say?

- Should one engage in farewells, or lend encouragement and hope?

The responses vary from denial of the possibility of loss to shock, paralysis, and repression, through to anxiety and even hysteria, and on to the start of grieving. This period is characterized by a great deal of ambiguity, as well as extreme reactions.

As is the case following loss, the adjustment during this period takes place on all three levels – cognitive, emotional, and functional. Due to the uncertainty and fluidity of the situation, the adjustment requires great flexibility. During the period of uncertainty, children can be prepared for the loss; adults can explain what is about to take place. Appropriate preparation will make it easier for them to cope if and when the loss occurs. During this period, "traps" are being set, which if not properly defused will exacerbate difficulties in the long term.

At this time, the child is dependent on the adults around him, who are supposed to be helping him. The adults on the other hand are directing much of their energy toward the threatened loss, and as a result they are often paying significantly less attention to the children. We now examine a few specific situations that can be problematic and have strong effects on children.

Unawareness and ambiguity

Unawareness and ambiguity regarding the situation leave the child with numerous questions that he will not be able to understand without the help of adults. In the absence of support, the child will find his own "explanations." He will fill the ambiguity about the future with his own futuristic scenarios. By having to resort to his own imagination and explanations, he may find himself in unrealistic realms. He may develop fears and anxieties that extend beyond what is warranted by the situation. Frequently, the child will not share his fears with adults, not only because he hides them but also because the adults are often *inaccessible* emotionally as well as concretely. They may be out of the house for hours on end, and when home they may not be emotionally available. The child gets the feeling and even the message that he is no partner to what is going on because he "won't understand" or "it isn't a matter for children." An even worse attitude is when the adults pretend there is no problem whatsoever.

During periods of ambiguity and uncertainty, many adults typically respond by being secretive and not telling the truth. They assume the child will not feel and will not understand what is happening. They believe that, given the situation, it is better not to "bother" the child. Since they themselves are not sure what will happen either, they easily justify telling the child any story that will temporarily "buy" some quiet. However, children sometimes know much more than what they are told because they can sense what is going on. They see through the lies and falsehoods, and learn not to rely on or believe adults.

Since the child can sense what is going on, his concern and anxiety spur him to seek information, explanation, and most of all solutions. He invents magical "ceremonies" and pins his hopes on charms and amulets through which he seeks to remove the threat of the loss. These "solutions" may be soothing to him, but they will drive him even further from reality.

It is critical that the adults explain the situation to the child while at the same time familiarizing themselves with the child's questions and feelings about the threat. Not only will the information provided by the adult make the facts clear, but it will also alleviate some of the child's anxiety because he will feel closer to the parent, and more confident that he can rely on him. Through his explanations and "open" communication, the parent will also be providing an example of how to handle a threatening, unclear situation. Adults should bear in mind several main principles when providing assistance to children during a period of uncertainty:

1. The child should be given full information, differentiating between what is known and what is not known.

2. As much as possible, the child should be made a partner in deliberations, decisions, and actions. Attempts should be made to find out what his feelings and requests are about the plans being made by the adults.

3. Clarification and reinforcement should be offered on issues pertaining to the child's basic security, daily activities and functioning, and family continuity. The adult should explain what might be expected in the future, as much as possible.

4. The child should not be saddled with exaggerated expectations of his maturity, or his willingness to make compromises or sacrifices.

5. The child should be enabled to continue his familiar routine as much as possible.

Rapidly changing situations

The period of waiting and uncertainty is usually characterized by rapidly changing situations. The patterns of life to which the child is accustomed become "fluid" and unstable, and the adults around him don't function as they used to. Behavioral norms become ambiguous, and he is uncertain of what is expected of him. There is a feeling that the boundaries of the family have "ruptured." Individuals who do not belong to the nuclear family suddenly become very involved in the family life: relatives, physicians, social workers, and others, many of whom the child has never met and does not feel close to.

This situation causes the child to feel insecure. A sense of stability and familiarity with the flow of life and the people who "belong" are critical elements for the child. He needs a framework and boundaries within which he can act, within which he feels protected. The uncertainty and ambiguity typical during this period will generate anxiety. The child sometimes reacts to an ambiguous situation by challenging and even tearing down the boundaries and rules, and through inappropriate behavior. He may seem to be exploiting the situation to attain benefits by no longer doing homework, going to sleep late, eating a lot of candy. The adults, whose attentions are focused elsewhere, do not have the energy to make sure the child follows the rules. Even if the child seems to be enjoying himself and taking advantage of the situation, he is actually feeling scared and threatened. This situation is especially hard on young children because they do not have the tools to set up their own rules for self-control, and are especially in need of the protective laws and boundaries set up by the adults.

It is therefore very important, even in situations of ambiguity, to set up a *stable and structured microcosm* for the child. It is important to clarify the present framework and rules, even if they will be valid for only a short duration. It is better to change the rules every so often than to leave the child without any framework at all. During this difficult period, the child lacks the support usually provided by the parent, which is his source of confidence and calm. A clear framework can provide a partial substitute that will give the child a sense of security.

During times of waiting and uncertainty, the adult may be in a crisis situation and behave differently than what the child is accustomed to. The child senses that his parent is having difficulties. However, because the truth is often concealed from the child, he or she is left frightened. Not knowing why the parent is behaving strangely, the child will make up his own explanations. He is liable to think he caused it, that he did something "bad." He experiences the estrangement of the parent as rejection.

Trust in adults

This experience gnaws away at the foundations of the child's faith in adults, at their credibility. His ability to trust them to tell the truth during subsequent times of fear and distress is undermined. In the future, it will be hard for the child to believe what he is told. He will suspect that some other secret is hiding behind the words; that something else is being concealed from him; that perhaps things are being said only to soothe him and make things sound more plausible. This distrust of the parent, and of adults in general, undermines the child's proper emotional function and further aggravates his insecurity, which already exists due to the possibility of loss. The experience that one cannot believe or trust will remain with him far into adulthood, and harm his capacity to trust other people. It will leave a shadow of fear of the uncertain. It will exacerbate the lack of confidence that has already been harmed by the loss, and reinforce the anxieties and fears that ordinarily develop in the wake of a traumatic event.

Children have the tools to adjust themselves to reality, bleak as it may be. As hard as it may be, if adults help them and explain as much as possible they will try to understand and accept the ambiguous situation. It is okay to tell a child that things are unknown or inexplicable, but it is inadvisable to lie. By letting the child know what is happening, adults open up two opportunities for him: the child is able to contribute his part and play a helpful role in the present situation, and can prepare himself for the possible loss. A child who is given the opportunity to take part in what is happening, who is given a chance to help out and express an opinion, will not feel so helpless and superfluous. He must be told how or where he can help or have an effect, and in which areas his capacity to help will be more limited. If he is aware in advance of the dangers that the future holds, and of the limitations on his ability to act or influence the situation, this will, it is hoped, free him from future guilt feelings over not having done enough to prevent the loss. A child whose father is ill should understand that his father's recovery is not dependent on him, and if the father eventually dies, it is not because the child did not try hard enough to be a better boy. When his parents are going through a marital crisis, he must know that it is not his fault, and that it is not in his power to prevent their divorce.

If the period of uncertainty is very long, it casts a long shadow. Life constantly hangs in the balance between hope and disappointment; everyone is living in limbo. It is very hard for the child to move on with his life under such conditions because he is not "free" in the emotional sense. Children whose parents for years threaten each other with a divorce, or whose parents are divorced yet do not "separate" in the emotional sense, live in such limbo. They cannot readjust their lives and their relationships with each of the parents because of the constant uncertainty and changes these relationships go through. They live for years in uncertainty about whether they need to separate and mourn the loss or can hope for a continued life together. Such children often report that this experience was even harder for them than the possibility of the loss. "Make up your minds!" they demand of their parents when they can express their feelings of anguish.

It is clear, then, that a period of uncertainty constitutes a very significant and complicated point in time that has to be attended to no less seriously than after an actual loss. The impact of the experiences that the child goes through during this period will affect his ability to handle ensuing events.

Foreseeable death as compared to sudden death

The response of adults to sudden death is different from their response to an anticipated death for which they were able to prepare themselves. The differences are primarily reflected in the initial period following the loss. The first months following a sudden death are often characterized by shock, whereas after an anticipated death acceptance of the reality may occur earlier, since its roots began in the waiting period.

Preparation

Awareness of the possibility of loss enables one to prepare for it, a fact that may bring unique properties to the process. The preparations will occur at both the concrete and emotional levels. The concrete adjustment makes it possible to devise possible solutions to anticipated problems, and prepare to take whatever actions may be required. The would-be mourner is able to confront the loss with greater control and confidence, and less alarm and helplessness. The mental preparation enables the individual to initiate internal separation, and provides an opportunity for dialogue with and separation from the person who will be leaving. This sort of dialogue provides an opportunity to "complete" issues of mutual interest, talk things over, clarify issues, bring up and discuss "unfinished business," and perhaps forgive. This kind of conversation will usually leave the mourner feeling calmer. Conversely, in instances of sudden death there is often a sense of missed opportunity – "If I had only had the chance to…"

All that we have described in terms of adults also holds true for children, especially children capable of understanding the primary qualities of death – finality and irreversibility. When the child knows there is a chance that his parent may die, although this knowledge increases his level of anxiety, it gives him time to prepare. The child will do so in his own way, in accordance with his level of cognitive and emotional maturity. Whichever way he chooses, he will experience a sense of at least partial control of an event that has been forced on him. He will be able to separate in his own way, demonstrating his love, asking questions, expressing anger, or any other emotion he wishes to vent before the death occurs. Each such expression provides more fertile ground for the subsequent processing of grief.

In the face of the wish to protect the child and shield him from knowledge of the imminent loss, one should bear in mind that even the child who is not told the truth may be able to sense it, and perhaps even hear about it indirectly. When it is clear that the loss is about to occur, it is best to explain this to the child and not allow him to harbor any illusions. It is important to explain to children the difference between a dangerous situation and a situation in which the loved one is undoubtedly about to die. The child that does not know this difference may be afraid that any dangerous situation in the future will end in death. It is important that the child understands that although adults may go to great lengths to prevent death, stronger forces sometimes prevail.

If the death was foreseeable and this information was not shared with the child, not only will he have been denied an opportunity to prepare and separate, but his faith in adults will also have been harmed. From his perspective, adults are supposed to know everything, and if they did not know that which could have been known, then they have failed. When the child eventually discovers that the adults did know but omitted to tell him the whole truth, this will damage his capacity to believe them and rely on them in the future. As we have already demonstrated in previous contexts, a child that has been "burned" in this way once will suspect in the future that the truth is being concealed from him, and this suspiciousness will exacerbate his fears. He will soon conclude that something bad is about to happen, and will not be soothed by the assurances of adults.

Sudden death

Sudden death leaves the child with a sense of catastrophe. The world of children is an optimistic place without any sense of danger, but sudden death is a dramatic illustration of the lack of existential security, now or in the future. It is liable to leave him with the feeling that nothing is safe. If the parent dies a sudden death, the child may live in the fear that something terrible is suddenly going to happen to the remaining parent and other people close to him. This anxiety will harm his ability to draw away in the healthy sense from those people who are physically and emotionally most important to him.

Suicide

The suicide of someone close is a traumatic event for adults. When the person who took his or her life is a close family member – a child, a parent, a sibling – the others must contend with harsh feelings that further complicate the ordinary mourning process. There are usually no clear answers to the irksome questions of "why?" Nagging feelings of guilt surface: Why didn't I read the signs of distress? Why didn't I do enough to prevent the deed? There are also accusations and anger directed at the person who committed suicide, and perhaps also at others who are thought to be "responsible," are thought to have contributed to what happened, or are accused for not having prevented it. The person who committed suicide abandoned the others, and in doing so made a harsh "statement" to those left behind. Adults try to console themselves by looking for the motives of the suicide victim, thereby reducing the "sting" of the accusatory statement directed at them.

Shame and bewilderment

To the child, suicide, especially that of a parent, is an extremely violent and emotionally loaded act. Since even the adults cannot understand it, the child surely lacks the tools to make sense of such an act. He does not sufficiently understand life to understand the torment of an individual who commits suicide. He feels shame and bewilderment, because he senses the ambivalent and perhaps even condemnatory response of his close environment to the act.

Rejection and abandonment

For the child, the suicide of a parent constitutes a horrifying experience of rejection and abandonment. The parent chose to leave him, to cease being his parent, to let him grow up alone. Why? Wasn't I a good enough boy?

Didn't I justify his wish to continue being my parent? Why didn't he want to live with me? Why didn't he love me? What did I do to cause it? What could I have done to prevent it? Maybe I'm to blame for what happened?

It is important for children to feel they are very important to the parent. This need constitutes an emotional existential basis for the child's development and growth. The suicide of the parent says to the child: "You weren't important enough to me for me to want to live and continue being your parent." This undermines the foundations of the child's existence. The suicide of a parent is a truncation of the thread of life and existence for the child himself. The younger the child, the more elemental the damage to his sensations. The child may feel that he does not deserve love, and even that he does not deserve to exist.

Blame, guilt, and anger

The child may feel that he is to blame for the parent's act, that he caused the suicide. He may think that the parent took his life because he was not a good child, because he was too heavy a burden for the parent. The irrational feelings of guilt are not necessarily due to limitations of the child's understanding; rather, they force themselves on the child even when there is no logical explanation. Guilt feelings usually constitute a substitute for the immense anger the child feels toward the parent who abandoned him, who did not love him enough. He is conflicted about the parent who abandoned him, since it is the same parent that the child loves and misses. The child cannot allow himself to be angry or hate the parent, and therefore transfers the blame to himself, cleansing the parent's memory from the stain of anger and disappointment, leaving him to be a "good" parent.

The child may blame the remaining parent for what happened, but even if this is the case he usually cannot afford to express this anger and accusation because he is worried that the other parent will abandon him as well. He has no other choice but to divert the feelings of anger and accusation to himself. The suicide of a parent causes serious narcissistic damage, with profound effects that need to be watched for many years afterward. The child needs corrective experiences through which he will feel that he is worthy of love and attention.

Suicide leaves the immediate family with the message that it is incapable of protecting and preserving its members; that it is not a good and safe place to live; that it cannot look after its members in times of trouble. These are lethal messages for a family, impacting and hurting everyone. The family feels guilty, tainted, broken. Even if the children are still too young to understand and express the experience, they sense it. They feel the fragility, the loss of security, the sense of shame toward the world. They have not only lost a parent but they also feel that the home and the family are in jeopardy.

The secret

In the instance of suicide, there is a common tendency to conceal the facts from the child. It becomes a heavily guarded secret within the family, a "time bomb" waiting to explode. Some adults believe they can conceal the facts of the matter forever. Others may claim that they are waiting for the right time to tell the truth to the child: "When he grows up, then he'll be able to understand." The adult buys himself time, buys a postponement of the moment when he will have to explain an act that he himself is unable to understand or accept.

Time passes and the child often finds out about the suicide in an indirect, coincidental fashion. Sometimes other children are the source of information, having heard the secret whispered by their parents. When the child hears about the suicide from other people, but it is still a secret at home, an even more convoluted situation is created. The child knows the awful secret, but is left to bear it alone. He has no one to ask about it or verify its truth, no one with whom he can try to understand it. He is left without any support, forced to confront alone the threatening and bitter truth that has come to light.

It is no doubt difficult for adults to cope with the needs of a child regarding a subject they themselves do not understand; one that leaves them helpless and in turmoil. Nevertheless, the child needs adults, needs the explanations, sense of comfort, and confidence they can provide. It is better that parents share their thoughts and feelings with the child, telling the child that they too are angry and bewildered, that they too do not understand, rather than leaving him alone and isolated with the same feelings and thoughts.

Murder

Children also lose parents in violent circumstances such as murder. When a parent is murdered, the initial experience – long before grieving sets in – is of absolute chaos, helplessness in the face of violence that is all-engulfing and against which there is no defense. It is nearly impossible to describe the situation of the children of a parent who murdered his or her spouse. Sometimes, when one parent murders the other, he or she also murders or attempts to murder other members of the family – often his own children. In such cases the child also has to deal with the fact that his parent wanted to murder him too. In some domestic murder cases, the murderer subsequently takes his or her own life.

Chaos

Such instances constitute an experience of total chaos for the child, a complete collapse of the family, and the disintegration of every basic principle of behavior and life. The most basic trust is crushed. Existential confidence is left with nothing to hold onto. The focus of attention is diverted from the process of grieving and separation to the act of violence, with all its implications: the sense of shock; the experience of ruin and chaos; the feeling that there is no defense or shelter from threat and danger; the sense of utter helplessness. There is also an overwhelming anger at the murderer, and the accusatory attitude toward whoever should have been on guard and prevented this from happening. The intense feelings of the child – fear, terror, and hatred – are beyond what the child is able to handle. In these circumstances, the child will be consumed by many difficult questions over a period of several years before he will be able to touch on the feelings of grief itself.

Authorities

Murder ushers the authorities into the child's life, including policemen, investigators, and welfare professionals. His own and his family's sense of privacy and intimacy are ruptured, and he is subject to the protection of external factors and unfamiliar figures. Sometimes the child is removed from the home, and the family ceases to exist. He loses everything, and feels that everything has been destroyed. He loses all sense of his defined and protected self, which had been part of his protective, sheltering parents and family.

Blaming

Blaming the murderer, blaming those who are thought of as being guilty for what happened, and blaming oneself for not having prevented the murder are only some of the questions and thoughts that will occupy the child's mind for years to come, and will torment him. It is hard to describe the tremendous burden of suffering and devastation, the sheer disappointment and utter loss of faith in love, hope, and humankind that will now be part of the child's psyche.

Vulnerability and isolation

When the murder was committed by one of the parents, the sense of chaos is further complicated by intense shame and the sense that society is casting out the parent who committed the murder as well as the family. The child lives with a sense of alienation and isolation. He feels stained by a social stigma. People might feel compassion towards the children, but often the children experience this as pity and aloofness. People talk about him and his family behind his back; he is unable to defend himself.

Rehabilitation

Whatever chance there is for rehabilitation will come from adults who can serve as alternate parental figures, and with whom he can build – with much patience and love – a relationship of trust. Acceptance, protection, and security are the milestones along a journey of healing that will eventually enable him to mourn his dreadful fate and the parent who was murdered. He will also have to mourn for the parent who committed the murder because that parent was lost to him as well.

Divorce

During a divorce, a great deal of attention is paid to technical aspects and changes relating to the new situation, such as division of property and the issue of child custody. The atmosphere is usually full of tension and anger.

We may not be accustomed to think of divorce as an act of loss, but in the child's experience it is. The child "loses" his complete family, since the family following the divorce of his parents is different, at times even temporarily "torn apart." He loses a part of his relationship with the parent who is leaving home, and at times loses part of his relationship with the parent with whom he lives, since the relationship between them has been altered.

Change in nature of family

At times the actual divorce is prefaced by a sometimes lengthy period of crisis between the two spouses, which is similar to the period of uncertainty described earlier. One of the parents may have left home or is seldom at home, reducing his or her involvement in the life of the child and the family. The atmosphere at home is tense, and there may be numerous fights and arguments. Many parents want to save their children from hearing about their problems, and do not share information or explain what is happening. They sense the tension in the air and are frightened. The children sense that one of the parents is growing more distant, and may take it as a rejection of them – the children.

When the parents divorce, the child experiences a profound change in the nature of the family. There is at least temporary uncertainty vis-à-vis the family framework. It is unstable, it is different, and its sense of unity and continuity are damaged. It is not clear how the family will continue, who belongs to it, how it will function as a family. The child is unsure on whom he can rely. The child's sense of belonging to a family, which is an important part of his identity and the way he defines himself to the outside world, is damaged. The child loses part of the support system that protected him. Numerous elements in the child's life are now cast in an unfamiliar and unclear light. Much of that which had been clear and familiar is lost.

As part of separation or divorce, one of the parents moves out. This constitutes a loss for the child because the parent is no longer with him. The younger the child, the harder it is for him or her to conceive that the parent is still there for him, even though he is not living at home. Often, though not always, he sees the parent less and is not as closely in touch with him or her. The uncertainty regarding the future relationship with this parent adds to the sense of loss. Even when the child is provided with explanations about the arrangements regarding his contact with the parent, he loses faith in the real parenthood of that parent. This feeling might prevail for a long while. He fears that the parent who drew away from the home and from the family will be "lost" altogether. As he experiences the new kind of parenthood, and assuming that it is a caring, loving, and consistent relationship, he will, it is hoped, return to feeling safe, loved, and cared for.

Relationship with remaining parent

The relationship with the parent with whom the child stays usually undergoes a change as well. Initially, the parent is usually preoccupied by anger, grieving, and readjustment to the new situation, and is therefore less emotionally available to the child, investing less parental effort in him and behaving differently. For the child, this experience is also mixed with a sense of loss, even if only temporary.

At times, the divorce leads to significant long-term changes in the quality of the child's relationship with the parent, be it the parent who left the family or the one with whom the child lives. These changes will be discussed in Chapter 4.

Ambiguity and instability

The changes and ambiguity concerning home and family life leave the child confused and frightened. The atmosphere of ambiguity and instability is usually temporary, and carries on until the family unit adjusts to the new situation, until the parents have adjusted and resumed stable functioning, and until the child's relationship with the parent who left has stabilized. However, the trauma of this period of insecurity and helplessness – during which the child experienced the loss of a familiar relationship with his parents and the loss of his safe, familiar family framework – leaves its mark. It is in any case a loss which he will need to grieve about and work through.

Sometimes there is no sense of finality in the separation of the parents. Uncertainty accompanies the life of the parents, and therefore also that of the child, for a long while. In some cases the divorce process drags on for years; in other cases the couple keep breaking up and coming back together. Some couples do not finalize the separation even though they are officially and legally divorced. They do not achieve emotional separation as they keep on fighting. In other cases even after the divorce there are ongoing attempts to mend the break-up, at least by one of the partners. In all of these instances, the child is left confused. The uncertainty of the situation prevents him from grieving over the loss while also readjusting to it. Instead of accepting the loss, moving on with his life, and adjusting to the new circumstances, he often is holding onto hope and is even busy with attempts to bring about a reconciliation between his parents and to "mend" the family. Often such hopes and efforts result in disappointment after disappointment. Valuable time is lost on these hopes and the pain of "failure" and disappointment becomes even greater.

Exploitation of children

One of the most serious phenomena in the break-up of a marriage is the exploitation of the children by parents in the dispute between them. They enlist the children in conspiracies against the other parent, use them to hurt the other parent, share their suspicions with them, slander and make accusations against the other parent. All of these actions make it hard for the child to maintain his independent relationship with the other parent. The child, who in any case feels hurt, abandoned, betrayed, and neglected, is further incited against the parent. This hampers his ability to accept the parent who drew away, and to maintain a positive relationship with him. Much has already been said about the importance of a parental image that enables the child to identify with it and internalize it. A "tarnished" image makes it difficult to carry on with this important process. The child's ability to accept the loss and advance toward readjustment is harmed. In order for him to continue enjoying a constructive relationship with the parent who left, the child has to accept the new situation. However, a child who is enlisted as an accomplice in a war being waged by the remaining parent, or when he is asked to identify with his parent's non-acceptance of the separation, will not be able to continue a nurturing and positive relationship with the other parent.

At the end of the divorce process, as the family unit readjusts to the new situation, the child requires a period of readjustment and adaptation. He is in need of a soothing and corrective process. As is the case after any loss, the child needs, first and foremost, to undergo a process of grieving through which he will be able to express the anger and disappointment, accusation and fear, and most of all the sadness and pain he is experiencing. He will have to "separate" from the previous family set-up, and only then will he be able to adjust to the new situation, and achieve emotional acceptance of the new reality.

If the parents themselves have not yet completed the separation and grieving process, it is difficult for the child to reach this stage on his own. It is very difficult for a child to advance further than his own parents in the process of readjustment following divorce. In addition, parents who are in a rut and unable to accept the separation, abandonment, and pain of divorce are not emotionally available to help their child accept the new situation.

Research studies that tracked the development of children of divorced parents describe the effects of this event in the short term, and on into adulthood. Some of the children are characterized by damaged self-image and a tendency toward depression. They may have difficulties forming intimate relationships, or may exhibit destructiveness where intimate relationships are concerned. It should be emphasized that not every child whose parents have divorced suffers long-term damage from the event. The factors that can mitigate the effects of this trauma are: preservation of the family framework and the sense of family continuity; continual contact with both parents who will continue to be nurturing parents – supportive and loving. It is important for children to be fully aware of their new life circumstances, and to be given a chance to be part of decisions that pertain to their evolving relationship with their parents.

Children should be granted the opportunity to express anxiety, concern, anger, grief, and pain. They need to be freed from any feelings of guilt or responsibility about the break-up and the continuing relationships between the parents.

Rejection and abandonment

The child who has been abandoned or rejected by his parent undergoes a traumatic experience, which includes the experience of loss. The act of abandonment can be concrete: the parent may disappear, or may distance himself from the family and break off contact. The abandonment can be "only" emotional: the parent seems oblivious to the child's existence; breaks off emotional contact with him; does not show any concern for or involvement in the child's life; fails to carry out the parental duties toward him; and most of all stops showing the child his love and care.

Rejection and abandonment have traumatic effects that extend beyond the loss. For the child, it is an experience of being "erased," in which he is given the devastating message that he is not loved and does not deserve to be loved. The emotional imprint left by abandonment is even more profound than loss since it is not an "act of God" but an act that is chosen, controlled, and desired by the parent.

Suicide

We spoke of how the suicide of a parent constitutes one of the most intense experiences of abandonment for a child. He has been "abandoned" by the parent in the boldest and most violent way possible. The suicide of a parent sends him the message: "You weren't important enough for me to want to live with you and be your parent," "I didn't love you enough to want to be with you." Nothing could be worse for the child.

Divorce

In some divorces, the parent who left home hardly sees his children or may even break off all contact with them. In other cases, such an abrupt physical detachment does not occur, but emotional distancing does take place. The child senses that he is no longer important to the parent, that the parent does not care about him and is not interested in a close regular relationship with him. The parent does not try to be involved in the child's everyday life, does not keep in touch, and is very "thrifty" in showing his love and caring. This sort of emotional abandonment is usually expressed in a tenuous relationship with the parent and a lack of stability or regularity of contact. The ambiguous and unclear messages sent by the parent cause the child to feel rejected.

The child who has seen his father reject or leave his mother, or vice versa, may be frightened that he too will be rejected and abandoned. The child's feeling is often reinforced by the remaining parent, who also feels abandoned. Consciously or not, this parent encourages the child to feel that he too has been left behind, and in so doing enlists the child to his side – for anger, excoriation, and blame. The child will pay a heavy price for this enlistment onto one parent's side: a painful distancing from the other parent.

Disappearance

There are instances in which a parent leaves the home and family and vanishes, without informing the family where he is, and if and when he will be coming back. The child veers between hope for the return of his parent and anger and despair over the parent's abandonment. The confusion and uncertainty make it very difficult to adjust to this situation. The child experiences abandonment, but throughout the period of ambiguity, which may be prolonged, he lacks any solid grounds for grieving over what happened.

Addiction

Parents who are addicted to drugs or alcohol are apt to neglect their children emotionally and even physically. The primary focus of the parent's life is his craving. The child is superfluous, constituting a burden and a disruption; the child feels abandoned and rejected.

Mental health problems

When the parent suffers from a personality disorder or other mental problems, the child usually suffers from severe lack of parental investment. The parent is concerned with his own emotional needs; the child and his needs are of little concern. Instead, demands are put on the child to cater to needs of the parent. The child lives in constant fear of "losing" the parent. He senses that if he does not meet the parent's needs and demands, he will be rejected and abandoned. His relationship with the parent is conditional, and is conducted under this constant threat; a threat that is often realized, especially in the emotional sense.

Abuse

Battered children and children who have been sexually abused or treated in some other violent manner by their parents also come under the heading of children who have experienced abandonment. Violence and abuse constitute an abandonment of parenthood. The abusive parent sometimes puts on an act of being a very loving parent – giving gifts to the child and sending messages that the child is very important to him. Submission to the abuse of the parent is the way the child is expected to pay back his parent's "love." The child is confused by the conflicting feelings he has towards his parent. He needs the feeling that he is so important and loved, yet it is the same parent who also hurts and abuses him. It is important for children to keep the "good parent," and they will therefore do whatever they can to keep their affection. If being a "good boy" includes suffering and submission to a parent's whims and demands, some prefer that to becoming a "bad" child and losing the "love" of their parent. In these situations children often delude themselves with the belief that in so doing they will prevent further abuse. They also often believe that they deserve the abuse because they were not "good" enough. In taking upon themselves the blame for the parent's behavior, they preserve the feeling that the parent loves them and is a good parent. It is easier for the child to take the blame than to "lose" his good and loving parent.

Acts of abuse, violence, and exploitation are often veiled and concealed not only by the parent but also by the child. The child does not tell anyone about them, either because he does not understand or admit the full extent of their meaning, or because he is ashamed and even thinks it is his fault. Exposing the parent, he fears, will hurt the parent and end in his loss. The experience, and all the implications thereof, remains concealed and unconscious for many years. Only when the child reveals that he has been abused, and understands that the parent has done him harm, will he be capable of encountering his emotions as an abandoned child. A child who has been abused has "lost" the good parent he deserved and needed, and has to mourn this loss.

Illness and handicap

When a parent has a serious and prolonged illness, the child may feel that the parent has lost interest in him. In certain instances, fulfilling parental duties may become a burden, demanding energies that are not available. Preoccupation with physical problems and needs might make the parent unavailable – physically and mentally – to the children. As a result they may experience the loss of parenthood.

In certain instances, the severe handicap of a parent, especially one that causes changes in emotional state and personality, may adversely affect the level of the parent's investment in the children and lead to an emotional distancing from them. Children of ill and handicapped parents "lose" the healthy parent they once had, and they grieve for that parent.

Parental crises and traumas

Crises and traumatic events that befall parents may rob them of all their energy, leaving the children feeling abandoned. For some orphans, the greatest source of hardship is not the death of a parent but the experience of abandonment by the surviving parent, who is consumed by grief and does not function as a parent.

Children whose sibling has died report similar sensations. Their brother or sister has died, but they have also "lost" their parents, who are totally overwhelmed by the bereavement and are functioning at a diminished level, often investing much less emotional effort in the remaining children. The remaining children feel all their parents' love "belongs" to the dead sibling and they feel deserted. This feeling sometimes lasts only during the initial period of mourning. In other instances, particularly in cases of prolonged pathological grieving, the feeling of having "lost" their parents may persist for years.

In some of the examples cited above, not only does the child feel abandoned, but a reversal of roles between parent and child takes place. The parent not only minimizes his parental investment in the child, but also "demands" that the child invest attention and support in him. Many children submit to the demands and expectations of the parent, becoming "parental children." They do so because they are left with little other choice: this is the only way to keep the family functioning. Unconsciously they may hope that this will repair the "loss" of the parent. They may hope that if they are "good kids" and care for the parent, perhaps they will also get to spend some "quality time" together, and resume being their parents' children.

There are some essential differences between the loss of a parent as a result of death and the experience of loss as a result of abandonment and rejection, as described here. In some instances of abandonment, there is no concrete dimension to the loss, since the parent is physically there. There are no dimensions of finality and irreversibility to the loss; instead there is a lot of ambiguity. The parent whom the child has "lost" is present, and the child seizes on the hope that he will resume being a parent. So long as the child does not relinquish this hope, he will not be able to start grieving for the "lost" parent. He will not be able to express and process his feelings regarding the loss he is experiencing as long as he is holding onto his hopes and investing his energies in "correcting" the loss. He will not be able to accept the reality of the "lost good parent" if he believes he will reappear.

Grieving and acceptance

Bereavement is the first step toward acceptance of the new reality. In the situations we have described, the child is so threatened by the rejection and erasure that he will often protect himself by means of *repression and denial*. It is difficult for him to accept the fact that the parent chose to abandon him. This admission is so painful that many children prefer to avoid it and deny it.

Abandoned children wait for the parent to come back, rationalizing the abandonment with imaginary excuses, denying reality, and inventing stories that hold out a less painful alternative. It is hard for them to let go of the same parent whose return they so strongly desire. Acceptance of the reality – admitting that their parent is not a good and loving parent, that the parent is willing to hurt him – will hurt the child no less than the abandonment itself. The child requires a nurturing and loving parent, and has a hard time letting go of that image.

In order to help the child process the loss, adults must first work with the child to see the situation for what it really is, and help him undo the duality in his relationship with the parent. Only when the child can stop his vigil of waiting for the "good" parent to come back, only when he no

longer denies that he has been abandoned, will he be able to start processing the grief. Only then will he be able to accept the painful reality and
learn to live with it. The encounter with the painful feelings of rejection
and erasure will facilitate processing of the loss and a process of rehabilitation.

The experience of parental abandonment undermines the deepest
foundations of the child's existence and development, causing *narcissistic
damage*. The message the child receives – that he is not deserving of
parental love, that he may not even deserve to exist – adversely affects him
at the libidinal level and the core of his personality. In research studies and
treatment records of children who experienced parental abandonment,
these children were found to have a high probability of ego function difficulties and personality disorder and pathologies. The child's sense of
self-worth sustains a great deal of damage. He feels that he does not
deserve any investment of love and caring. His dominant sensations are of
degradation and emptiness. The internal object is damaged, lifeless, and
empty. The typical defense mechanisms employed in this situation are
intense and rigid idealization, denial, and repression.

Sometimes the child compensates for his inner sensation of emptiness
and nothingness by means of grandiose self-perception and massive
investment in self, which serves to fill the immense internal void. Rejected
children call out for recognition, acceptance, and unconditional love, but
do not know how to internalize them, and lack faith in the ability to attain
them. As a result, they often adopt *aberrant modes of behavior*. These children
may exhibit an inability to show human empathy. They may be abusive of
others, suffer from depression, give in to addictions. They may exhibit
unrestrained anger, uncontrollable lying, criminal behavior, and sexually
deviant behavior. As adults, they may seek ways to fill their internal void
through obsessive shopping, unbounded profligacy, or use of addictive
substances that are supposed to "fill" them with a good feeling and dispel
the sense of emptiness, self-contempt, and degradation.

It is difficult for such individuals to form or have faith in relationships,
and they typically avoid intimate relationships. This behavior is dictated
by fear of abandonment and loss. They have a strong tendency to be the
person who abandons, ending relationships before they have a chance to
mature. This "helps" them preserve their sense of control, preventing

dependence on another person and the resulting vulnerability. Their behavior also reflects a subconscious need to be the one who abandons – to hurt others and take revenge for everything that was done to them.

It should be emphasized that when the other parent who continues to raise the child is caring, supportive, and loving, he or she can provide the right counterbalance to the damage described above, and give the child a firm foundation for continued growth and strengthening. Such a parent will give the child not only a correcting experience of a stable unconditional love, but, it is hoped, will also allow the child to grieve for the "lost" parent and support him in this difficult process.

Previous and cumulative losses

Anyone who has experienced traumatic loss is more sensitive and reacts more strongly to any subsequent loss, actual or potential. He already knows the impact of such a harsh experience, having already been "burned" before. When a child experiences repeated losses, the cumulative effect causes the repercussions to be especially severe. The damage to the mental development of the child leaves scars that will be more difficult to heal.

Vulnerability

A child who has experienced the death of a parent is in a more vulnerable state when he experiences any additional loss of a parental figure. The child whose father abandoned him will react strongly when his mother's boyfriend leaves her, and him. A child whose mother was taken ill and had to be hospitalized for a long period will be especially anxious if his father has to be hospitalized. Often, adults do not understand why a child may exhibit such intense anxiety when faced with seemingly simple situations. The child's overreacting has to do with the traumatic memories that immediately surface whenever he gets close to a situation that contains elements of a potential loss and separation. For children who have already experienced traumatic loss, even the beginning of a situation that involves a risk of loss will stir up the deepest fears and anxieties. Their sensitivity and fears are more acute than those of "normal" children who have not been hurt. They already know the taste of loss-related pain, and bear the old emotional scars.

Loss of grandparents

The illness and death of a grandparent may at times be an extremely threatening trigger for these children. Grandparents sometimes serve as alternative parental figures for a child who has lost a parent. The child becomes very attached to the grandparent, finding love, acceptance, and security. When he becomes aware that he may lose the grandparent, or when the grandparent dies, this is a traumatic event for the child. His response may be no less serious than when he lost his parent. This surprises the adults, who assume that the death of an elderly ill grandparent should not be taken as an unusual tragic event. But for the child, it is a repeat experience – another loss of a person who raised and loved him. Emotions that were repressed and not expressed after the initial loss now flare up, inundating the child. Since he is older, he is more aware of his emotions and fears, and can express them clearer.

Coping abilities

The responses and coping abilities of the child to additional losses depend on several variables that have to do with how he experienced the initial loss:

- Did he receive support and reinforcement at the initial loss, and was it helpful?
- To what degree did the first loss damage his ego strength?
- What defense mechanisms did he adopt to cope with threatening situations?
- What has transpired since the previous loss?
- Has he had good and strengthening experiences since then?
- Has he had to deal with additional hardships, emotional as well as concrete?
- Does he have a loving and supportive parental figure?

- Does he have a supportive environment around him, a support network of grandparents, uncles, and aunts, and/or friends?

Although the child who experienced a previous traumatic loss is sensitive and vulnerable, he may also be more mature than other children his age, and possess the mental tools that will enable him to cope better than the child who has not experienced any previous trauma. He is already well versed in dealing with the hardships of life.

Loss of two parents

Some children lose both parents. Sometimes they die or are killed at the same time, as in a car accident. In other instances, the loss of the surviving parent occurs some time later. These are two different situations, but both are particularly harsh and complex. When a child loses both parents at the same time, the sense of calamity and loss is absolute. The child's entire world is instantaneously shattered, and he feels he is left alone in the world. Suddenly, he goes from being an ordinary child with parents and a family to one who has nothing. He feels as if he does not belong to anybody, that there is no one to care for him or look after him, no one to guarantee his well-being and love him, no one to "be there for him." It is difficult to describe the utter dislocation and loss, absolute loneliness, and dreadful nothingness.

When there are other siblings in the family, the sense of loneliness is a little less pronounced because the siblings have each other. The ages of the siblings are significant. If at least one of them is older and can serve as a protective, mature parental figure, or if some of them are already at an age at which they can support one another, then the sense of disconnection and dependence on the outside world is slightly mitigated. When there are adult siblings, they will attempt to reorganize and continue to function as a family unit, helped by one another. They will usually try to divide the parental duties among themselves.

The death of both parents brings about the intrusion of outside people into the family: close relatives and good neighbors as well as teachers, social workers, and other institutional personnel who want to help, or are compelled by law to intervene. This intrusion undermines the family's autonomy, and raises the concern among the children that they will have no control over what happens to them from now on. Numerous decisions about their lives and future pass into "alien" hands, and they feel forsaken, given to the mercies of other people who make the decisions that affect them. They do not want to live under the patronage and kindness of others, but this desire does not always withstand the reality of the situation. In many instances, they are placed in the care of a custodial or foster family, or are forced to take in outside figures that wield parental authorities. The change is supposed to protect them, ease their plight, furnish more normal living conditions, and answer their basic needs. Nevertheless, although their existential needs are resolved, they feel disconnected and rootless, as if there were no one backing them up. In many cases it takes years before they settle and feel they "belong." In addition, when children are removed from their home, even if they move in with relatives such as a grandmother, aunt, or other family member, they experience another traumatic loss – the loss of their home.

The simultaneous loss of both parents is therefore an experience of such intense and multidimensional trauma that the processing of loss in its wake is significantly more complex than anything described above. It is not only an absolute loss that leaves the child without a sense of belonging or emotional support, but it is also accompanied by numerous other losses. The trauma adversely and intensely affects every area of the child's life. It causes a deep wound that he will carry throughout his life. Many years may pass before he finds a way to rehabilitate the sense of belonging, equilibrium, and confidence he requires. It will be a long time before he dares once again to build a close and trusting relationship with someone close to him.

Due to the enormity of the blow, the child must readjust and enlist the energy and defense mechanisms that will enable him to continue with his life. He cannot allow the trauma to permeate his life with full force because it is too threatening, too all-encompassing. Only after the passage of several years, after he has reassembled his life and built up the internal strengths and external relationships on which he can rely, will he be able to allow himself fully to touch on the deep significance of the calamity and the pain, and process them.

Loss of the remaining parent some time after loss of the first parent

Such a loss constitutes the fulfillment of the nightmare that the child has feared the most, ever since the initial loss. This is proof of the utter lack of security and control over life. It represents the "victory" of the loss that has already hurt him once. As noted above, the individual who has been hurt by one trauma becomes more vulnerable if an additional trauma occurs. The manner in which he responds, and his capacity for coping with the situation, are highly dependent on the resources at his disposal and the burdens upon him: What has happened since the initial loss? Has he had positive experiences through which his strengths increased? Which mechanisms has he employed to cope with the initial loss? All of these factors will influence his ability to cope with the new blow. The additional loss presents a new emotional burden that is heavier than the first, by virtue of the fact that it falls on "saturated" ground.

The rehabilitation of children who have lost two parents depends, first and foremost, on them finding *substitute parental figures* who will not only look after their physical needs but will fill the emotional roles of parents – imparting unconditional love, protection, and nurturing. Under these conditions, the child will be able to restore his trust in the world and heal his hurting internal world. Nevertheless, the loss of two parents will leave a deep hurting scar which will always be there.

Gender of the absent parent and the child

The issue of gender has already been mentioned in the course of discussing how the gender of the child vis-à-vis that of the parent can influence the child's response to situations arising in the aftermath of the loss (Chapter 2). The issue of gender was particularly stressed in the context of tasks associated with the Oedipal phase and adolescence.

Gender roles

Children learn gender roles first and foremost from their parents. They learn the instrumental roles that pertain to gender – how to bake a cake or how to fix a leaky faucet. With the help of the parents they develop traits that are related to male/female identity. Their parents have a crucial role in the process of developing their sexual identity.

We have cited the importance of the age of the child when he lost his parent. We have also shown that age-linked tasks and sensitivities will be influenced by the loss. We have emphasized the importance of helping the child complete the missing tasks concerning the development of his sexual identity and gender roles. We now survey and briefly summarize the four situations: a son who loses his father; a son who loses his mother; a daughter who loses her father; a daughter who loses her mother. The characteristic effects of loss of a parent in each of these situations are described. Our description of these scenarios assumes that the child is growing up without an alternative parental figure. For if the remaining parent forms a new intimate relationship and the child grows up with an alternative parental figure who is part of the family, the scenario can be very different from that which is described. An alternative parental figure who fulfills the gender roles in the family and the child's life will enable the child to go through the common developmental phases.

It should be emphasized that the situations described here are based on traditional stereotypical gender roles. In the light of changes in western society regarding gender roles and the relationship between the sexes, we can also anticipate variations in this realm among children growing up without one parent.

The son who loses his father

The son who loses a father will miss the masculine figure with whom he is supposed to identify, and from whom he is supposed to learn male traits and roles. The boy will naturally seek alternative male figures with whom he can identify. Many young boys tend to identify with very masculine figures such as Superman or Tarzan. Adolescents choose a rock star or an athlete. Younger boys who have lost their father are inclined to choose superhuman heroes who often exhibit power-driven and even violent behavior through which they channel their feelings of anger about the loss, and towards their father who is not there, and their desire for control, as compensation for not having had control when the loss occurred. The unrealistic figure with which they identify increases their preoccupation with omnipotent fantasies that can give them strength. In general, young boys are attracted to omnipotent fantasies, but boys whose fathers are not there in reality will lack a real-life individual to counterbalance the fantasies and keep them in check.

In the quest for filling in what he is missing, the child also casts about for an alternative father figure. Young children "adopt" uncles and family friends. Adolescents sometimes find the figure they are seeking in their youth movement counselor or army commander. A masculine figure who can fill some of the functions of a father may serve as an important resource, contributing toward the child's development.

The absence of a father leaves the son feeling that the Oedipal "stage" is free and that he is his mother's "man." This opens the door to possible manifestation of unconscious fantasies and urges. Meanwhile, there may be no one at home to set up boundaries to the child's "manhood." The boy's endeavor to assume the male role may even suit the needs of his mother, who lacks a spouse. We expand our discussion of the dynamics involved in this scenario in Chapter 4, but at this point it is sufficient to state that such a situation can increase confusion and anxieties vis-à-vis the child's developing sexual identity and experiences of gender roles.

The sense of omnipotence and absence of boundaries that the child experiences may also transfer to other areas of his life, and might be expressed in behavior marked by an absence of boundaries or inhibitions, discipline problems, defiance of limits and prohibitions, risk taking, and clashes with individuals who represent rules and limits, such as teachers, policemen, and army commanders. The masculine identity that is forming within the child is unbalanced. Often there are difficulties in making a healthy separation from mother. When he reaches adolescence and early adulthood, he may exhibit difficulty forming relationships with young women. Choosing a mate might be influenced by problematic needs. In some instances, there is an unconscious need to make the separation from the mother through the mate, creating a situation that causes confrontation and defiance toward the mother. In other instances, the choice emanates from an unconscious desire to preserve the mother's image, and not to separate from her. The chosen mate resembles the mother; at other times she is always left as second best to the mother.

Fatherless sons may also have a difficult time choosing a profession. Some have a hard time accepting the authority of male superiors. These two areas are related to male self-image and the boy's experiences with the male world. These difficulties were elaborated in the discussion of the effects of loss on young adults in Chapter 2.

The son who loses his mother

When a son loses his mother, he will miss the experience of maternal warmth and love, the "soft" and embracing love that the child especially needs in his first years of life. Boys who lose their mothers often feel emotionally alone. Fathers tend to express their love through physical and existential concerns, but sometimes have a hard time bestowing maternal warmth and softness on their children. The son who is "left" by his mother may crave his mother's love, but also harbor a great deal of anger toward women. He is attracted to women – most frequently to women older than him – because they are a substitute for his missing mother. He is also threatened by women, for fear that they too will abandon him.

In order to seek and find a suitable mate and form a healthy, adult relationship with her, he must first separate himself from the yearning for his missing maternal love, and free himself from the fear of being abandoned by a woman.

The daughter who loses her father

When a daughter loses her father, she loses the man who was supposed to be her first suitor. The father's adoration and wooing of his daughter are the basis on which the daughter begins to feel and experience her femininity. A girl who has no father is left with the feeling that her father has abandoned her. She is left with an unconscious fear that men will not love her enough, and that they will leave her too. She has a strong need for a man who will offer the paternal experience of love, admiration, and courtship. She is unsure of herself, unsure that she will be able to earn the devotion of a man who will protect her. When she does find someone willing to form a relationship with her, she often needs him to be hers and hers alone – as a sort of compensation for what she lost as a child. She needs to be assured that she will not be left alone again. Subconsciously, she is angry with men, but she is also in great need of them. She tends to develop unrealistic romantic expectations. She is looking for the ideal man who will pick up where her father left off. Anyone who does not fulfill these high expectations will be discarded. She may eagerly court a man whom she desires, to the extent of negating her own self-worth.

When a fatherless daughter is attracted to unavailable men, it is evident that she is still waging the uncompleted struggle for her status as a woman – one more battle in the uncompleted Oedipal campaign to "win" her father. Her father's absence left her in an unfinished competition with her mother. The competition with her mother may have been even further reinforced – and unfinished – by her mother's new suitors. Perhaps she competed for them, but was denied a chance to resolve this Oedipal issue because her mother's suitors did not fulfill the father's role towards her.

In order to prepare herself for a healthy, adult relationship, the daughter must complete her search for a substitute father. And in order to eventually grow into a mature woman who can enable her own daughter to grow up and "compete" with her, she must grow out of the need to compete with her own mother.

The daughter who loses her mother

When a daughter loses her mother, she loses her primary role model for feminine roles and traits. She was supposed to learn from her mother not only how to clean and cook, dress, and put on make-up, but also "feminine" traits such as softness and warmth. She will feel her mother's loss a great deal when it comes to needing advice on various feminine subjects, including relationships with the opposite sex.

The loss of a mother means the loss of the maternal, protective warmth, the loss of an emotionally inclusive partner; a role model for such relationships, which she will need to learn for her own functioning as a wife and a mother. By the nature of things, a daughter who has lost her mother will turn to her father in hope of finding answers to her needs. The special relationship that characterizes the connection between father and daughter takes on additional layers of emotional dependency, further reinforcing the ties between the father and daughter. It is not hard for her to view him as her "partner." This strong relationship will have to be unbound later in her life, when developmental separation is required. The absence of competition with her mother prevents the daughter from accepting the developmental demands by which she must gradually relinquish her father as suitor and partner. This may harm her future ability to form emotional relationships with age peers of the opposite sex. She will tend to "compare" them to her father, whom she often conceives as the perfect man and partner. In order to develop healthy relationships with other men, she has to break free of the special bond with her father.

Due to the unique place her father fills in her life, it is also difficult for her to accept any new intimate relationships which her father might form, viewing them as competition and hurtful to her. She will probably express her feelings of jealousy through acting out. If she is an adolescent, she may fight for her "rightful" position through provocative behavior, which will be primarily sexual in character.

Siblings

The effects of gender on the child who has lost a parent are influenced – sometimes balanced – by the child's siblings. The situation of a daughter who only has brothers is different from that of a daughter who has other sisters. The situation of a boy who has only sisters is different from that of a boy who has other brothers. The way the family handles the loss within the context of gender roles is different for each one of these combinations.

A fatherless boy who has brothers can identify with them, and with their help can develop his masculinity. The natural competition between the brothers for the mother's affections will moderate the development of an excessively strong connection with the mother. The situation is different for a fatherless boy who only has sisters. He is the "man" in the family, surrounded by women. His models for imitation and identification are all feminine, and he is probably assigned the role of "man of the house," an object for courtship and competition.

A motherless daughter who has sisters will have opportunities for feminine relationships. The sisters can serve as role models, they can provide a shoulder to lean on and a source of advice given from a feminine perspective. The girl's relationship with the father is different when she is not the only daughter, and has to "compete" with her sisters for his love and attention. The case is different for a daughter who only has brothers. She is the sole woman in the house, the "princess" of the family, for both her father and brothers. She is accustomed to receiving a great deal of attention and being spoiled because of her femininity.

In conclusion we need to emphasize again that the influence on the gender themes is greatly affected by the existence of other male–female figures in the child's life – relatives, friends of the family, new mates of the parent, teachers, etc.

The relationship prior to the loss

There are always unique dimensions to every parent–child relationship: the father with whom the child used to play chess; the mother who used to arrange picnics and outings, and taught the child about every flower and bird. In the absence of the parent there is now a void. The child is missing that special essence that imbued his parental relationship with a unique flavor. This essence will be particularly missed because it will be difficult to find a substitute for. Each parent also has his or her distinctive emotional and spiritual "roles." A father may have passed on traditional values; a mother may have preached tolerance, compromise, and love of one's fellow man. The child's feelings of pain and yearning take on a special hue because of the absence of these unique characteristics.

Good relationship

The quality of the relationship that existed between the child and the parent prior to the loss will affect the process of bereavement and readjustment following the loss. When the child had a good relationship with the parent, the parent will of course be missed very much. However, the positive experiences and memories leave the child with an internal imprint from which she will continue to draw strength and love, even in the parent's absence. The child will continue the internal dialogue with the internalized figure of the parent, which will carry on serving as a valuable, helpful source for the child. Children carry on "conversations" with the missing parent, thinking about what he would say, how he would react, what advice he would have given. The image of the parent is maintained as a loving and supportive internal object that continues to provide strength in difficult, troubling times.

Young children who do not yet understand the full meaning of death will at times fantasize that they have a real connection with the parent. They may believe that mother can "hear" them, even "answers" them and "sends" them signs. This belief enables them to summon the loving and protective image at times of distress and strong yearning.

The child who had a good relationship with his parent prior to the loss will also be able to make room for alternative relationships. The positive experience has imbued him with a sense of trust, and an ability to forge other supportive and intimate relationships. He will accept an alternative parental figure and will seek ways to form a satisfactory relationship with him or her.

Poor relationship

Things are more complicated when the child and parent did not have a close or nurturing relationship prior to the separation and loss. In such cases, the child faces several obstacles: the internalized image of the parent is not a positive one, and the child lacks the protective and constructive internal resource it should and could have provided. If the relationship with the parent was characterized by indifference, lack of love, or even violence and abuse, the child is left with the memory of a castrating, hurtful image. Not only is it not constructive, but it also leaves the child with many unresolved issues and angers.

The loss of the parent leaves the child in a sharp conflict. On the one hand he misses the parent and wants to remember him as a positive figure; on the other he has anger and other negative emotions that may have left him with feelings of revenge. In extreme cases the child might even feel a sense of relief. This will in turn arouse feelings of guilt. He may even be led to believe that the loss occurred because his thoughts assumed magical powers that caused it. The loss eliminates the possibility to express these negative emotions and open a dialogue with the parent. The child is stuck with his difficulties, which may thwart his progress through the various stages of mourning. He will have a difficult time experiencing symbolic separation and internalizing the parent as a constructive internal object because of his preoccupation with harsh memories and unresolved issues.

In order to extricate himself from the conflict and the feelings of guilt over his negative feelings, the child may convert his feelings of anger and pain into self-accusation, taking on himself the blame for what happened between him and the parent, tormenting himself for not having been a good son or daughter. In so doing, he cleanses the image of the parent from the negative connotations. It is important to fully address and resolve the unfinished business of the child's relationship with the person he has lost. The difficult memories can consume a great deal of mental energy. The discharge of this burden will enable the child to move on with his life and, when the time comes, to be a better parent to his own children.

Influence of cultural and socio-economic factors

Children respond to loss within the cultural and social context in which they grow up, and in accordance with the expectations of the adults and the society around them. We have discussed the cultural factors that affect the way children relate to loss, and particularly death. These influences are part of the socialization process that each individual undergoes as a child. The child receives his model of grieving behavior from the society in which he grows up. He adjusts himself to the mourning practices he sees around him: screaming and crying by mourners at a funeral; or at the other end of the spectrum, quiet and impassive reserve. Even if the child has a hard time with the social patterns, he knows that this is the accepted norm, and is therefore not alarmed by them, as might occur to someone unfamiliar with the customs.

A child who grew up on a kibbutz, and was subjected to its emotionally restrained society, learned that it is unacceptable to cry, and that he is expected to be strong. A Palestinian child who grew up during the Intifada learned that someone killed while rioting is a martyr, and the raised cry for him is a social–political–religious outcry rather than an expression of personal grief. A child who spent months or years escaping from Ethiopia knows there is no time to cry over those left behind because he has to conserve his strength for his own journey and survival. A child raised in a religious community accepts death as an incontestable judgement of God; he is comforted by the belief that the deceased has passed into a better world.

The practice of lighting candles and putting flowers at the sight of a disaster or other public place which is "chosen" in a spontaneous manner can be observed in many western cultures. It is an expression of collective mourning, especially by youth. It is an example of a mourning custom and norm that developed to give an answer to psychocultural needs which had no answer in modern society. As stated earlier, modern society leaves children and young people with little or no role to play in loss-related situations. Many adults are bewildered and do not know how to relate to the grieving child. They are not sure if and how to help children express what they are feeling. The cultural and social vacuum that exists insofar as mourning customs in modern society are concerned makes it difficult for parents to provide an all-encompassing framework that is supportive of their children's grief. As a result, often the grieving child is frequently passed on to external professionals for fulfillment of his needs. The alarmed aunt asks if the child has been referred for psychological treatment; the teacher expects the guidance counselor to have a talk with him; even the mother hopes that the social worker will answer his difficult questions instead of her.

Every loss is labeled by society; the nature and circumstances of each loss will influence its social "acceptance." The particular values and ethics of every society will influence how that society regards anyone connected with the loss, including the child. Society's attitude may vary from esteem and prestige to stigma and culpability. The child of a man killed in military action is the child of a hero, and will be viewed in a prestigious light. But what social status is accorded to the child of a man who died of illness? And are the children of a father who committed suicide stigmatized as well? How does the society relate to divorce? What are people saying behind the back of a child whose mother left the family and moved in with another man?

The stigma or prestige conferred on a particular event will influence how the children cope with it. At times it will make things more difficult, at times it will make things easier. Children are very sensitive to social messages, even those that are seemingly hidden and concealed. Not all children enjoy the special attention, even if it is positive and prestigious. This is even more so the case for children who are ashamed about what happened. Among their peers, especially among younger children, these social "messages" are often delivered in a rather brutal manner.

Children themselves have many dilemmas regarding their expectations of society. On the one hand, the child wants his suffering to be recognized, wants people to know what he is feeling and the difficulties he faces. He wants them to take his situation into consideration. On the other hand, he does not want compassion, does not want to be "marked" in any special way or regarded as different. The child gets angry when people point at him and cause him embarrassment. However, he is also angry with people who do not pay sufficient attention to him and to his feelings. He is confused and sends confusing messages to the people around him. He often feels very alone in his social environment and hides his true inner experiences and anguish.

Chapter 4

The Remaining Parent and the Family System

Research studies and empirical evidence indicate that the most critical factor affecting how the child copes with his loss is the parent who continues to raise him. Difficulties of children after the loss are primarily related to difficulties in the functioning of the remaining parent. Adults who have suffered loss as children report that the difficulties of their remaining parent harmed them sometimes even more than the loss itself. Conversely, when the child's needs are appropriately met by the remaining parent, he is able to continue progressing along a normative pattern of life and growth. It is therefore important to devote a chapter to understanding the modes of response to the loss and behavior of the parent and their implications for the child. We discuss this issue by way of looking at two parameters – how the remaining parent handles the loss; how his personality attributes might affect the way in which he handles his life after the loss – and how these factors might in turn influence the child's life and growth.

Since the family is the primary field of activity of the child's relationship with the parent, and the place where the child lives and grows, by gaining an understanding of the function of the family in wake of the loss we will get more clues to understanding what happened to the child after the loss. We describe the functioning of the family through two aspects: by pointing out possible coping mechanisms of families after the loss; by pointing out parameters that describe the functioning style of families in general and how these might be relevant to understanding the effects of the family on the child in the years to come. The combination of all these elements provides an overall picture. The various elements are related to one another and influence one another.

How the parent copes with the loss

Both the initial grieving responses of the child and how he copes with the loss in the years to come are closely linked to the parent's responses to the loss. The parent raising the child is the individual who provides the *modeling* and example of how to cope with the loss. The child may react to this modeling by imitation and participation, "balancing," or resistance and distancing. It is the parent who can help the child express his grief, or can block and prevent it. It is he who can help the child to cope, or deny him a healthy coping process.

Often children serve the needs of their parent. Children can take it upon themselves to comfort the parent, to "compensate" him for the loss and even care for him. The child is highly attuned to the needs of his parent, and often acts out of a desire to answer these needs. The younger he is, the more dependent he is on the parent's response. The older he is, the greater his emotional independence and his ability to formulate his own understanding of the situation and therefore be able to formulate a more independent response to the loss.

As background to our discussion we must remember the differences between adult and child mourning. Not only are we talking about differences in the understanding of what happened, but also differences in the "rhythm" of their responses. While adults dwell in the mourning for months and years, children "overcome" the primary shock in a relatively short period. Adults' responses usually go deeper and deeper, whereas children go in and out of them, seemingly "forgetting" what happened and often hiding their difficulties. These basic differences cause a natural lack of synchronization between the process of the parent and that of his children. The gaps need to be "bridged." Parent and child have to work on understanding and accepting each other's different style and rhythm so as not to find themselves alienated and angry with each other.

In some instances, the parent tries to force his own way of mourning on the child. A sense of emotional alienation results because the child is forced to adopt a grieving style that is unsuited to his needs. If the parent does not recognize the need of the child to resume his life, the child feels guilt for wanting occasionally to disengage from the mourning and enjoy a game or a movie. He is ashamed at not being loyal and devoted to the remaining parent and to the mourning for the absent parent. The parent has the right to mourn and cope with the loss in his own way, but it is important that the child be allowed to follow his own unique path, one that is attuned to his needs.

In our description hereafter we make a somewhat artificial distinction between the parent's response to the loss and the parent's personality traits that may affect the response. In addition, we distinguish between the responses of the parent during the initial period following the loss – the first years of mourning, readjustment, and adaptation – and ensuing years.

The parent is the primary model and support for coping

The ability of the parent to be in touch with and process his own pain and emotions, and readjust to the new reality after the loss, serves as the primary model for the child. A parent who is in touch with his emotions and able to express them genuinely in the child's presence "invites" the child to join in and do as he does. He sends the message that expressing emotions is an intrinsic part of coping with the loss. He enables the child to express what he feels, and offers him a supportive, containing, calming environment to do so. This provides a relieving opportunity for the child. The parent is the most natural and most important partner of the child's emotions, especially those of distress.

Young children are not conscious of their emotions, but when given the opportunity they express them directly for the most part, without intellectual obstructions and diversions. The older they are, the more they develop adult-like defense mechanisms. They too become afraid of the emotional intensity and harsh thoughts they are experiencing. The example and supportive presence of the parent makes it easier to vent these feelings and cope with them. The child needs his parent's support to help him process the grief. He draws on the adult's resources of maturity, sense of balance, life experience, and existential confidence. The younger the child, the greater his need for these sources of support.

The expression of one's inner feelings must undergo "working through." The parent should not only offer the modeling to this ongoing process, but also offer the child a leading hand and a soft shoulder. An intellectual, controlled processing is lacking the main ingredient in the "working through" of the loss. Without the ability to encounter and express emotions, it is difficult to fully process them. Parents sometimes speak with their children about the loss, albeit with utter reserve. They "lecture" them as to how to understand and how to act; they explain with rational concepts. When the conversation transpires without any real venting of emotions, essentially it loses its credibility. Stripped of real emotional expression, the conversation lacks emotional integrity and cannot therefore give the right response to the needs of the child.

If it is difficult for a parent to be in touch with and express emotions, or if he is unaware of or in denial about what is happening to him emotionally, then he cannot grant the child the help he needs. The child senses the parent's fear of being inundated by emotions, and will avoid their expression in the parent's presence. Such a parent may also, perhaps unconsciously, try to thwart any such expression by his children. The encounter with the child's emotions, and even more so with an emotional outburst by the child, "endangers" the parent. Many parents claim that although they had a hard time expressing their own emotions, they encouraged their children to do so. It is doubtful, however, whether these good intentions were in fact realized, since the child has a hard time expressing emotions and feelings that his own parent is unable to encounter.

Emotional acceptance and adjustment

Just as much as the child needs the support and encouragement of the adult to express his distress, he also needs him as a model at the stage of emotional acceptance and adjustment. The child needs the example of a coping parent. He needs to get the message that it is okay to resume life. He draws strength from the "permission" given by his parent to go on with his life.

Children have a natural ability to adjust to reality, painful though it may be. But if the parent is stuck and cannot accept reality, he leaves the child confused, and alone to cope with the situation. A widower who is unwilling to part with his wife's belongings, a divorcee who refuses to accept the finality of her husband's leaving home, these parents will not be able to help their children accept and cope with the loss. The parent's non-adjustment holds the child back from making progress, and readjusting emotionally and behaviorally. Unconsciously or not, the parent "demands" that the child remain by his side and not accept the new reality.

A parent who is still mired in questions of why, or who has intense feelings of anger and accusations, cannot help his child cope with these questions, process them, and advance beyond them. A parent who viewed the loss as an act of rejection will not be able to furnish his child with the tools and strengths needed to experience the loss without sustaining damage to his "self." It is only natural that the parent is also confronting questions related to understanding the essence and finality of death, the meaning of life in spite of the loss, and how to cope with the unique circumstances of the loss. Only if he is willing to confront these issues will he be able to help his children cope with them.

Some adults feel they ought to have the answers to the questions before they dare to confront the children's questions, but they are wrong. The child has to see that the parent is capable of grappling with the questions and difficulties. He should see that the parent does not become paralyzed and helpless, and that even though he has no answers to some of these difficult issues he continues to cope. The child does not have to receive solutions and answers to each question. The fact that the parent is brave enough to encounter the questions sends the message that it is possible, and at times necessary, to be inundated by questions, even if satisfactory or soothing answers are not at hand. The mere raising of the questions constitutes an important catharsis and "allows" the child to share his with the parent.

Defense mechanisms

Just as much as children learn from their parents' coping skills, so they might also copy their defense mechanisms. Intellectualization, denial, avoidance, repression, and projection are some of the typical defense mechanisms employed by adults. Their use is a reflection of how hard it is to cope with intense emotions and distressful situations. It is critical that parents be aware of the mechanisms they employ. Their replacement by healthier mechanisms constitutes a healthier modeling for the child to copy.

The grief process of the parent

In the initial period following the loss, the parent is hurt, preoccupied by the loss, inundated by intense emotions, troubled by questions that cannot be answered. The parent is without the support and reinforcement of a spouse to which he was accustomed. He needs time to himself. Occasionally it is hard for him to find the time to address the emotional needs of his child and provide support and reinforcement.

After the turbulent initial bereavement period, most adults readjust by strengthening themselves from within and by locating external sources of support. They gradually resume their duties as parents, and once again invest in their children. Nevertheless, various research studies indicate that even years after the loss a significant percentage of children continue to suffer from deficient parental investment. The cloud that hangs over the parent, the depression, anxieties, and fears, the still unresolved matters regarding the loss, the worries, the burden of single parenthood are all factors that may hamper the parent's ability to invest in his children, imbuing them with a nurturing vitality and energy.

Pathological mourning

In extreme cases, the parent wallows in pathological mourning and fails to rehabilitate himself – in terms of emotional function – for an extended period of time that may develop into years. In this case, other adults should be aware of possible damage to the child's development. A parent who is immersed in his own grief and emotions is unable to consider the emotional needs of his child. He will not help the child to separate from the grief and invest in life. He will be detached from the child's need for growth and development. The child "loses" the remaining parent, and is emotionally neglected or even abandoned.

Children are afraid of the feeling that their parents are "falling apart." It is difficult for them to see their parents weak and in pain, but they can adjust to this situation if they know it is for a brief period. The child has to be told that "Mama is sad," and that is why she is not so patient or available to him right now. Nevertheless, the child is threatened by the feeling that his parent cannot cope or does not want to go on with life, and is afraid he will be losing him too, losing the support and care he needs so much.

Supporting a continuous relationship with the absent parent

One of the roles of the remaining parent is to help his children maintain a relationship with the absent parent. If it is a dead parent, the child needs to continue to "know" him or her through stories and anecdotes. If the parent has left home, it is important to help the child keep in touch. The ability of the parent to help his child depends on his ability to be "in touch" with the image or the person, without projecting his own difficulties on the child.

A father who is unable to mention his dead wife because it is too painful will not be able to let his children hear stories about her. An indignant divorcee who is angry at her spouse for abandoning her is fostering a negative parental image, making it harder for her children to experience their father as a positive parental image.

Existential confidence of the adults

The loss undermines the existential confidence of the adults, especially during the initial period, at which time numerous aspects of life are up in the air: concerns regarding economic and other daily problems; apprehension about social status; the burden of the responsibility to the continuing smooth life of the family; the fear of additional losses. Sharing such problems and concerns with children is a natural and even healthy mode of behavior, but this must take into account the child's ability to understand. Parents who describe the problems and concerns while they themselves are in a turbulent state may leave the child with the impression that the difficulty is too overwhelming to deal with. Due to the child's lack of knowledge and familiarity with life, he may not have his own way to judge and therefore may be very alarmed; this must be taken into account. Sharing problems with the child should be supplemented by a soothing message about how the parent thinks or plans to handle the situation. It is important to find out if the child understands what he has been told. When the parent says that he does not know where he will find money for the family to live off, he must delineate the boundaries of his concerns. If he did not intend to say that the family could be hungry and homeless tomorrow, but only that they must watch their expenses and avoid luxuries, then this should be made clear. A parent who says he "doesn't know what the sense is in going on living" must make it clear to the child that he does not intend to commit suicide.

Double burden on the remaining parent

Loss of a spouse places a double burden on the remaining parent. From now on, he alone is responsible for the economy of the family, its physical operation, and its social and emotional well-being. Some of the difficulties of the parent following the loss may be attributed to this heavy burden. When the parent struggles to withstand these burdens, the children suffer as well. The burden of being a single parent is particularly onerous during the initial period. While preoccupied by his grief, he must invest energies in the reorganization of the family. The parent may be required to immediately address pressing financial or housing concerns. At the same time, he must help his children through the process of their grief and coping. He has to handle all of these problems single-handed, without a spouse to share them. Under these conditions, he may ask his children for support and aid. To a certain degree the help and support of children is a healthy part of the family's coping and reorganization after the loss. Yet the parent's over-reliance on his children might be harmful and hindering to their growth and proper development.

Parents who have lost a spouse are very afraid for their children, fearing another loss, another blow. Sometimes they restrict their children's activities, and increase their fears. Fear becomes a central issue in the parent's life and the life of the family. Demands are put on the child to adjust his life accordingly. The fears of the parent fall on fertile ground, since the child who has undergone the trauma of the loss is probably also more afraid. Consequently, he will not put up much of a fight and will relinquish his needs for independence and other age-appropriate behavior.

The child who has lost a parent is also worried; he is mainly afraid of losing the remaining parent. He is afraid of something happening to the parent – illness or accident – or that the parent will be drawn away from him by a new intimate relationship. Fear adversely affects the child's ability to break free and distance himself. He remains close in order to "protect" the parent. These "realistic" fears might develop into experiencing more general anxieties, which are of a more overwhelming nature. Whatever the case, these children are burdened in ways that may hold back their normative behavior and development.

The remaining parent can and should try to reduce these fears and anxieties. As mentioned, some parents are well served by the dependence and fear of their children. In such instances, the parent promotes the fears in order to satisfy his own emotional needs and to foster the child's dependence on him. A child who has already lost a parent is much more dependent on the remaining parent, and is therefore also very sensitive to the parent's emotional needs and moods. The parent must be conscious of the messages he is sending. He can and should help the child break free of this dependence and from the caregiver role which the child may have taken upon himself.

Personality of the parent and how it affects coping: implications for the child

The personality of the parent, and his previous and present life circumstances, affect his coping with the loss, both in the short term as well as in the long term, and have important influences on the upbringing of the children. Psychodynamic theories and family-system approaches describe the development of the child's personality within the context of the parent's attributes and behavior. Parenthood reflects these attributes. The ability to cope with loss depends and reflects the personality structure, the mental balance of the individual. The theme of separation is a primary issue in both the development of the personality as well as in coping with loss.

We have also emphasized the issue of separation as one of the most important axes along which the parent–child relationship develops; critical developmental tasks take place along this axis. From the moment of birth, the child "distances" himself and separates from the parent on his way to becoming a separate, independent individual. Psychodynamic theories emphasize the process of separation–individuation, through which the developmental task of separation takes place as the child develops his own self. The process is initiated during the first years of childhood, and is reprocessed during adolescence. The parent is the primary facilitator whose task is to enable the child to carry out this task. His ability to help the child undergo this developmental process depends on his own personality structure and his mature ability to contain the separation from him.

Following traumatic loss, the parent may have a hard time facilitating the separation, because he is also hurt, and wants to keep those important to him close at hand. The parent's instinctual impulse is to prevent and avoid additional separations and "losses." Nevertheless, if he has a healthy personality he will "overcome" these needs, and permit his children to go on with their needs for growth and independence. During the initial period after the loss, it is natural that the parent will have difficulties allowing his children to distance themselves much, but over time, with readjustment and reassurance, the parent's inner forces will, it is hoped, be restored and he will be able to contain and even encourage the continuation of his child's natural development process.

As we have already noted, tasks of developmental separation are more difficult and complex for a child who has experienced traumatic loss. He requires a great deal of reinforcement and assistance from his parent to advance through this process. However, when the parent is also threatened by the child's separation from him, not only will the parent fail to reinforce the child and ease the process for him, but the parent will usually make things even harder for him. A widow threatened by loss will not encourage her young child to go out and play with other children, will not push her adolescent son to take trips and engage in activities with his peers, and will do what she can to prevent her son from volunteering for army service in a unit far from home.

Immature personality or personality disorder

Parents with immature personalities, especially those with borderline personality or with a personality disorder, will have a much harder time bearing up under situations of loss. The experience of a traumatic loss constitutes a threat to their most basic emotional existence and triggers regressive and even pathological defense mechanisms. Previous conflicts rise to the surface. Their emotional ability to cope with separation and loss is very limited, sometimes non-existent. As a result these individuals cannot face or "process" their loss. Instead they respond to the harsh reality by employing defense mechanisms such as projection, replacement, and denial. They resort to mechanisms of splitting and intellectualization, and may experience feelings of paranoia. The reality after the loss is full of threats, and they lack the mental tools to cope constructively with the new situations.

These parents require a great deal of external nurturing and assurances. They cannot provide their children with the support and containment to help them through their own mourning and loss processing. Not only will they be unable to help their children cope with the loss, but most probably their function as parents that facilitate growth will deteriorate. In such instances, even prior to the loss, it was no simple feat for these parents to enable their children to distance and separate. Before the loss, the other parent – their spouse – provided a counterbalance in soothing, supporting, containing, and enabling the children to set out and go on with their own lives. Now the remaining parent is both alone and traumatized from the loss and becomes more vulnerable and susceptible. He seeks and sometimes finds "solutions" to his needs with his children. Not only is that parent's ability to help the children through their loss very limited, but it is very likely that he or she will make things even harder for them.

The parent's inability to facilitate separation is apparent not only on concrete issues such as giving the child permission to physically distance himself, but also in throwing up obstacles vis-à-vis emotional and symbolic distancing. The child's building of emotional independence and eliminating the bonds of dependence is perceived by the parent, usually unconsciously, as a threat to his own existence. The child is required to remain loyal and close to the parent. The parent nurtures the child's dependency on him. Parents with such personality requirements unconsciously "use" their children and "subjugate" them to their own mental needs. The children have to carry out the work of mourning and their process of growth under the heavy pressure of their parent's pathological needs.

A widow with a borderline personality may feel threatened and worried every time her son develops a close relationship with a girlfriend. Her son's distancing from her leaves her feeling emotionally "abandoned" and she will often act out her fears and create "reasons" for him to "return" to her. She might fall sick, she might threaten to stop her financial support. She will create situations in which he will be put under pressure to return to her. The parent's personality dysfunction is often expressed in other ways as well: the manner in which the parent manages family life, the quality and type of relationship with the extended family and surrounding society, the new intimate relationship he chooses, his ability to hold a job, and his general rehabilitation and realization of himself. Failure to function properly in these areas will affect the quality of his children's lives. Because of the many demands of life after and as a result of the loss, his abilities to handle life in a mature way are repeatedly put to the test. His poor mental–emotional abilities will also have their grip on his children.

Instability and change

Instability and constant change may characterize the "solutions" adopted by the faltering parent. He may frequently change places of residence, dragging his children through numerous changes, and thereby increasing the instability of their lives by forcing more losses on them. He may frequently switch intimate partners, causing confusion and bewilderment to his children. Although they may need and even welcome another parental figure, they will nevertheless be wary of establishing emotional connection with figures that come and go. Every additional separation from a parental figure is painful to them. In some instances the opposite situation occurs: the parent lacks sufficient flexibility, and is unable to carry out the needed readjustments that will make it possible to embrace needed changes. His inability to move on makes it difficult for his children to do so.

Parental life history of loss

Another source of parents' emotional difficulties results from their personal life history, especially if this history includes traumatic experiences of loss. Parents who themselves lost a parent when they were children, who went through the holocaust or lost part of their family in it, who migrated from another country and were raised in conditions of distress and loss, or who grew up in difficult family circumstances, are vulnerable adults whose mental function might probably be very distressed by any additional traumatic loss. The additional loss is at times the straw that breaks their back. Sometimes these are individuals who have not fully processed the previous loss, and the current loss therefore floods them with unresolved issues from the past. The emotional burden with which the adult is coping is not only related to the recent loss, but to the latent emotional baggage he still carries from the distant past.

Parents in this situation have a hard time helping their children through the process of bereavement and coping because they themselves are straining to cope. The parent who did not process his loss when his mother died will have a hard time coping with the experiences his children undergo as a result of their mother's death. His wife's death will re-ignite the harsh memories from his childhood and the painful and unprocessed feelings. The encounter with the emotions and difficulties of his children will bring him back to his "unfinished business." He will probably project his difficulties upon his children. If he cannot contain their experiences, he will do whatever he can to avoid encountering their emotions and hardships. As a result he cannot be helpful to his children in processing their loss. He may also make it difficult for them to go on with their growing independence and separation from him, because the loss of his wife has now added one loss too many and he will have a hard time enduring more separations and "losses." Very often these phenomena are taking place while the parent is unconscious of them and "covers" them up by claiming it is his children who have the difficulties.

Roles the child might fill due to lack of spousal support

All the parent's emotional difficulties take on a new hue because he is now without spousal support. Prior to the loss, he probably had the support that helped him deal with his special needs, thereby relieving pressure from the children. A parent with such difficulties often seeks help – and often finds it – among his children. As such, personality difficulties of parents, which are exacerbated by the experience of loss, may lead to such phenomena as the "parental child" and the "spousal child."

The *parental child* is a child who has been "enlisted" to emotionally protect and "raise" his parent. It is common to find parental children in cases where previous to the loss the spouse took upon himself "parental" roles – to protect and care for his spouse. With the loss this task is given to one of the children.

The *spousal child* is a similar phenomenon, in which the child serves as the parent's partner. The spousal child is given the roles, as well as the privileges, of a spouse. He is an equal partner in decisions and is given much power in the life of the family. Often the parent declines new intimate relationships. Eventually he or she will also make it hard for the son or daughter to form separate intimate spousal relationships of their own.

Parental and spousal children also benefit from their status. They are assigned a special place in the family, with special privileges and attention.

They exert power and control over the parent and over their siblings; their Oedipal fantasy is realized. These benefits are "perks" that are hard for them to relinquish. The child will therefore develop an interest in maintaining the situation. They will understand and "pay" the high cost of these privileges at a much later stage of life. Due to the loss, the remaining parent has an ostensibly legitimate reason to expect and even to demand special investment and loyalty from his children. These demands usually become even more adamant as the children grow up. The threat of "losing" them becomes more tangible. The parent will claim that the child is "everything I have left in life." He will invoke the "after all I've done for you" argument. These legitimate "requests" are often done with an emotional "blackmail" undertone and take advantage of the child's emotional susceptibility and dependence on the remaining parent.

In contrast to the many potential difficulties we have described, healthy coping by the parent can make it easier for the children not only cope with their loss, but also to go on with their growth and development and to live their lives in a full and normative manner, in spite of the loss they have experienced. No other figure in the child's life can be as beneficial and helpful as the remaining parent.

Coping with loss within the family

The family is the grieving child's "home" in more ways than one: with the other members of the family he shares the loss and the long voyage of coping. Here is where he is surrounded by the people closest to him, the people who are supposed to support and protect him. In modern society, mourning focuses primarily on the members of the immediate family; most of the burden of coping with the loss is borne by the nuclear family. Although the extended family and the community may offer support and attempt to provide assistance, especially in the initial phase, they are significantly less involved in the life of the family and its individuals than was the case in traditional societies. In the long run coping with the loss and its aftermath mainly happens within the confines of the family.

The child will negotiate the rough terrain of adjustment to the loss — both in the initial stage and in ensuing years — as a member of the family. He will draw his energy and strength from the family, and within its safe confines he will be able to express what he is going through. Important changes that result from the loss, as well as the wide-ranging changes one encounters in life, will be experienced within the family framework. The manner in which the family handles these affairs will have strong influences on how the child faces his life tasks.

The quality of the family's response and behavior following the loss is closely related to the character of the family prior to the loss. We now describe the main factors that characterize the family's attempts to cope with loss and correlate these factors to general attributes of the family system.

Family mourning process

Similar to the individual, the family entity undergoes a process of mourning. This is a parallel process. The family experiences the same stages of grieving as does the individual. In the initial stage, there is a sense of shock and trauma. The family is unable to absorb what has happened and reacts on an external–technical level. In the second stage, emotional responses increase, as the family encounters numerous situations that underscore the meaning of the loss: the first family dinner without; the first holiday observance without; even the leaky faucet that no one knows how to fix. The family responds both at the emotional and concrete levels, and in so doing begins to internalize the new family situation. Eventually, the family reaches a stage of adjustment to the new reality.

The process intermittently advances and retreats, and this is evident in terms of how the family functions. At times, the reorganization of the family seems to continue apace, and it appears that the change has been "understood" and adjusted to. At other times, emotions may gain the upper hand. A sense of confusion sets in and sadness and other emotions become dominant again. This may cause each individual family member to seclude themselves in their own private realms. The family may find it difficult to function as one unit.

Ordinarily, after the initial period of readjustment – approximately a year or two – the family will reach a new equilibrium that reflects the changed reality. Just as the loss does not disappear from the life of the individual, neither does it disappear from the life of the family. It remains present and makes itself felt throughout the long years of the family's existence. Changes and shifting circumstances in the normal course of life will repeatedly confront the family with the repercussions and implications of the loss, and will demand continued changes and renewal of the family equilibrium. Coping with the loss is a shared "mission" adopted by the family. Following the loss, there will be many additional changes that will require the family to readjust and adopt a shared response.

The means by which the family copes, and the changes it is required to make in the short as well as long term, are the child's "backdrop" and "stage," which influence him and are in turn influenced by him.

Every family has its own mourning customs and grieving style, and its own ways of coping with the loss. Each family has its own way of expressing pain, anger, longing, and sadness; its own manner of remembering the missing person; its own rhythm by which life resumes its ordinary patterns; and its own modifications and adaptations of the family routine.

Changing needs of the child

We reiterate that the child's needs change over the years, including those needs that are related to continuous coping with the loss. In this process, he will require the assistance and cooperation of his family. A child who was a baby when his father died needs his older siblings to tell him how he played football with Dad; he needs his sister to tell him about the time Dad drove her up to summer camp; he needs Mom to talk about her courtship with Dad. Family conversation and sharing can help to fill the void the child has.

As he grows up, the child's position in the family will change, which will also influence his role in the family in relation to the loss. The child will again and again change his particular role in the family effort of coping with the loss. If the child was a baby when his father died, as he grows up he can and must become more active and a partner in determining the observance of the anniversary of his father's death. The family has to make "room" for him, and provide him with an opportunity to express his emotions and opinions. In this manner, he will become a partner in shaping the family memory, and building his own individual relationship with his father's loss.

Every family member will undergo personal changes and life-affected changes: the mother will take a different job; the brother will enlist in the army; the sister will embark on an extended trip to India. Every new situation demands readjustment by the family; every change leads to the repositioning of each individual within the family system. There is a continual need for mutual support, and a need to devise emotional coping patterns appropriate to the new reality. The child is not only an important partner in shaping these changes, but frequently a cause of them as well.

Family traditions concerning loss-related issues

Sometimes there is "fixation" in the manner in which the family addresses loss-related issues. A family "tradition" has been forged and no one "tampers" with it: when the dead person is mentioned and when not; how they go about the yearly memorial day; which "stories" are told and which are "hashed." Such traditions "protect" the family members from delving too deeply into the painful subject. It is easier to handle it in a rather "mechanical" manner and so leave the sensitive areas "closed." It is because the situations are handled so "mechanically" that events and occasions pertaining to the loss take on a sensitive hue. There is no real sharing of what each individual member is going through. Individuals are not permitted to question, or express a desire to change. There is no family dialogue and therefore no real emotional sharing and collaboration. The family does not openly work on finding a new formulation that would meet the needs of every member of the family. This situation fosters emotional alienation within the family. The children do not have a way of expressing their needs and wishes and are therefore left "alone."

During the first few years, the family members need a great deal of *emotional support.* The family is an important resource of energy for strengthening, and can be a prime factor in regaining a sense of security, rehabilitation, and proper function. There is a great deal of *emotional dependence* in families that have experienced loss, in the immediate term as well as in subsequent years. The situation places a heavy burden on the family since during the first years each individual member is preoccupied with his own grieving and coping demands. In subsequent years too, when changes occur and sometimes more difficulties arise, further mutual help will be required and the family members will need one another. Because of their common trauma, they are more dependent on each other, yet they might also be more disappointed. As the child grows up, he will repeatedly return to the loss-related tasks. He will need familial support and containment in order to carry out these tasks.

Roles within the family

In the wake of the loss, roles develop within the family in response to what occurred. Some are *concrete roles* and some are *emotional roles*: one may vent emotions, another may stifle them; one may mourn and reminisce, another may move ahead, wanting to go on living; one supports, another always needs and demands support; one expresses pain, while the other is preoccupied with anger and accusation. Every member of the family plays a part in this dynamic drama. It is important to make sure that sufficient flexibility exists, such that at various periods different family members can fill different emotional roles. Those who are strong can at times be weak; the supporters become at times the needy. The role of "mourner" need not always be assumed by the same members of the family. Rather, the role can and should be alternated among the members of the family as they go through more difficult or less difficult periods. The shift in roles should match the changing situations of each member, so that the family members enable one another to rotate from one role to the other as the need arises.

Children's roles

Children have roles too. They frequently bear the most difficult roles of all: those that the other members of the family have opted not to accept. In emotionally stunted families that do not encourage the expression of grief and emotion, it is not uncommon to find a child who makes repeated attempts to reinstate the "forbidden" expression of emotion. He may cry a lot, or he may close up into himself and be sad. When the family is not sufficiently united or supportive, the child attempts to unite it through "inappropriate" forms of behavior, sounding an alarm that brings the family together around a common theme. When the parents are immersed in their grief and do not function, it is often the child who calls for their readjustment and resumption of normal life and parental function. Through his behavior, the child expresses not only his personal needs but also the needs of the family as a unit that must continue to function.

Changing roles and stability

The ability to change roles, and the restoration of balanced relationship between parent and child, will enable the child to continue his development, and enable the parent to go on with his life. Lack of flexibility blocks individual and familial development. If the widow who devoted all her time and energy to looking after her children during the initial years after the loss does not allow herself to change her own order of priorities and devote more time to her own well-being, or if her children make it difficult for her to do so, fixation will ensue and both her life as well as that of her children will not fulfill their potential for growth.

Instability in family life

Reality remains fluid for a long period of time after the loss. Instability in family life and the lack of clear knowledge regarding the future that are typical to this stage are not beneficial to the child, who needs a familiar, regular framework. The family frequently undergoes a great deal of change: concrete changes, such as changes in financial status and place of residence; changed relationships with the outside world, close family as well as friends; change in the social status of the family. These changes affect the children greatly; "losing" their sense of security and belonging confuse them.

Children need stability, especially in the wake of loss. They need the sense of security that comes with familiarity. The child is able to get along in a world he knows. In new and unfamiliar circumstances, he is confused and anxious. He does not know the rules, does not know what tomorrow will bring, cannot anticipate how those around him will act, or what is expected of him. The rapid-fire changes now overwhelming him will force him to continually relive the intense feelings he experienced at the time of the loss. In order to calm down and adjust to the new situation, he needs quiet and stability, a secure framework, and set clearly defined rules of the game. A family that offers stability and quiet will provide these vital conditions.

The child whose parents have divorced has to know when and where he will be able to see his father. Frequent changes in the schedule of visits will compromise his already undermined sense of security in his future contact with his father, and frustrate his attempts to build a new secure relationship with him.

Some changes are forced on the family, while some are adopted by choice. Whatever the case, decisions must be adopted regarding how to act and how to behave. It is important that the familial response take into account the child's needs for stability and his ability to adjust to additional changes. He has to be afforded the opportunity to express his wishes and his problems. Adaptation of the familial solutions to the needs of the children is likely to ease their adjustment significantly.

The more the family can avoid additional shake-ups, regain its equilibrium, and re-establish stability and clarity in family life, the better able the child will be to readjust and rebuild his world, and return to investing his efforts into growth and development.

Family equilibrium

Since numerous changes take place in the family during the initial years after the loss, the family must exhibit *flexibility and openness* in order to continually ascertain whether the existing patterns are suited to the new conditions and evolving needs: the needs of the family as well as the needs of each individual member. Families that are locked into certain patterns, and which are unable to examine themselves and change, will find themselves unable to provide appropriate responses to the changes affecting their members.

As children grow, their needs require the family to make infinite changes. It is very important that the family system be able to make the appropriate changes and offer suitable responses to their needs. Not only do the children in the family require changes; the parent will also want to make changes in his life. Inflexibility and inability to change will thwart the parent's continued development, growth, and rehabilitation.

Following the loss, the equilibrium of the family changes. The loss leaves a void not only at the individual level, but also a void in the life of the family as an entity. This void forces changes on the family. Years will pass before the family finds a way to fill the void and re-establish equilibrium. This equilibrium will be reached following a long round of "negotiations" on the various aspects of family life that were affected by the loss. The equilibrium pertains to technical tasks like who takes care of the household chores as well as, and even mainly, the emotional roles: melancholy vs. energies of life; anger vs. acceptance; sadness vs. happiness, etc. Children have a great deal of influence on the family equilibrium. They are keenly sensitive to circumstances in which there is a lack of equilibrium, in which case their own function is negatively affected. They often take it upon themselves to "balance out" the family.

Not every family has an equilibrium that is healthy and growth ensuring. When a family already has a tendency toward *pathological relationships* prior to the loss, it is easy for the parent to "exploit" the emotional dependence and fragility following the loss, and further reinforce these patterns. The mother who used to foster a relationship of guilt by putting herself in the position of family "martyr" will exploit her widowhood to nurture this role even further, and promote guilt feelings among her children. It is she who suffers the most; therefore they need to be more attentive and "good." Such disequilibrium in the emotional roles does not leave the children much "space" for their own emotions and needs to develop. The family circles around and is bound to the suffering of one member, without rebalancing according to the changing situations and needs of everyone.

Family response to loss

Members of the family "encounter" the loss in a variety of ways and at varying intervals of time, yet they must also formulate a "familial response." Is it okay to mention the name of the missing person? If so, when? How? Is it only permissible to refer to the missing person with feelings of sorrow, or may the subject also be approached with humor and laughter? Is the dead person portrayed only as having been perfect, or can the family also challenge, express anger, criticize him?

Various occasions necessitate a "familial response." At each year's anniversary of the date of death, how will the event be observed by the family? Conversely, how will the family act on holidays and other festive occasions? Will they celebrate? How? With whom? Will the loss be mentioned on such occasions? With whom do children of divorcees spend their holidays? Who "gets them" for Christmas or Passover? Are they allowed to express their wishes in these matters? To what degree does the familial response reflect the needs of the individual members of the family? Does it leave sufficient room for individual expression? Is there enough room left for divergent responses by different members of the family? How are the family "negotiations" held? Is there an open, true dialogue, or are the "familial" solutions imposed and dictated by one dominant member?

These questions present the many delicate issues at hand. It is to be hoped the family is able to furnish a response that represents a reasonable answer to the needs of everybody, including the kids. However, adults do not always "hear" the needs of their children, do not always give them an opportunity to voice their opinions, and do not always include them in family decisions. The child may remain alienated from a process that must include him and provide a response to his needs as well. At times, he will have to "shout" in order to be heard.

Good little girls and boys

Children from families affected by loss are frequently "good little boys" or "good little girls." They are very considerate and can sense when "Mama's in a bad mood." At such times they downplay their own needs and adapt themselves to the parent's sensitivities. When bereaved parents decide to hold a holiday dinner at home rather than take part in the extended family celebration, the child/sibling does not put up a fuss even though he would have preferred to be with his cousins at the large family dinner. He "understands" that his parents are going through hard times and accepts that he has to make the sacrifice.

Communication

The vulnerability and sensitivity following a loss can strain the open, honest lines of communication in the family: there is a fear of hurting one another, and it becomes hard to express real feelings and needs. Each member of the family is preoccupied with trying to understand himself and his own needs, and has to make an effort to clearly express these needs to the others, in addition to trying to ascertain what the others are feeling. As a result, the messages are often non-verbal and cryptic. The family invests a great deal of energy in attempts to simultaneously "decipher" one another and protect one another. It is difficult to share the specific thoughts and feelings that consume each person: feelings of pain, yearning, and anger, or thoughts that have to do with accusation and blame; feelings of guilt, fear, or questions about the meaning of life. "Ordinary" families are not accustomed to sharing or communicating on such personal and complex issues. In order to contend with these multiple sensitivities, openness and creativity in the lines of family communication are required, thereby permitting the family to contain and exchange the complex feelings and thoughts of individual members. The post-loss situation requires the family to overcome these difficulties and create the sense of sharing that each member requires, providing a genuinely protective and containing environment.

External resources

External resources are an important source of support for the nuclear family. Grandparents, uncles, aunts, close friends can provide assistance: concrete assistance such as helping out with a lift when the family car doesn't start on a cold winter morning; or fixing the flat tire of a bicycle when a child wants to go riding with friends. But primarily, this consists of emotional and social support: an invitation to a holiday dinner or a joint vacation with another family; a shoulder for the remaining parent to lean on during times of crisis; a "replacement" father or mother figure to identify with for the child. Some families lack external relationships that can provide support and assistance. Other families thwart the attempts of outside support systems, and close up inside themselves. In such cases the child is deprived of those resources that could have supported his growth.

The relationship with the family of the missing parent is especially important. This family can not only provide a source of support, but also a source of "connection" with the missing individual. Through the members of the extended family, the child will be able to get to know the missing parent better. Through them, the child can gain a sense of continuity between the past, present, and future; keep up the connection with themes related to the parent, and reinforce his sense of family belonging. Sometimes there may be a strained relationship with the family of the missing parent. Tension, accusation, disappointment, and anger may threaten to disrupt the continuity of the relationship, and may sometimes even sever the child's connection with the parent's family. Problems emanating from past tensions, wars over inheritance and money, attempts to dominate and dictate, non-acceptance – all of these factors can foster feelings of antagonism, hatred, and suspicion, and lead to "punishment," neglect, and disconnection. The child is the victim and pays the price.

Aspects of the family system that influence coping with loss

Every family, like every system, has its own particular patterns of behavior. These will also affect how the family copes with the loss. By familiarizing ourselves with the characteristics of the family systems, we will gain a sharper understanding of what transpires in families in the wake of a loss.

Emotional expression and emotional sharing

Does the family have open emotional communication channels? Does it have a tradition of sharing individual difficulties and personal struggles with one another? Is it considered acceptable to express feelings and emotions within the family, be they distress, weakness, anger, sorrow, confusion, and helplessness; or conversely, happiness, encouragement, enthusiasm, and humor? How do members of the family respond to these admissions – through listening and acceptance, and providing emotional support? Or do they hasten to dole out advice and/or criticism, disregarding what has been said, or not responding at all? Effective emotional communication will enable all family members, children included, to share difficult loss-related emotions with each other.

Open lines of communication

Open lines of communication within the family allow members to vent disagreement, anger, and disappointment with one another. These may be difficult emotions to contain, but in families whose members are confident of the love and acceptance of others, in which every member has his or her own special space, it is permissible and even desirable not to agree, and even to be angry with one another. The family that is coping with loss and with various readjustments has to be able to contain the differences of opinion that invariably exist among its members. The mother may already feel the need to find a new intimate partner, whereas her children are not yet ready for change and will therefore be angry, considering it a betrayal of their father. Is the family capable of enabling each member to express his true feelings, even if they are intense emotions that clash with what another member of the family is feeling? The child who is given an opportunity to express himself in a frank and candid manner and share his true feelings and thoughts with other members of the family will be given the important opportunity to process them.

Emotional closeness

To what degree do members of the family genuinely reveal themselves, sharing their inner selves with one another and expressing closeness, caring, and support for each other? To what degree are they emotionally accessible to one another? How supportive are they of one another, willing to contain, able to be emotionally accessible to eachother's needs? In response to loss, there may be a tendency to draw away from and shut off the outside world, although there may be an equal and opposite need for closeness and support. Families with a pre-existing pattern of closeness will be able to overcome the obstacles and respond to individual needs of closeness. Younger children have a particular need for closeness, since they still lack the ability to express their feelings in words and thereby create a sense of emotional companionship.

Family unity and cohesion

Family unity and cohesion give a measure to the mutual support within the family, and reflect acceptance and love, caring and commitment. Unity and cohesion are the source of energy for members of the family; the "backbone" that imbues the individuals with a sense of confidence regarding their place not only in the family, but also in the world. It strengthens them both internally and toward the outside world. At times of crisis, families that had previously been united will become even more united; it will be even more noticeably lacking in those families that had not been as strongly united prior to the crisis. If the family lacked closeness and unity prior to the loss, it will be exceedingly more difficult to develop them now, when everyone is licking their wounds.

In the absence of family unity, each individual is isolated – an isolation that is even more difficult and painful to bear following a loss. The additional emotional burden may at times trigger a sharper sense of distance and alienation within the family, and in extreme cases will even give rise to the sensation that the family is disintegrating. Some families only become conscious of their lack of mutual support and closeness after the crisis hits. The enormous need for support may motivate them to alter the pattern, encouraging the families to work at improving their internal communications and learning to provide support and reinforcement for one another. In fact, the experience of loss may be a critical factor in the enhancement of family unity.

Emotional closeness and unity are important resources that imbue the child with the feeling he is not alone; that the family is capable of joining together and shouldering the difficult burdens now placed on it. Cooperation and containing furnish the child with a sense of security, a sort of guarantee that no matter what happens in the future, the family will be there for him. Armed with the knowledge that his family is solidly behind him, he will be able to withstand the tough times.

Personal space

The personal space that is made available by the family grants each member the freedom of independent thoughts and feelings, empowering him to relate to his own personal needs and desires. He should be able to consider the feelings of fellow family members out of choice, rather than through coercion or emotional blackmail. When individual members of a family enjoy this sort of freedom, each member is able to cope with his grief and troubles in his own particular way.

Children are in need of this personal space as well. It is important that they feel that the choices and decisions they make are relevant to their own intrinsic needs, and that they are not necessarily dictated by the demands of their parent and/or family. Yes, the child must learn to consider the needs of his family, but not at the expense of altogether abandoning his own internal world. A family with "space" will enable a child to get in touch with his own needs and feelings, permitting him to seek the solutions most appropriate to him.

The flexible family

A flexible family affords its members the opportunity of *differential response*. The various members do not necessarily have to respond or act in the same uniform manner. A mother who is angry at her husband for abandoning the family will enable her children to choose how they wish to relate to their father, rather than dictate what their feelings toward him should be. Parents who have lost a child and are still immersed in their grief will understand and allow their other children to move on with their lives – travel, marry, or move to another city for their studies.

Families that lack such freedom "strangle" their members and dictate what is considered acceptable and what is not. They are ruled by rigid conventions that dictate how the members of the family ought to feel and act. In such families, there is always at least one person who dominates and dictates to the others. Sometimes it is a parent; it may be one of the children who forces the rest of the family to follow his directives. The pressure tactics and attempts to restrict individual freedom come in different ways. They are not always blunt and forceful; at times the pressure is concealed and implicit, expressed through emotional "blackmail." The widow blackmails her children into relinquishing their own personal needs and desires by always reminding them how lonely she is.

The family that has already experienced loss exhibits greater sensitivity, which can in turn be used as a pretext for expecting and even demanding that family members take these sensitivities into consideration and make the appropriate concessions. The sense of space and freedom offered by the family reflects the family's ability to contain symbolic "separations" that enable each member to form their own selves. When a family does not enable separations, any act of distancing will constitute a threat to the well-being of its members. In the wake of a traumatic loss, this sort of family will make it even more difficult for its members to distance and to separate. The family members will make things harder for one another and not permit individuals to take distance from the group. Distancing will be conceived as a threat to the wholeness of the family, an act of "betrayal" and abandonment, rather than an opportunity needed by each member for his or her own personal growth. Such families will not only fail to offer support and approval for processes of individual growth, but they will impede it. The child will be deprived of the proper conditions for the growth and development of self and of independence.

Pathological equilibrium

In some families there is a pathological equilibrium. An unhealthy dependency develops among the members of the family, and pathological responses are offered to family members in need. Such families encourage emotional dependency, frown upon flexibility and individualized responses, dictate how family members respond to each other, and use guilt and other emotional pressures to instill control. The family discourages individuation and personal space – emotional as well as behavioral. Intergenerational boundaries are often blurred. In the wake of a loss, these sorts of families are fertile ground for the development of pathological behavior, since emotional needs – both of the individual and the family – are pushed to the extreme and the members of the family are now more dependent on each other.

Boundaries

Every family system is characterized by boundaries. These boundaries are both within the family and between it and the outside world. Intergenerational boundaries must be preserved within the family, between the parent and the children, and between the nuclear family and the extended family such as with the grandparents. The boundaries between the family and other individuals that surround it – friends, neighbors, etc. – must also be maintained. The loss often upsets the functioning of the family, and therefore "invites" intrusion and rupture of these boundaries: grandparents become overinvolved and take upon themselves parental roles; the widow lets her children "decide" whom they approve as a new partner for her, etc.

Immediately after the loss, there may at times be increased involvement of outsiders in the life of the family. The use of these external resources is considered normative and may even be necessary for the initial maintenance of the family, which has to contend with the initial state of shock and crisis. However, if the stepped-up involvement of these outsiders is extended over the course of time, it is evident that the family is not preserving its boundaries. In families that had been characterized by blurred boundaries prior to the loss, there is a greater chance that the shift in equilibrium after the loss will lead to even more indistinct boundaries. Unclear boundaries confuse the child: it is not clear to him who fills which role in his life. Children need to know and experience clear roles and boundaries in the functioning of their parents and family because it is in relation to these that they learn to define their roles and behavior.

The reverse situation is one in which the family completely blocks out the outside world. No one is allowed to know what is going on, no one is allowed to "interfere." This situation also undermines the functioning of the family. Families that prevent any influence by others block the possible contributions of external resources that might enrich and reinforce the family. Such families are often also incestuous, symbiotic, and even enmeshed. Growth and change – individual or familial – are oppressed. When loss occurs, the family is in need of reinforcing resources; the tendency toward isolation and seclusion will prevent it from taking advantage of such help. A closed family will prevent support systems and mechanisms from fulfilling their critical function. The widow who insists that only she can provide for the needs of her children will prevent their enrichment through contact with other people. She will not allow her son to attend a soccer game together with a neighbor, or will refuse to let her daughter take a trip with her friend's family.

Family myths

Myths are an important part of family life. They help to establish continuity between the generations and an understanding of the significance of family relationships in the past, present, and future. Myths represent goals and values that are shared by all members of the family, and play an important role in sending messages and educating children. They feature stories about figures with whom family members can identify, and whose ideology can be emulated. Through the myths, the dead and those who no longer have an active part in the family life continue to have an important role in the family tradition. For the children they are an important source for learning and identification. It is important therefore to learn how the "story" of the loss and the figures involved are integrated into the family myths. Is it considered additional proof of an existing myth? A family with

a tradition – and the attendant myths – of bravery and sacrifice will integrate the death of a son who died in battle into its heroic tradition. The
death will assume a positive meaning and further reinforce a family myth
that encourages its sons to uphold the values of devotion and sacrifice to
one's nation.

Conversely, families may also have negative myths in which the family
believes in its bad luck and that its members are hounded by forces beyond
their control. The current loss could be taken as an added sign of such a
myth and further perpetuate it, be it about the men of the family dying
young or about marital difficulties and divorces.

For children, family myths are an important resource for building their
self-identity. It is important that children hear all the details of the myths,
thereby enabling them to assimilate those aspects with which they may
choose to identify. Nevertheless, it is dangerous when myths are presented
to the child as an unalterable fate over which they have no control. If a tradition of bad luck continues to haunt the family, the child will be anxious
that his own fate has already been decided, and will feel he has lost control
over his future. It is therefore important to clarify just how the child views
these myths and what they mean to him. It is important to make sure he
does not consider the myth to be a force that controls his future, even if the
recent loss seems to corroborate the myth's veracity.

Family secrets

Every family has secrets. Some secrets relate to present circumstances and
some to the more distant past. Secrets are not only from the outside world
but also within the family. Healthy secrets are those that maintain the
boundaries of the family against the outside world, and concern issues that
only members of the family know about and need to know about. On the
other hand, when the family has many secrets, and when there are strict
internal rules about concealing things from outsiders, the family will "construct walls" to prevent outsiders from getting a look inside. The family
will delegitimize contacts between the children and the outside world out
of fear that secrets will be revealed. Often the secrets concern issues that
threaten the parents with fear of criticism and interference. Family secrets
may be about difficult subjects such as violence, abuse, parental dysfunction. Secrets can also be about the poor relationships among family

members. At times, the circumstances of the loss itself constitute a secret, such as in the case of suicide or a disease to which stigma is attached. The children know which family secrets "endanger" the family, and will usually maintain them zealously.

Because the situation after the loss often makes the family feel different and even "abnormal," it increases its secrecy vis-à-vis the outside world. Some parents lose confidence in themselves or even know of their dysfunction. It therefore threatens them that others should find out what is happening. The secrecy binds the children too and makes it very hard for them to share their hardships with the outside world and to seek external help. When a secretive family pattern is observed, one should exhibit heightened awareness for hidden distress signals from the children.

Secrets can also be within the family: secrets that some family members know about but others do not. Most often, these secrets are concealed from the children. Children usually sense when things are being hidden from them, and will try to find ways to discover the secret. Children who feel there are many secrets in their family will lose their sense of trust in their parents, and live in anxiety and fear of an ominous unknown. We have mentioned the tendency to hide from children those subjects that have to do with impending or actual loss. Planned changes in family life may also constitute secrets held back from the children. The child may discover that his father intends to remarry or that his mother is planning to move to another city. He is surprised and once again caught unprepared, as was the case with the initial loss. He loses his sense of trust in the parent who has not shared information with him, and is left with the feeling that he always has to fear the unexpected; that something bad is invariably going to happen to him. This feeling is compounded by the trauma of the loss, and the fears and insecurities brought on by it.

As shown, family-related factors have much influence on the life of the child after the loss. They can contribute much toward the child's positive readjustment and continued healthy growth in spite of the loss, but they may also make things more difficult. Through the family system, it is possible to influence most of the crucial processes, and make things easier for the child. Intervention and treatment through the family is often the best way to help the child.

Bereaved siblings

Judaism defines brothers and sisters of deceased siblings to be full-fledged mourners. Nevertheless, modern society has not devoted sufficient attention to the grief and suffering of bereaved siblings. Much attention has been devoted to the bereaved parents; they are at the focal point of the drama of losing a child. This means that in many instances the bereaved sibling is cast to the sidelines. There is a tendency to view siblings as those who are there to assist their bereaved parents, even "save" them, and not as mourners in their own right who are in need of consideration and attention. The parents often also feel they are the primary victims, and as such fail to pay enough attention to the grief and suffering of their children. They do not always "grant permission" to the siblings to engage in their own grief. Furthermore, the child's right to pursue his life in spite of the tragedy is adversely affected as a result of the obligations to his parents and his need to compensate for the deceased sibling.

In recent years, there has been greater recognition of the grieving needs of siblings, and understanding of the unique problems they face. We now consider some of these unique aspects of siblings' grief and the difficulties they face. It should be emphasized that many of the phenomena outlined in this book that refer to the effect of loss on children apply equally to siblings who have lost a brother or sister. Here we refer only to the unique experiences and difficulties of children who lose a sibling.

Before delving into the detailed aspects of the effects of loss, we describe the general dynamics of sibling relationship, which are relevant to understanding the responses of the bereaved sibling. Siblings fill various roles for one another, and their relationship is characterized by a complex network of mutual influences. The deep implications of the loss of a sibling derive from these roles, and are expressed not only in daily life but also in more distant realms and extended periods of time, including the development of the personality and the self.

Intimacy

Siblings usually share a great deal of intimacy. They grow up together, spend long hours in each other's company, and are "exposed" to one another in many ways. Even when siblings wish to maintain privacy, the physical closeness and contact forged by growing up together makes this hard to do. There is a great deal of interaction between siblings in many realms, from sharing the same bedroom and playing Monopoly together on winter nights, to the deep emotional involvement in each other's personal and social lives. The special relationship each of them has with the parents is strongly influenced from the roles in relation to his brothers/sisters. They grow up together and go through life's passages and changes together. They know each other inside and out, from the day they were born.

A wide variety of powerful emotions are shared by siblings. There is closeness and love, as well as jealousy. There is deep friendship, but also rivalry and even hatred. There is a sense of mutual aid and involvement, but competition and resentment as well. These intense feelings coexist in a whirlpool of emotions, and are the source of much ambivalence in the relationship between siblings. One should bear in mind that siblings accompany one another in the process of growing up. Each undergoes numerous and rapid-fire changes and the mutual relationship frequently takes on new and different aspects. The loss prematurely ends this process. Various factors may affect the sibling relationship, beginning with objective variables such as age differential, birth order, and gender, and individual factors such as personality features and the unique relationship each one has developed with the parents.

Age differential

When siblings are close in age they grow up together, with all which that entails. They may be close and share a great deal in common, but jealousy and competition often strongly influence the relationship. In the case of loss, a deep void is experienced because the everyday companionship and conflict are suddenly truncated. When brothers are far apart in age, there is a tendency for the older one to be the revered figure, an object of emulation, even a "parental" image. If the older sibling dies, his absence is felt in many similar ways to the absence of a parental figure. When a much younger sibling dies, his older sibling often feels as if he lost his own child because in many of these cases the older brother was highly involved in raising this child.

Birth order

The birth order influences the behavior and even the development of each child's character. It "dictates" roles. The firstborn always enjoys a unique position in the family, due to the special relationship with his parents, who usually have very high expectations of him. This special status affects how he will relate to his siblings. They look up to him. He serves as an example, and at times fills a "parental" role. He may also be the object of jealousy and even hatred. The younger brother is given the status of being "the little one": sometimes the spoiled child who is coddled not only by his parents but also by his siblings, who are often jealous of him. The middle child is often engaged in a struggle, jockeying for position against his older and younger siblings. He is suspicious of the others and often feels he gets the least of attention in comparison to his brothers. The middle child competes with everyone, and often keeps to himself.

The death of a sibling alters the roles that are influenced by birth order. If the firstborn is no longer there, then his "position" as senior becomes "available." If the youngest child is gone, the role of the cared for and spoiled child is now vacant. If the loss occurs when the children are still young, this shift in roles constitutes a sort of fulfillment of their latent fantasies, even hidden wishes. The "realization" of these will leave the sibling feeling guilty. He might even believe it is his omnipotent power that brought about the death of his brother or sister.

Gender of the siblings

Boys and girls have different status and roles. An older sister develops a different relationship with her younger brother than does an older brother with a younger brother. She is maternal toward her brother and pampers him, whereas he will educate and teach him to "be a man." Among brothers there is an alliance on masculine issues; among sisters there is a partnership on feminine issues. The opposite is also true: the brother uses his closeness with his sister to learn about relationships with girls; the sister looks up to her "cool" brother, who helps her learn about relationships with other boys. Such unique relationships – and their benefits – are abruptly cut off with the death of a sibling.

Family climate

The relationship between siblings is also affected by the family climate. Close, sharing families will help the siblings live in harmony with one another, and enable the children to solve their natural disputes in a good-natured manner. A family that is full of tension and competitiveness will encourage rivalry and jealousy between siblings. A family that is not accepting of its members will not give role modeling of tolerance and acceptance among siblings.

The family climate determines if each child can find his special place in the family, and if he will be able to develop in his own personality and way. This personal space will allow for individuality without too much competition among the siblings and without losing the love and support each needs. If this is not the case, much unfinished business accompanies the mourning over a brother or sister.

Unique parental relationship with each child

Parents have a unique relationship with each child, and this has an effect on the sibling relationships. If a parent seems to prefer one child over the others, his siblings will be jealous of him. If a child feels rejected by a parent, this may impair his standing among his siblings or, conversely, they may compensate him for the parental rejection. Siblings often hear their parents describing their connection with a deceased son as having been "a very special relationship." Whether this is realistic or only conceived as having been so after his death, such statements exacerbate the already existing sensitivity among the siblings regarding their own special status with the parents. When a deceased brother is accorded unique status, his siblings have little chance of competing for this special "place" with the parents.

The relationship between the parents affects the relationships among the children. Parents who are consumed by their own relationship, be it for reasons of support or friction, leave their children with a deficit of parental attention, and the children frequently find solace in stronger sibling relationships. In other instances they each find comfort outside the family, in which case they also grow apart from their siblings. Such tendencies often become stronger after the loss. Siblings fill roles that will in turn affect their brothers and sisters: one may provide a positive role model for achievement and good conduct, as opposed to another, who provides a negative role model, and who may even lead his siblings to behave in an aberrant manner.

The grieving sibling

As to grief-related behavior, the same principles that have been described for children's bereavement hold true for siblings as well; their response depends first of all on their age and stage of development. Nevertheless it is worth re-emphasizing how critical it is that siblings understand the circumstances and reasons that brought about the death. Clear explanations about the disease and under which conditions it might cause death may help elevate some of the child's fears that the same fate is awaiting him. It is vital that siblings be allowed to take part in the grieving and coping process along with the rest of the family.

The grieving of the sibling is very intense since he or she is left with the sense that they have lost part of their identity, lost someone who was a part of them. The sadness and pain are overpowering, the sense of loneliness is great. Following the loss, there is a strong tendency to try and preserve the sibling's presence by wearing his clothes, listening to his favorite CDs, carrying on imaginary conversations with him, considering what he would have said or done if he were here, and even seeking ways to make contact with his spirit. There is a strong sense of missed opportunity. Often, there is remorse for things that may have been said or done, memories of little fights that now seem so ridiculous and petulant. There is a strong desire to go back and fix things. There is a yearning for what was supposed to be a shared future – all the things the siblings were supposed to be doing together throughout their lifetime.

Loneliness of the siblings becomes even more intense because often, at least during the initial period, the siblings are also "abandoned" by the parents. With the loss of a sibling, the bereaved sibling also loses part of his own life, since among many bereaved families life changes significantly, primarily during the initial mourning period. The bereaved parents are inundated by a deep sense of grief, and often lack the strength or even the interest to fulfill their parental duties toward their remaining children. They shut themselves off and are enveloped by their grief, leaving the other children on their own. The children are left feeling unimportant to their parents, that only the deceased child was and is important. They feel that their parents do not care what happens to them, and in extreme cases even feel they ought to have died rather than the child that did.

The younger the child, the more a sibling's death will leave him feeling at greater risk, threatened and confused. Children are not supposed to die. If it happened to his brother it could happen to him too. Subconsciously, he is threatened by the fact that his parents did not succeed in protecting his sibling. If something bad happens to him, will his parents not be able to protect him too?

Older siblings are often given a message by society that it is now up to them to take care of their parents. They are not given permission to grieve because they are expected to "be strong" and "be good" for their parents. They are expected to assume family roles, and function in an adult and even "parental" manner toward their parents. They are not allowed to mourn as siblings; neither are they permitted to be children. These sorts of messages create "scars" that will remain for many years after the loss.

In addition to the pain and loneliness, the bereaved sibling also has anger – anger at the dead brother who is not there, who left him with such intense pain, who "spoiled" life for him. It is difficult and even forbidden to express the anger. No one will accept it; certainly not the parents. The child feels guilty for harboring such feelings, for being angry with a sibling who is now dead, a sibling he himself misses. Children, especially younger children, often fear that the bad thoughts they had are what caused the tragedy. Siblings sometimes do and say nasty things to one another during a fight or in the heat of the moment. "I wish you would drop dead" is commonly uttered during fights among children, and bad thoughts are even more frequent. When they come true, the sibling is panicked by the "knowledge" that it was he who caused the tragedy. Usually he will keep this "secret" to himself, and it will burden him very much. Some of the more common modes of behavior among bereaved siblings are now described.

The "good" child

The sibling is given a message by his parents that they do not have the strength to deal with any more problems now, and he therefore has to be "good." This message means that he cannot expect his parents to devote any attention to him or deal with his problems or needs; they are preoccupied by their loss. In the child's perspective, his parents love his deceased sibling more than him, or, even worse, they only love the deceased sibling. He is afraid that if he isn't good, he will lose them to an even greater extent. However, by adopting exemplary, grown-up behavior, the child is doing himself a great disservice because it gives additional "proof" that he has no needs or difficulties of his own, and that from now on his role is to be the "good child."

The void that remains

Bereaved siblings feel that a void has formed; a life partner is no longer there. There is no substitute. Sometimes in the initial period they cling to their other siblings in the hope of filling the void. But not every child has a sibling, and even among those who do there may be drawbacks such as age disparity, siblings who no longer live at home, or strained past relationships. These factors can limit their ability to forge emotional partnerships that will compensate and comfort them in times of need. The void left by the deceased sibling remains in any case.

Identification

Identification and following in the footsteps of the missing sibling is another way to blur the sensation of void and loss. A younger brother may volunteer for the same army unit where his brother served and got killed. Following in the same footsteps may be an unconscious way of dealing with the guilt of being alive while the brother is not, a way to continue his life "for him." If it was an older brother, he was often the subject of admiration and following his example keeps his "path" real.

Parental expectations

The parents send overt and implied messages regarding their expectations of the remaining siblings. On the one hand they make it clear that no one can ever fill the void left, while on the other they expect the siblings to "compensate" for the loss. Sometimes they want another sibling to assume the deceased sibling's role and be just like him, although they will simultaneously make it clear that there is no possible way for anyone else to be like him. The messages are ambivalent and confusing. The remaining siblings have the feeling that no matter what they do, it will not be enough.

The void and the needs of the parents create a new dynamic among the siblings: Who will be "asked" by the parents to fill the role of the missing sibling, and who is "not good enough"? Which child will be pressured to stay close to the parents, and who will be given the freedom to go on with his life? Who remains devoted and close, and who is distancing himself, freeing himself from the emotional duties to the parents? Some siblings take upon themselves the role to "compensate" for their brother and let the parents put on them the expectations they had of the deceased sibling. They choose the same line of studies, engage in the same type of music or sports activities. Such behavior often harbors a latent hope that the child will earn the affection of his parents, which he feels only the deceased sibling gets. Such hopes often end up in disappointment if and when the child senses that his parents' emotions are not aimed at him, but rather at the image he has taken upon himself. Sooner or later the realization comes that he cannot fill the place of his deceased sibling.

In some extreme cases, the bereaved parents may decide to have another child who, they hope, will fill the void. This child is conceived – literally – into the role of compensating for his sibling's loss, and will have to work harder than an ordinary child to forge his individual self.

Circumstances of the loss

Many siblings fear that a similar fate will befall them; that there is something "contagious" about what happened to their sibling. It is an ominous belief that derives from anxiety and fear, and perhaps from unconscious feelings of guilt and an unwitting desire to atone for the fact that fate did not take them. They may feel that they require some sort of magical protection to ward off the evil eye and avoid the same fate as their sibling.

The circumstances of the loss can have unique implications for the siblings. If a brother died of an illness, his siblings will be afraid that they too might get the same disease. If the disease is hereditary, the fear has realistic roots that cast a cloud over their lives. If the brother died a hero in the course of military service or in other heroic circumstances, the siblings sometimes feel a need to continue in his footsteps, and embark on a similar military career in order to prove that they too are willing to take risks. If the brother's life was cut short by a car accident, they may fear that a similar fate awaits them.

If the brother committed suicide, the siblings are left with severe emotional distress and intense guilt. They feel guilty for not having anticipated or prevented the tragedy. They feel betrayed, since he did not come to them with his problems, and did not tell them of his intention to take his own life. They may blame their parents for what happened, but cannot verbalize this accusation since they do not want to hurt their parents even more. The suicide is usually not an open subject for discussion. No one dares to speak openly and find out what happened, for fear that painful accusations may emerge. The family, which in any case feels it is falling apart, is unable to contain any further controversy. The scar tissue left by the suicide will remain sealed. The parents fear that another child may also decide to commit suicide; they will lose confidence in their own parenting abilities. The children sense their anxieties and concerns, and therefore cannot process their feelings, thoughts, and anxieties openly with their parents.

In some instances the suicide is related to problems in the family and exposes flaws in the parental behavior. Such behavior is often a secret that the children know they are supposed to keep. After the suicide they have to work even harder to disguise the truth. Sometimes the suicide is the realization of fears anticipated; the problems were known but not successfully addressed. After the suicide it is even more difficult for the family to cope with the problems that have come to light. Defense mechanisms may be employed even more intensely than before, and prodigious effort will be invested in placing the problems and family secrets back under lock and key.

Open dialogue

Many bereaved families lack an open dialogue between parents and children, all of whom are grieving. The parents are preoccupied and inundated by their own emotional state, which hinders their ability to handle the real needs of the siblings. Given their state of mind, they cannot "hear" their children.

Decline in scholastic achievement, isolation, introversion, and even depression have been observed among bereaved siblings. The symptoms usually appear during the more advanced periods of mourning, and not necessarily during the initial stage. They stem from the child's inability to express and process grief, difficulties in his relationship with his parents, lack of parental attention and investment, and the child's feeling that there is no legitimization for him to go on living.

Aberrant behavior

Aberrant behavior, especially destructive conduct and taking risks, is a "solution" to the bottled up emotions. Such behavior is a means of expressing the immense anger which the sibling has no "permission" to vent: anger at what happened to his life; anger at the sibling that died; anger as well as a desire to hurt the parents who have abandoned him and devoted themselves to mourning and doting on his deceased sibling. It is also a way of provoking fate and seeing if something bad will happen to him. Finally, it is a way of diverting the parents' attention back to him and his needs.

Expression of bereaved sibling's feelings

In most cases however, many years will pass before the bereaved sibling allows himself to fully express his feelings. That occasion often arises only after a period of depression or after encountering difficulties in different areas of life, such as studies, employment, or romantic involvement. It often comes to light only when they are already adults. For the most part, siblings do not attribute these difficulties to their brother's death and its aftermath. Only a process of inner reflection, at times facilitated by professional therapy, will eventually lead to the realization as to connection between their problems in the present and the loss of their sibling and its intense aftermath, which may have happened way back in childhood.

Shift in parental role

The death of a child may lead to a significant shift in how the parent perceives his parental role and relationship with his other children. The loss underscores their importance to him. He feels a sense of having missed an opportunity with his deceased child, and will adjust his priorities in order to devote more time and energy to the other children. In such instances the family is strengthened, and the remaining siblings benefit from a more qualitative parental investment. In spite of their great emotional difficulties, most parents try and make a great effort to continue with life. This does not come easily, but they are aware that it is the only way in which they will be able to give their children and themselves any sort of quality of life.

Patterns of response

Still, there are some patterns of response that make things very difficult for the siblings. Parents who do not bring their other children into the circle of grief leave the family in a state of artificial "business as usual." The family functions reasonably well, but much of it is happening only on the surface: the deceased brother is not mentioned; the family does not share the grief. Often the parents explain this pattern by claiming that they want to save their children the suffering they themselves are going through. The actual result is the opposite: because they are unable to share their own emotions with the parents, the siblings are left alone and isolated with their anguish. The deceased becomes an unapproachable ghost spirit.

Some parents exhibit "ownership" of the grief. They conceive themselves as the sole victims of the loss, and do not recognize the suffering of the siblings. They do not recognize the legitimate grief of the siblings, thereby preventing them from having their right and opportunity to mourn. On the other hand, when the siblings express a desire to resume normal life, they are accused of not caring. The parents use the siblings' need to go on living as evidence that they did not suffer at all from the loss.

At times there is excessive idealization of the deceased child, and the other siblings have little chance of measuring up to him. The remaining children feel that they are less successful, less important, and less loved than their dead brother. This feeling exists not only during the initial mourning period, but may and often does pursue the siblings far into adulthood. The response of the parents and the idealization of the deceased sibling may give rise to the pervading feeling that anyone still alive has no value. The child reaches the seemingly obvious conclusion that the parents would perhaps prefer that he would have died instead. He envies his dead sibling for the outpouring of love he receives; perhaps it is better to die and be the recipient of all this love.

Because parents are fearful of any additional tragedy, they sometimes place strict restrictions on their children. In an attempt to prevent anything else bad from happening, they do not allow them to stray beyond the tight reins of their control. The child is prohibited from taking any risks. Even normative behavior for his age is considered a risk to which the parents do not agree, such as going off on a trip with the guys, driving at night, or serving in a combat unit in the army. "We've gone through enough," the parents will say, asking their child to be considerate of them, and to adjust his life to their sensitivities and fears.

Overprotectiveness also reflects a need to fix what happened. The loss is conceived as their failure to adequately protect their child; the result of bad, irresponsible parenting. They are determined to do all they can to prevent such a situation again. They need to prove to themselves that they are good parents who protect their children. Some parents allow themselves to demand that the other siblings live their lives according to the parents' expectations and sensitivities: "How could you do this to us?!" "How can you even think of riding a motorcycle?!" "You know how hard we worked so all our children can study!" The pressure may be direct and obvious, or alternatively exerted through indirect emotional maneuvering and guilt feelings: "Okay, do what you want to do, our lives are over anyhow." "You are our only hope, and our sole reason to go on living. But go ahead." In exchange for relinquishing their desires, the parents may offer the sibling hard-to-refuse enticements such as financial inducements: "If you don't go away to college, we'll buy you a car."

The child's understanding that it is up to him to give meaning to his parents' lives puts a heavy burden on him, but can also be an emotionally rewarding seduction. After the loss he felt abandoned and unloved; now he feels satisfaction knowing that his parents need him. In exchange, he is willing to give up his independence and freedom to make his own life choices. In some instances, even as an adult he will be unable to summon up the strength to withstand his parents' pressures and manipulations.

Some bereaved parents live with the feeling that their lives are over. They lose interest in life; it feels empty and meaningless. Their children are aware of this emptiness and consciously or not take it upon themselves to give it meaning. They do their best to be good students, try hard to succeed and notch up achievements in various fields of endeavor. Siblings can also lend significance to their parents' lives through negative behavior that demands their attention. They fail examinations, misbehave at school, and even become involved in deviant or dangerous activities. In so doing, they keep their parents busy, forcing them to once again be involved in their lives and at least partially "separate" from their grief. They rekindle their parents' relationship by providing them with concerns and objectives they must share.

In conclusion, we describe several concrete examples of what takes place in some of the homes of bereaved families, and how the lives of the siblings may be affected from these phenomena.

The home as a memorial shrine

Some bereaved parents fill the home with photos and objects that commemorate the dead child. They sometimes devote a room to his memory, or even make his presence felt in every area of the home. Siblings may feel they are living in a temple dedicated to the memory of the deceased. Their own presence is symbolically minimized. By leaving the deceased sibling's possessions as they were and preserving his bedroom as it was prior to his death, the other children are left with a feeling of non-separation; that life has gone into suspended animation. Since they feel guilty for living and for wanting to go on with life, they dare not ask for the room or his other possessions for their own use.

In some bereaved homes, there is an abiding message that there is no place for happiness, nor will there ever be. Happiness is forbidden; laughter has lost its place; having pleasure from music is frivolous; enjoying a television show is foolish. Nevertheless, children need happiness and pleasure. They are capable of mourning for a sibling and also going on with the pleasures of life. If happiness and satisfaction are taboo at home, the child will seek them elsewhere. He will visit friends more frequently than is common, spend more time at the youth movement or teen hangout, and will go out to discos and movies more than he used to. He will not bring his friends home as he knows his friends will not feel comfortable. Since he may also be embarrassed if his friends see what goes on at home he will refrain from inviting them. Some bereaved parents are insensitive to the fact that they are placing an especially heavy burden on their children by preventing them from having an ordinary home life, and by not putting in enough effort to make it a place where their children can continue to grow up happily.

Self-image

Research studies and long-term observation of bereaved siblings indicate that they sustain damage to the development of their self-image. The aftermath of the loss harms many aspects of the siblings' healthy growth: the lack of attention and love; the need to satisfy the needs and expectations of the parents, therefore forego own wishes and needs; the traumatic loss which threatens the sense of security; the hopeless "competition" with the deceased brother. All of these reactions undermine his sense of self-worth and therefore harm the development of the "self."

Bereaved siblings sometimes report that only at a fairly late stage in life did they begin to feel the full grief over a sibling who died years earlier. Only when they reached adulthood did they understand the immense price they had paid, and to what extent the experience of loss and its aftermath disrupted their continued development and normal life. Only when they passed into adulthood were they able to heal some of these wounds so they could resume being their own selves, rather than continue living under the shadow of being "bereaved siblings."

New beginnings and other changes in life

After a big loss, it is normal to feel that the world has stopped spinning, that nothing is important anymore. Hope for a good life often seems out of reach. Nevertheless, life does go on, and changes, many of which are enhancing and good, are part of the normal course of life. The child moves from one grade to the next, transfers to another school, gets new teachers, and changes friends. There are many changes that are brought on by the loss itself: the parent finds a new partner; the family moves to another town. We now describe some of the characteristic changes that occur as a result of the loss, and how these changes challenge the child. We point out the possible connection between the initial process of adjustment after the loss and the manner in which the child will respond to and cope with further changes.

For the most part, children adapt well to changes, and are flexible enough to adjust to new situations. Whenever the child exhibits difficulties and opposition to change, the source of the problem should be examined. It should not be immediately assumed that he "does not want" to adapt himself, or "doesn't try hard enough." There are reasons for failure to adjust to change among children who have experienced loss.

Primary changes

The primary changes in the child's life have to do with his family. The changes are usually initiated by the parents, based on needs that arise in their own lives. The need to change jobs may require the family to move to another area of the country, which entails change of school and change of friends for the child. A new intimate relationship will not only mean the introduction of a new member to the family, but can also lead to the expansion of the family, adding new children – the new spouse's children and/or the birth of new siblings. Marriage and a larger family sometimes lead to the need for a new house, moving to a different area, and even another city.

The changes may be unavoidable necessities, or they may take place through the initiative of a parent who wants a fresh start and a new opportunity. For someone who has experienced traumatic loss, change is a means of taking distance from the memory of the loss, a way to end the bereavement, to start something new and rehabilitate himself. Changes and beginnings are usually an opportunity to do something different, to lend hope and energy to life. Yet by the same token they are also frightening and pressuring. They always entail separation and therefore they are also a loss. There might therefore be ambivalence in regard to them.

Changes, even if seemingly positive, are liable to arouse dormant, unresolved issues stemming from the past loss. It is natural for a child who has experienced a traumatic loss which he could not control and which left him scarred and hurting to be wary and even fearful of additional separations and losses. This child already knows the feeling of lacking self-confidence. He is no stranger to loneliness or sadness and fears that the impending change will re-expose him to this suffering. A new situation will again confront him with uncertainty and unfamiliarity, jeopardizing the continuity of the safe and familiar which he so much needs and cherishes.

A child who is being asked to accept his mother's boyfriend is subject to numerous fears: Will he like me? Will mother continue to be "mine"? Will mother's boyfriend be my father from now on? And if so, what sort of father will he be? Must I now forget my biological father? And is this a betrayal of him? The child wants his family to be normal, just like everyone else's. He wants someone to go to football games with, just like his friends. But he is also afraid of all the side-effects that go along with such a change.

The timing and essence of the change may suit the parent, but not necessarily suit the child, and may even be at odds with the child's needs. The degree of readiness for change and the need for a change varies for each member of the family. The widowed father feels he is ready to start a new intimate life, but the child has not yet completed the process of bereavement for his mother. The divorced mother wants to move away to make a new start in life, but the child is in need of a sense of familiarity, a sense of belonging, and is not ready to move far away from his father because he still feels very unsafe in his relations with him.

Some of the changes seem to the adults very trivial and "obvious" and therefore they think there is no need "to fuss" about them. They do not understand why the child is so sensitive and overreacts. The child's ability to respond and adjust to change has to do with the question of whether the parent has informed the child of the planned change. Did he explain the reasoning behind it? Did he solicit the child's opinion? Did he consider the child's requests and/or difficulties? Parents are sometimes afraid to let their children take part in planning changes, for fear of countering opposition. They prefer to present the child with a fait accompli, exploiting the parental privilege of authority and decision-making power. However, merely listening to the child's response to the proposed changes does not mean that the parent must act on the child's demands or requests. It offers an opportunity to prepare the child, to understand what is troubling him, and perhaps, without much effort, to adjust the plan to fit his needs and wants.

Hidden issues and unresolved problems

Sometimes the parent takes note of the child's difficulties only after the change has already occurred and the child starts to "make trouble." Through this behavior, the child brings his problems to the attention of the parent and places on the agenda unresolved issues that concern him and his ability to get on with life. The problems might seem irrelevant to the loss itself, which has seemingly been forgotten because it happened so long ago: troubles in school; aggressive or impudent behavior; acting out; introversion; drawing away from the parent; spending much time away from home.

These forms of behavior are characteristic of children in distress. It might seem that the issue under discussion is only the present-day change: difficulty making friends in the new neighborhood, getting accustomed to the new teacher and new school, having a hard time accepting mother's new boyfriend who "isn't so nice." It is important to ascertain whether the present-day concrete problem is not actually a cover for hidden issues related to the loss and to the unresolved problems that derive from it.

The ongoing processing of the loss which accompanies the growth of the child will cast its shadow over every new adjustment the child needs to overcome. The more the child has processed the loss, the greater the chance that he will "permit" changes and new relationships to grow. The child's willingness to take risks and invest his energies in building up new relationships of love and emotional dependence is heavily influenced by the extent of the "scab" still remaining from the loss. We now describe several common changes that take place in the wake of a loss, and illuminate typical responses of children which are likely to result from the loss.

Changes in the family

Some time after the death of a parent, or after a separation and divorce, the remaining parent may begin to consider establishing a new intimate relationship. The first change will occur when the parent starts dating potential partners, some of whom may visit the family at home and even participate from time to time in family events like meals and birthdays. This constitutes a harsh change for a child, even if there is no indication of permanence about it. The change confronts the child with the possibility that sooner or later someone will form an intimate relationship with the remaining parent and thereby "enter" his life too.

Vagueness and uncertainty as to what will happen next is typical of this period: the child is unsure how he should act toward the new adult who is the parent's partner, but who as yet lacks any role or status in the family. The child puts the new "candidate" to the test in an attempt to decide whether he likes him, seeking to determine if it is worth forming a relationship with him. The child grapples with the question of whether he is ready for a "substitute" for the missing parent. The situation is fraught with doubt, fears, uncertainty, and ambivalence.

When a permanent relationship is formed – along with the stronger although not yet final commitment to a spousal relationship – the partner will in one form or another be added to the family. The closer relationship includes the assumption by the new spouse of a "parental" role vis-à-vis the children. At this point, the child has to grapple with the real acceptance of the new partner and possible parent. The next phase of the relationship is a committed, long-term intimate relationship that may include marriage. This phase will permanently fix the position of the new "parent" in the child's life.

During all of these stages, the "chemistry" between child and adult is put to the test, as well as the child's readiness to accept a new parent. The child's emotional readiness for this change is very much the result of the previous phases: how the loss was worked through and accepted; what are the relationships with the missing parent; which new patterns of relations have been established with the raising parent. The more unfinished business and unresolved issues that exists, the harder the process of adaptation and acceptance of the changes. The child is tormented by guilt feelings, anger, longing to go back to the old and familiar. As a result, at best he will be emotionally ambiguous. More often he refuses to open up to the new and will do a lot of acting out to oppose it.

Things might become more difficult because the new family set-up includes new "bothers or sisters," the new spouse's children. Also, new children may be born into the second marriage. The child worries about his "place" in the family, worries about the time and love he will be getting from here on. Emotions of jealousy, anger, and fear are very prevalent and need to be attended to. Additional siblings represent a shift in the family equilibrium to which the child has grown accustomed. He may be happy about having a new sibling; his hope of having a big brother or a little sister may be realized, but the change also poses a threat. Sometimes his position in the family is indeed strongly affected and he is in need of extra emotional reinforcement and love.

The behavior of his parent has critical influence, and constitutes a weathervane for the child. If the parent makes an effort to have his new partner accepted into the family and builds a relationship of closeness, trust, and intimacy, he provides an example to his children, promoting the idea that new relationships are worthwhile and rewarding – in spite of the inherent pains and risks. Alternatively, if he himself is conflicted, his children will remain conflicted as well. In some instances the parent does not "invite" the new spouse to fill any parental role with the children. Alternatively, sometimes the spouse may show little interest in getting involved in family life. Either scenario would leave the child feeling insecure. The age of the child will affect his response: usually the young boy who is looking for a father will form a relationship with a new figure faster than an adolescent.

There is a difference between a child whose parent has died and a child whose parents have split up. The latter may feel that his relationship with the biological parent is at risk due to the introduction of a new "parent." He is liable to feel that he is being asked to choose between them and to prove his loyalty, which will make him feel guilty and conflicted. He does not want to betray his biological parent, or lose even more of him. But he does want a normal family in which his father or mother has a husband or wife. Whatever the case, the child who has already experienced the loss of a parent goes through a difficult process to accept an alternative parental figure and to establish a close and trusting relationship with him or her. During this process a wide variety of responses is to be considered normal and acceptable, each reflecting the previous experiences of the child and his present needs:

- *Enthusiasm and hope:* the child who has been yearning for a parent is happy that his wish and need have been fulfilled. He nurtures a fantasy that the void left by the loss will now be filled. He believes the family will once again be "normal." The child hopes the new parent will make up for various deficiencies in his life: the new father can take him out to a football game; the new mother will make a delicious home-cooked meal.

- *Anger and non-acceptance:* the child refuses to accept the new spouse. He is angry about the change that has taken place in his life and expresses his anger through troublemaking.

- *Reserving judgment and keeping distance:* the child may not be enthusiastic, but neither does he raise serious objections. He is conflicted, and subjects his parent and the new spouse to a long, drawn-out test. He refrains from forming a true relationship, opting to keep a safe distance. If the parent has gone through several intimate relationships which broke down after a while, the child has experienced loss again and again, and will therefore be very careful in allowing himself to build another intimate close relationship with yet another person who will any way disappear.

In some instances the aches and pains of the loss even increase during the period of change as the child is inundated by unresolved issues. Unresolved, emotionally charged issues that were left unaddressed, such as anger, questions and accusations, unexpressed disappointments and intense feelings related to the loss and its aftermath, are aroused by the triggers of change. They have remained dormant and hidden until now. They were not dealt with because of fears and in the hope that they would "disappear" on their own. The change awakens these dormant issues.

When a child is still angry with his mother for having gotten a divorce from his father, he will be unable to accept her decision to begin a new intimate relationship. A child who thinks his father has "forgotten" his dead mother will not "permit" another woman to take her place. After the child and parent have communicated their emotions and worked out their difficulties, the child will be able to accept the change, grant his "permission," and even enjoy its benefits.

In order for the child to be able to accept a new parent, he has to "assign" the absent parent to a safe, secure position that will not be threatened or compromised by the new figure. Even the child who earnestly seeks a new father has to and wants to preserve the memory and "place" of his biological father. To that end, he needs to undergo various tasks, especially the processing of the loss and the development of an internalized relationship with the absent person.

When a parent is involved in changes, and especially in a new intimate relationship, he may at times pay less attention to his children. The child feels neglected or even abandoned, which in turn revives the memories and feelings he experienced after the loss. When the new intimate relationship follows a long period during which the child has acted in some capacity as the parent's partner, he will feel betrayed.

Moving to a different home

A child's home is his castle. Changing one's home constitutes a separation from familiar walls, disengagement from the place which stores important and cherished memories, including the times before the loss. Moving means leaving all these memories behind and there is a fear that they will be lost. Anyone who has lost a person dear to him or her fears that the memory will also grow distant and fade away. Children harbor these fears even more than adults because they have not had enough experience of "carrying" their memories within. The child cherishes the memories surrounding his home because they constitute an important part of his identity: this is were he was a baby; in this yard he played basketball and won. Here are the "footprints" of his past that has been disrupted. Moving to a new home might mean exchanging a protective place for an unfamiliar and perhaps unsafe one.

Generally speaking, moving to a new home also means transferring to a new school. This translates into leaving good friends behind, no longer having the teacher who understood and liked the child, no longer enjoying the same status and position in class and school. All of these are normative losses and present any child with fears and worries, but for the child who carries the deep wound of a traumatic loss and who already "knows" how the experience of loss feels, this normative change is much more threatening. While the change may also offer new opportunities to the child – a fresh beginning complete with new horizons – the doubts and fears are paramount in his mind. Will he make new friends? Will he be as well liked as he had been? How will he get along in school? Faced with a new, alien environment – teachers as well as students – he will have to prove himself, establish his position in class and with his peers. Will he tell them his father is dead? Will he reveal that his parents are divorced? He does not want to be perceived as being different. It is important to him to be like everyone else. He certainly does not want to attract negative attention, or have anyone pity him.

Children often oppose change only because of their fear of it. If the child's questions and fears are respected and responded to, if he is offered possible solutions to his problems, then his cooperation can usually be attained. If not, the change might become yet another trauma for him and for the parent, who will have to invest a great deal of energy in overcoming the objections and difficulties thrown up by the child. The parent is often preoccupied by the change and may therefore neglect to make himself available and help the child through. He may believe that his good intentions and his belief that the change will improve the life of his family are sufficient.

It is usually hard for parents to admit to their children that the change they are initiating is being made first and foremost for their own benefit. They do not allow themselves to say "It's my turn now. I'm going to take care of myself and get my own life back together." The child might not accept this sort of sentiment with love and understanding, but being ignored and disregarded is much harder still. It is difficult for parents to let their children know about extenuating circumstances and difficulties that have compelled them to make the changes. However, if the child does not understand the reason for change, he is denied any opportunity to enlist in the cause and do what he can to help.

Attentive listening, sharing of feelings and thoughts, support and love are the "tools" of help that members of a family, especially the parents, can offer their children. They may not be able to do what the child wants, they may not be able to solve all the symptoms of distress the child experiences, but it is critical that the child knows they are aware of his difficulties, that they understand and care. When viewing the childhood of a child who has suffered a traumatic loss, it is important to note the changes that have taken place in his life after the loss, and to understand the effects they had. Were they experienced only as another hardship, or did they turn out to be a beneficial experience through which the child grew stronger?

The changes undergone by the child after the loss are an important part of the "story" of the loss and rehabilitation. They can "wrap" the traumatic event with hope, growth, and happiness.

Chapter 5

A Few More Things That One Should Know

Dos

The following is a list of recommendations as to how the adult can best help a child following a loss:

1. Remember that it is the adult who provides the *example and modeling* to the child how to respond, and that it is his "permission" which allows the child to act.

2. It is most important that the adult who is closest to the child – first and foremost his parent – continues to be the *primary caregiver* after the loss, even if he has difficulty functioning in this role at this time. If the parent has a hard time coping with all his duties, he should receive help and assistance in carrying out his other tasks, preserving whatever energies he has to care for his children. It is he whom the child trusts and from whom the child needs love, closeness, and support. If the parent draws away, this will cause extensive harm to the child, amplifying his sensation of loss.

3. *When the parent is not available,* it is best for the child to be looked after by people he knows, people he feels close to, who love him.

4. Following the loss, the child should remain as much as possible within his *natural, familiar environment,* at home, with family and friends, at school. He needs the comfort of familiar things, and

the support systems that he is accustomed to. It is not advisable to remove him from home or to leave him for hours on end with other caregivers. At home, he should have his own safe zone, complete with the toys and games he is used to playing with. He should be given opportunities to meet with his friends and spend comforting distraction time with them.

5. *Let the child grieve in his own way.* Every child will find his own way to express his emotions, whether through crying, anger, shutting himself off in his room, or listening to music.

6. Allow the child to work through his *mourning at his own pace;* allow him to go out and play, watch television, or do anything else that relaxes, occupies, and distracts him.

7. Find ways to help and encourage the child to *express* his emotions and thoughts. Talk to him in his own "language" through games, make-belief role play, painting together, or any other medium that fits his personality, emotional, and mental level.

8. Give the child a *personal example* of how to express thoughts and feelings. The expression should be as *balanced* as possible: making room for weakness, but also making the effort to find strength; expressing grief, but sometimes also holding back; expressing fears and worries and also giving place to confidence, trust, and hope; expressing sadness, but also making room for humor. Such a balanced example of attitude and behavior will enable the child to find his own balance.

9. *Provide explanations and answers* to all of the child's questions. The answers should be adapted to the cognitive ability and mental level of the child. They should be detailed, lucid, and clear. An effort should be made to determine if the child fully understands, and supplementary explanations and examples should be furnished if needed. Only the truth should be told and – if conditions permit – all the truth, and in real time.

10. Furnish the child with *information* about what has happened and what will happen in the near future. The information should

relate to how events will affect his day-to-day life and that of the family. The explanations should be brief, concrete, and simple.

11. Inform the child of *proposed plans and changes* and give him a chance to express his opinions and desires. His requests should be honored as much as possible.

12. Allow the child to exercise his *freedom of thought*, and let him feel safe and secure in doing so. Adults close to him should "contain" his emotions, fears, anger, and anxieties. It is important to *listen* to him; "lectures" about how he should behave should be kept to a minimum.

13. Give the child a *sense of confidence* – existential confidence. He should be given the feeling that the adults, and especially his parent, will do everything possible to protect him, look after his needs, and prevent additional loss and hardships. It is vital to get across the message that the world has not devolved into chaos as a result of the loss; that in spite of what happened the parent and even the child have control over what will happen in their life. This should be demonstrated through concrete examples that are relevant to the daily life of the child.

14. The child is in need of a great deal of *warmth and love*. Do not be sparing of words and do not hold back on the hugs. Remember that loving physical contact is the direct way to his heart and his feelings, even more so than spoken words.

15. Bestowing one's love on a saddened, hurting child does not mean breaking down rules and boundaries. Clearly outline the *"rules"* to the child; he needs to know what is permissible and what is forbidden. Flexibility and common sense should be employed. This is not the time to start educating him, nor is it the time to be overly strict. Conversely, the child should not be allowed to unburden himself in whichever way he sees fit. It is important to maintain the laws and rules of conduct as they have been practiced until now. Lack of boundaries cannot compensate for the feeling of pain. On the contrary, a child who has experienced loss and the devastation of his secure

world has to feel that some things remain stable and unchanged, allowing him to regain a sense of confidence and order in his world.

16. Find out which issues are of greatest concern to him in the wake of the loss, and how they impact on his daily life, which issues he has difficulty handling. It is important that the child be given *opportunities to tell about his troubles*, and offered the help, advice, and support in choosing the most appropriate solutions for him.
   Here are some typical issues that may trouble the child: how to tell friends what happened; whether or not to attend a party with classmates; who is going to be picking him up from basketball practice; whether the family will have enough money to live on.

17. Give the child *concrete tasks to perform*, and allow him to fill a role in family life. In so doing, he will feel that he too is able to contribute toward an improvement of the situation, that he is more than just a helpless little boy who is dependent on adults.

18. Children have abundant natural abilities. It is the duty of adults to provide the conditions to nurture those abilities. Faced with loss, a child finds himself in a state of distress, and should be given the *tools to cope* with it. The work cannot be done for him, but he must be given all the love and support he needs to see it through. He can and should undergo this process by himself, in his own way. The child who is coping with loss-related difficulties gains by learning how to cope, and by acquiring the knowledge and confidence that he is able to endure hardship.

Don'ts

In addition to the aforementioned list of important things to do, below is an equally important list of things not to do.

1. *Don't lie*. Do not distort facts. Do not impart information and explanations in ambiguous language the child is liable to misinterpret.

2. *Don't assign the child the roles of an adult.* Do not assign him impossible and foolhardy tasks such as: "From now on, you'll take care of Mom"; "From here on, you will have to be a good boy"; or "You have to be strong."

3. *Don't put blame on the child.* Do not encourage or reinforce any feelings of guilt he might have about the absent person, or about you, the remaining parent. Do not give him the feeling that he bears even the slightest responsibility for what happened, or for what will happen.

4. *Don't remove a child from his home* if at all possible, and don't leave him in the care of strangers.

5. *Don't make major changes.* The period immediately after the loss is not a propitious time for any other major changes. This is not the time to move the child to another school, or to move to a new home. It is best if the remaining parent can maintain the same routine and schedule as before. Changes require coping and readjustment, and investment of emotional energies. The child does not have extra emotional resources to call upon right now, and requires every ounce of energy and strength to cope with the loss and its implications. That which is familiar and comfortable helps build back the child's confidence and will provide the basis for adjustment.

6. *Be conscious of yourself.* Do not project your world onto that of the child. Study your own emotions and inner world closely, and take care to differentiate between yourself and the child. Adults are liable to transfer their own fears, needs, and difficulties onto the child. They will defend this, arguing that they are only trying to protect the child. All too often this has nothing to do with the child's world or his needs, but only with the difficulties of the adult.

7. *Do not project onto the child.* Adults who have experienced the trauma of loss as children have to be particularly aware of their own sensitivities and the defense mechanisms they employ, and make the effort not to project them onto the child.

8.   When the child is behaving peculiarly, do not ignore it hoping it will "go away by itself." *Acting out is a distress signal.* It is important, first and foremost, to check with the child himself, talk to him, ask and listen to his explanation.

9.   The parent can then also consult with others who know the child, such as his teachers. It is sometimes advisable to *consult with professionals* – psychologists, social workers, or other counselors. Those who are emotionally reeling from the loss are liable to respond in an over- or under-exaggerated manner. Consultation with a professional can help to determine whether or not the behavior/response of the child is to be considered normal and appropriate under the circumstances. If it is determined that the problem requires intervention, it is best to take care of it as soon as possible.

A few myths about children

- Children do not understand.

- Children do not need to know the whole truth.

- The sensibilities of children are less developed; children are not as sensitive as adults.

- Children only care about those things that are of interest to them, such as television, sports, friends, etc. Children don't care what is happening beyond what concerns them directly and have no interest in the problems of adults.

- Adults should not talk with children about issues that belong to the adult world such as death and divorce.

- There is no need to explain things to children; all they need is to be told.

- Children forget quickly.

How to respond: some practical suggestions

Adults who care for children during the initial stages of loss commonly ask the following questions. I have offered answers, but before reading them may I suggest that the reader try and come up with the answers that seem most reasonable to him or her. I am sure that many readers will discover that by listening to their own intuition and common sense they will be able to come up with the "proper" response. At times, due to the sensitivity of the subject matter and because of our concern for children, we lose faith in our own ability to know what to do. When we find ourselves in the stressful stage that immediately follows the loss, when everything seems so difficult and perplexing, we adults are sometimes baffled, and lose faith in our own powers of judgment.

As a rule, I do not believe in set formulas for solving problems. There is no one "correct" way. There are basic principles, which have already been discussed in this book. Here I shall summarize some of the important ones. But there is another essential underlying principle, which is that each answer and solution has to be in accordance with the specifics of each and every situation. This means that we must take into account the following main factors:

- age of the child
- his or her level of mental development, character, and ability to handle difficult situations
- the history of his or her life
- the pattern of behavior and abilities of the parent
- how the family reacts
- what is available to the child and his family in terms of supporting environment
- the cultural and social dictates, and many other relevant factors.

Therefore, although I have furnished answers to some typical issues and questions, I strongly recommend that the reader make an effort to determine whether they are suited to the specific circumstances he is dealing with.

Should the child be prepared for an anticipated loss, and if so what should he be told?

The reader would be well served by reviewing the section in Chapter 3 on the period of uncertainty and ambiguity, which points out the main principles of effectively handling a situation in which loss is anticipated. It is important to prepare the child for an eventuality of expected loss. The plain truth of the situation should be explained to the child, including the degree of risk involved. The adult should ascertain what questions the child has, and offer comprehensible answers. In the event that the adult does not know, it is best to admit this fact to the child.

It is important to soothe the child's anxieties as much as possible, especially as regards the implications of the loss on his life. It should be made clear who is caring for him. He should be assured that his caregivers are aware of his needs and will see that they are met. It is vital that during the period of uncertainty the normal course of the child's life is maintained as much as possible.

Who should tell the child what happened? When? What should he be told?

As soon as the loss occurs, the child has to know about it. The news must be given *as soon as possible*. The parent or parents are the ones who should tell the child what happened, even if they are in an emotionally frail state during the first few hours.

When a parent dies, it is best if the remaining parent informs the child. Only if this is not possible should he be informed by another individual close to him, who will see to it that the child sees the remaining parent as soon as possible. Talking with a parent who is in emotional turmoil is still better than talking with a distant relative or family friend. Being physically and emotionally close to the parent at this difficult time is more important than the manner in which the news is given.

A parent who feels he cannot be alone with the child at such a difficult time should ask someone else to be present and help out – a grandparent or aunt, a good friend or a professional.

It is important to create opportunities for additional discussion with the child in the days following the event, in order to fill in information gaps, explain what happened, and answer the child's questions. When the issue is a couple's decision to divorce, it is critical that both parents be present when they inform the child of their decision.

It is preferable to talk to the child at home, and better yet in his own room. Should this be unfeasible, it is important that conversations take place in pleasant, intimate surroundings in which the child feels secure and free to respond; a place where he can cry, show his anger, and express his turbulent inner feelings.

Should children attend the funeral?

Whether or not a child should attend a funeral depends first and foremost on his age. There is no reason to have a child attend a funeral when he does not yet understand the concrete meaning of death. A child should not be forced to attend a funeral. If he wishes, he may be permitted to attend, but only after some preparation. The child should be given a description of what a funeral is, and what happens at funerals. The description should be as factual and graphic as possible. After these explanations have been given to him, the child should be asked if he wants to take part.

An attempt should be made to determine if the child actually *wants* to attend the funeral and if his decision is not done for the wrong reasons: he thinks adults expect it of him; he wants to "hold onto" the remaining parent; he is afraid of staying home alone while everyone else is at the funeral. The child should be asked if he wishes to take part in the memorial service in one way or another, such as by laying a wreath or reading something he wrote.

Throughout the funeral, there must be an adult who is responsible for being with the child, accompanying him and looking after his needs. This role cannot be entrusted to the remaining parent, who will be in a state of deep turmoil at this time. It is important that the adult who looks after the child is someone the child knows well and feels close to. The person accompanying the child should be in physical contact with him or her, hold his hand, embrace him in a warm hug. The physical contact will give the child a feeling of warmth, protection, and support.

The child's responses during the funeral must be closely monitored to determine if and when he wishes to draw away from the center of activity, or, alternatively, allowed to come closer. The sights and sounds of the funeral rites, and the expressions of grief of the mourners, might alarm the child. He should be allowed to express his own responses in his own way.

Who should be informed of what happened?

Should the school be informed? Should the classmates know what happened? Anyone who has anything to do with the child's everyday life should know about what happened, and the sooner the better. School can be an important source of support for the child. His regular teacher, the guidance counselor, or other teachers with whom he might have a close relationship should visit him at home, just as classmates can and should. One should be sensitive to the child's privacy. He should not be made into a "public" figure and his event into everybody's business. Only people who are really close to him should offer their companionship during the initial period.

The child's teacher has the duty of explaining what happened to his classmates, assuring friends' visits, and preparing the class for the child's return. The teacher can also help to schedule the visits of friends so that they do not constitute a burden on the child and his family. Prior to the child's return to class, the teacher should be in touch with the parent to find out how the child is doing. He can further ease the child's return to school by holding a preliminary one-on-one discussion with him.

Should children be brought to the cemetery?

If the child wishes, he can be taken to visit the grave soon after the funeral. The sight of a grave covered with earth and flowers is much less frightening than the scenes of a funeral; the atmosphere is calmer and less alarming than the funeral itself. The burial site, not yet with the stone, allows the child to realize in a pragmatic way where the body is, and therefore to get further explanations as to what was done during the funeral.

It is important to take children to the cemetery to see the grave. The first time a child visits the cemetery, it is recommended that the parent take him there separately, and not as part of a formal memorial ceremony. Steps should be taken to ensure that the visit be held in a relaxed atmosphere. It can be suggested to the child to bring something he wishes to put on the grave. During the visit to the grave the child should be given a chance and even encouraged to ask questions and say what's on his mind. The sooner the child sees the burial site, the more tangible and understandable death will be for him. Henceforth, he can be brought along on subsequent visits to the cemetery, in accordance with his own wishes. Many adults attach great importance to frequent visits at the cemetery, especially during the early stages of mourning. For the child the cemetery visit does not have the "social" or "have to" connotations. The visit for him or her is very personal and can have a variety of meanings. It is important that adults be attuned to the child's feelings and what the encounter with the grave means to him. It may be a very harsh confrontation with the fact of the death, inundating the child with a wave of sorrow and sadness. In which case the child might prefer not to repeat the experience. By the same token, the tangibility of the grave might conceivably give the child a feeling of greater closeness to the deceased and therefore he might wish to visit there from time to time.

For small children who do not fully understand the concept of finality and irreversibility, visiting the grave might be a way "to make sure" the dead person has not arisen, a way of checking that he did not leave his grave. If a child does not want to visit the cemetery, it does not mean that he is not mourning, or that he has forgotten his loved one.

When should life be resumed at its normal pace?

It is important for children that their normal lifestyle be resumed *as soon as possible*. Children require a familiar framework: regular daily schedule, regular school and after-school activities, including playing with friends, eating normal meals at regular hours, regular bedtime, and if possible for the young ones, a bedtime story.

The return to school should also be as soon as the child feels he is ready for it. Some children wish to go back to school the day after their parent's death. This seems odd to the adults. It is true that the child wishes to "escape" to school, so he does not have to be at home where everything is sad and upset. Such an escape gives the child a sense that not everything in his life is disrupted. It does not mean he does not understand what happened; on the contrary, he does, and therefore tries to escape the harsh reality. Children should be "permitted" to escape back to their routine. It gives them a sense of security. It does not mean that they do not understand or do not care. It does mean that they feel threatened by the harsh new reality.

In the case of divorce or a parent leaving home, the child should know what is the routine of meeting the parent, talking to him on the phone, and spending time with him on weekends and vacations. Clearly known rules of the game reduce the child's unrealistic expectations, anxieties, and disappointments. It is to be hoped the child will not interpret every non-contact with the parent as rejection and "he does not love me any more." He or she will know that love and attention will come his way during the prearranged meetings and therefore will train themselves to wait rather than be anxious all the time. The sooner children get back into a familiar and set schedule, or one that is new but clear and well arranged, the sooner they will be able to start to readjust and regain their sense of confidence and inner peace and get back to functioning as kids.

There are many more issues and questions that parents confront regarding their children. When in doubt it is advisable to *seek advice and counsel* from a friend, a teacher, a family member, or a professional: first, because it is important for the parent to reassure himself and act with confidence; second, there is a chance that the decisions of the parent will be heavily influenced by projections of his own needs and emotions. As such they will not be attuned to the needs of the child and might even harm him. Outside counsel can balance such a situation.

Good signs

Behavior that indicates the child is successfully readjusting includes the following:

- The child resumes his previous eating and sleeping habits.

- The child is active and energetic, and has regained his joie de vivre. He is enthusiastic and inquisitive, and schedules activities.

- He renews his social contacts and activities, and forms new, healthy relationships.

- The child regains the level of independence he enjoyed prior to the event. He seeks less the proximity of adults and is back to playing and spending time with his friends. He handles his tasks independently.

- Conversations with the child reveal that he understands the finality and irreversibility of the new situation. The plans he makes and the hopes he expresses indicate that he is reconstructing his life to conform with the changed reality.

Warning signs

Adults should be conscious of certain telltale modes of behavior that might indicate distress:

- complete disregard – total denial of the loss and its repercussions
- intense, constant fears, anxieties, and panic
- complaints of pain and poor health, with no medical evidence to support the claim
- continual sense of guilt
- chronic condition of apathy and/or depression
- chronic mood of anger and condition of aggression and acting out
- frequent and prolonged periods of offensive temper tantrums
- expresses himself in an abusive manner
- initiates fights with other children or adults
- acts in a disobedient or rebellious manner, disturbs those around him
- prolonged period of drastic behavioral change and instability
- stops doing his homework and paying attention in class with a decline in level of studies and grades
- permanent condition of distancing and closing out friends and family
- dramatic, continual changes in sleeping and/or eating habits
- resumption of bedwetting and/or poor bowel control

- use of alcohol and/or drugs
- suicidal thoughts and/or actions (including the taking of exaggerated risks)
- clashes with the legal authorities
- adolescents who exhibit unusual and inappropriate sexual behavior and substance abuse, high risks in their driving.

These indicators are not necessarily solely signs of distress to do with the loss. One should take into account the child's age and compare his behavior with the normative behavior of his age peers, as well as his own behavior prior to the loss. If the irregular behavior goes on for a prolonged period, a professional should be brought in for an opinion and give his recommendations on how to address the problem.

Psychological treatment

One of the questions that occupies the minds of many parents and other adults close to the child is if, and at which point, the child requires psychological treatment, and what sort of treatment is warranted? The answer is very complex, and must take into account numerous factors related to the child and his immediate world: his parents, family, and environment. Since the issue is so complex, there are no ready formulas, but here we provide a general rundown of several fundamental principles, and a survey of possible types of treatment.

One of the most frequently asked questions has to do with timing. How soon after the loss is it recommended to begin treatment? Is it best to start treatment immediately after the event? Will immediate treatment prevent future problems?

Initial period

Although adults sometimes opt to promptly transfer responsibility for the child's mental well-being to a professional, this is not recommended in the majority of cases. During the initial period, children, like adults, are going through emotional turmoil. They need time, love, and the assistance and support of those closest to them, especially their parents. For the most part, they do not need psychological treatment. Premature treatment sends the child the message that there is something wrong with him. It is important that the child feels it is okay to be "not okay": that it is fine for him to react in whatever manner suits him best. If he is sent for treatment too hastily, he is being given the message that "you've got a problem" as opposed to "there is a problem." It also gives the child the message that "you are a problem for us." He will feel that he has been sent to pour out his emotions and troubles to the therapist because the parent does not want to listen to him or cannot handle his difficulties.

Subsequent periods

During subsequent periods there is greater probability that the child will require special assistance. Throughout this book, we have emphasized the extent to which the loss will continue to affect the child how he will be required to process it again and again; how the loss is liable to exacerbate his normal developmental tasks. Abnormal behavior and acting out may at times indicate that the child is having a difficult time coping psychologically. Employment of rigid, inappropriate defense mechanisms provides a warning sign that the child is in trouble. When such indications are present, the source of the problem should be determined in order to see how the child can be helped. Psychological treatment is one of the tools available.

Adults may harbor widely divergent attitudes about psychological treatment. Some are quick to seek it out; they may be alarmed by their child's behavior, feel they lack the proper tools for understanding and treating it, and hope that psychological treatment will solve all the problems with the wave of a magic wand. Conversely, other adults are mistrustful of psychological treatment, afraid to admit the child has a problem, wary of the stigma of being in therapy (mainly in their own eyes, though they will claim that it is society that is judgmental). Others are concerned, perhaps subconsciously, about the revelation of dark secrets about their child, themselves, or the family. Whatever the case, the adult projects his own difficulties on the child, thereby preventing objective determination of the need for treatment. Obviously, this is not in the best interests of the child.

It is advisable to consult with professionals who have a pre-existing relationship with the child – his teacher, guidance counselor, family doctor, or any other individual who knows the child – whenever any suspicion of difficulty arises, or if the child or parent feels that treatment is required. These individuals can assist in determining whether the problematic behavior is indeed not within the normal and expected range. Throughout this book, we have stressed that some modes of loss-related behavior are considered normal for these children, even though they may be abnormal for children who have not experienced loss. Such behavior does not necessarily indicate a need for psychological treatment. When the child is old enough to verbalize his feelings, it is important to share views and emotions with him and to ascertain whether he is troubled or whether he feels he is in a state of distress. In considering therapy the child's cooperation must be enlisted.

We shall now sum up several fundamental principles to be observed when seeking treatment. It should be stressed that these are general statements that are not intended to be fixed formulas or absolute truths. The decision to seek psychological treatment has to be based on knowledge of all the facts relevant to the child and his specific case, and not on the notion that treatment "can't hurt."

Most children who undergo traumatic loss do not require psychotherapy. However, quite a few may be helped by therapeutic or other professional care at one time or another. Only some children need and must undergo psychotherapy. Following diagnosis, the most important questions are whether to treat and what to treat. In other words, on which issues does the child need extra help and what is the goal of the treatment. Not every difficulty the child faces needs to be resolved through psychotherapy. Some problems are healed by time, resolved or minimized through life experience. Many loss-related processes require time, and cannot be rushed or alleviated more quickly through psychological treatment.

In previous chapters we have placed a great deal of emphasis on the value and need of the child to have a parent and family with whom he can go through the grieving process as well as other processes related to the many changes he and the family will experience. Therapists cannot and should not constitute a viable substitute for this sort of vital, family-oriented sharing and closeness. Nevertheless, in certain instances they offer a therapeutic alternative to processes that should have but have not happened naturally as part of the child's relationship with the parent and the family.

The difficulties of a child who has experienced loss can be expressed through a wide variety of issues: some are directly related to the mourning process and the acceptance of the loss, with all its implications; more profound influences concern the development of a healthy self and personality. In severe cases, pathological defense mechanisms might emerge. Problems of children often surface through behavioral issues, poor school and learning performance, and inadequate social adjustment. The diagnosis should be based on a very wide holistic overview which takes into consideration not only the current difficulty or symptom but the whole life history of the child, and of course the loss, even if it occurred a long time ago. The professional must study not only the child but also the whole system in which he grows.

One of the most important decisions is *who* should receive therapy/counsel. We often see a child sent for treatment because "he has problems" or because "he's making trouble." Yet often we find that the child is the "warning light." Through him other problems surface concerning the functioning of the parent and the family. The parent might not be aware of the real problems underlying the child's symptoms. In some cases the parents may conceal the real difficulties they have. The child becomes a convenient "scapegoat."

Much has been written in this book about the difficulties of the parents in working through their grief, coming to terms with the loss and its implications, and enabling their children to express and process their own grief. We have also spoken about parents who are not coping with the loss in ways that may bring about progress, acceptance, or rehabilitation. When this is the case, the parent's difficulties are liable to be projected on the child, making it even harder for him to cope. In such instances, the child comes or is brought to therapy "instead" of his parent or the entire family. In other instances, the child can be best helped through his parent. In these cases the parent receives counsel and is the "agent" for bringing about the change in the child.

It is therefore crucial that the therapist ascertains who is the genuine source of the problem and whether he or she can be brought in for therapy. He should determine whether *individual, spousal,* or *family therapy* would respond to the needs of the child, or whether it would be better to offer the child direct therapeutic aid so that he can process issues that are not being adequately addressed at home. At certain times, the child is psychologically inaccessible and psychotherapy is inappropriate, such as immediately after the loss when the intense emotional turmoil does not allow room for treatment of deep issues. There are times when it is more important for the child to engage in subjects other than the loss and its implications. If feasible, treatment should be postponed to a time at which the child will be able to gain from it.

Here are some additional issues that have a bearing on determining the specific treatment regimen:

1. *Duration of treatment:* is short-term or long-term treatment recommended?

2. *Frequency of treatment:* how often should the therapy take place – once or twice a week?

3. *Gender of the therapist:* should the therapist be a man or a woman?

It is impossible to reply to these and many other questions regarding the choice of treatment within the framework of a book. These questions must be raised and decided upon by the professionals and must relate to the specifics of each individual case.

Often adults are confused by the need to make a decision about which professional should be selected: psychologist, social worker, psychiatrist, counselor, art therapist, dance therapist. All work in this field and offer their particular method as the method of choice. This is not the appropriate time and place to explain the unique qualities of each of the aforementioned practitioners. However, it is vitally important to stress that the chosen professional not only has experience and know-how in treating children and their families, but in particular has experience in treating individuals who have suffered loss and trauma. The professional should possess a versatile "toolbox" of treatment approaches and skills, so that the treatment can be adapted to the needs of the child. The following is a brief description of several types of treatment and the unique qualities of each therapeutic method in relation to the typical needs of children who have undergone the trauma of loss.

Individual treatment

An individual treatment of the child makes it possible to use the specific techniques that tailor to the child's particular situation and needs. Using game therapy and expression through arts are two examples that are particularly suited to the treatment of younger children, and can offer appropriate answers to loss-related issues. Other techniques are used to treat adolescents.

As mentioned often before, many children suffer from lack of emotional attention after the loss. At times it was "only" neglect and in others there was distortion of the child's real emotional needs. Individual time with the therapist can "correct" some of the damage and give the child or adolescent a second chance to work though "forgotten" and long-neglected personal experiences and issues.

When the parent receives individual treatment, he not only helps himself to cope with the difficulties, but also helps his children, since his therapeutic processing of the loss and other personal issues will improve his parenting abilities, and better equip him to furnish the needs of his children.

Family therapy

Therapy within and of the whole family constitutes an effective and highly recommended framework for those coping with the hardships of loss. It enables a family to work its way together through issues that require emotional sharing and collaboration of the whole family. It enables the family to hone the coping skills and tools at their disposal. The therapist helps the family through the process it had difficulty carrying out on its own.

Couple therapy

This therapy enables the couple to sort out the difficulties between them, and formulate the parental behavior that is best suited to proper management of the family and its children. Such treatment is recommended in the case of difficulties in establishing a smooth relationship between the remaining parent and his or her new spouse. Resolving the difficulties between them will "save" the children from being the innocent victims of the hardships the new couple have. Couple therapy can help bereaved parents discern what the loss has done to their relationship, as well as how other factors – exposed or exacerbated by the loss – affect them. In so doing, the couple can solve their problems without projecting them onto their children. When couple hardships are ignored, often the loss-related issues get overemphasized and the children become the victims.

Group therapy

There are many variations of group therapy, each of which can make its own unique contribution. The most important and unique advantage of the group as a therapeutic experience is that it allows individuals with similar problems to share what they are going through, and to realize that it is "normal." After hearing how other members of the group handle and solve their problems, each can formulate his own alternative course of action.

Thanks to the shared situation and issues at hand, members of the group often feel they are better understood in the group than by others who have not gone through the same experience. They are therefore also willing to "take" more from their peers, be it non-coercive observations or confrontation and pressure to cope. The group empowers its participants, encouraging them to deal with their difficulties and do more to change and rehabilitate themselves. Group therapy carries less stigma than other therapeutic methods, and participants are less apt to feel there is something wrong with them.

The groups described below contain therapeutic elements, but also have other important aspects that are very effective for inducing rehabilitation after loss: sharing and self-help, deductive, educational, and sometimes even social, and supportive friendship.

GROUP OF CHILDREN

These groups usually have between four and ten participants, within the same age range. Most have a planned duration of a few months up to a year. With groups of younger children, therapists frequently use means of activation, and expression through arts. In these groups, children are given opportunities to express what they are going through. The expression of their inner world is vital. Often this is the first opportunity the child is given for such an open and holding experience. This may be the first time he dares express emotions, fears, and tormenting thoughts and questions. The therapist will encourage and empower the children to do the same with their parents and family.

GROUP OF CHILDREN AND PARENTS

This is a new and very effective model that is as yet not widespread. The entire family – parents and children – takes part in a larger group, giving the various families an opportunity to tackle the numerous issues that have been on their minds since the loss. By seeing how other families handle the same issues, and realizing that their problems are similar and they are therefore not an "abnormal" or "bad" family, the family gains an experience that cannot be replicated by any other form of therapy. With this heterogeneous group, the children naturally branch off into a subgroup that provides a source of support, identification, and emulation; a similar subgroup of adults will also form. These subgroups contribute toward advancing each participant's personal and family processes.

GROUP OF PARENTS

Parents of children who have undergone loss can be aided by a group in which the participants have undergone similar events, and are grappling with similar situations and problems. Here too there is an opportunity to share difficulties and to learn coping techniques from others. Instead of sending the child for treatment, the parents improve their own position: both through therapeutic experience that will personally help them process the loss, and through study and enhancement of a repertoire of behavior modes they may apply with their children, as well as the management of their family as a whole.

To sum up the subject of therapy, we should emphasize again that although therapy is sometimes essential and often helpful, time has its own healing power. One should not underestimate the coping and healing abilities of children as well as adults. It is important to allow for the natural capacities to take their turn. One should accompany the child with patience and confidence. One should be there for him, offering a sensitive ear and a soft yet supportive shoulder. He needs these along all his years of growth. He also needs to know and experience that he can cope on his own.

Glossary

The definitions given in this glossary are based upon the following volumes:

The Corsini Encyclopedia of Psychology and Behavioral Science (2001), Edward W. Craighead and Charles B. Nemeroff (eds). Hoboken, NJ: Wiley.

Dictionary of Psychology (1985), Arthur S. Reber. London: Penguin.

Longman Dictionary of Psychology and Psychiatry (1984), Robert M. Goldenson. New York and London: Longman.

The Family Encyclopedia of Child Psychology and Development (1992) Frank J. Bruno. Hoboken, NJ: Wiley.

The Gale Encyclopedia of Psychology (1996), Susan Gall (exec. ed), Alan J. Feldman (ed). Farmington Hills, MI: Gale Research.

acting out   Irrational impulsive behavior. Outbursts of uncontrolled unconscious impulses, often aggressive and sexual. Exposure and presentation of emotions that were restrained and repressed, often unconscious or subconscious, through acts and behavior that expresses and represents them. The term is often applied to antisocial or delinquent behavior in general.

adequate behavior   Relating and behaving in a manner that fits and is adequate to the situation.

avoidance   Withdrawing, taking distance, in thoughts, beliefs, and emotions from an object, physical or metaphorical, usually because it is threatening. The individual moves away from unpleasant stimulus.

borderline personality disorder   A person with a borderline personality functions on the thin border between normative adaptive behavior and a dysfunctional and inadequate response and behavior. The typical symptoms are: irritability, lack of stability in general and especially in interpersonal relationships, extreme emotional shifts, impulsive anger, frequent eruptions of anger and rage, a damaged self-image, impulsive destructive behavior towards the self and others.

catharsis   A therapeutic release or discharge of emotions. Expression of anxieties, fears, stressors, complicated emotions, and other mental materials, conscious and unconscious. Their expression is by talking or other mediums of expression such as art, writing, drama, etc. Such expression brings about relief and healing.

cognitive development   The process of the development of the ability to think. The process of collecting information about the world and digesting it to logical mental formulas. The development of the thinking processes of all kinds such as perceiving, remembering, concept formation, problem solving, imagining, and reasoning. Each developmental stage is characterized by the specific cognitive abilities that develop at that time.

concept formation   The learning process through which a new concept and understanding is acquired. The development and understanding of concepts; that is, ideas based on realities or abstract phenomena.

containing   This term describes the situation in which one person feels that another person contains him, his feelings, thoughts, etc. in the metaphorical sense. The "contained" person feels he is not alone, somebody shares with him the burdens of his life and especially his internal world. This person therefore feels more protected and safe. He feels that his emotions and thoughts are legitimate and therefore he has "permission" to express and share them. The feeling of being "contained" stands as an opposite to feeling judged, rejected, ignored, etc.

defenses, defense mechanisms   Any action a person pursues in order to defend themselves, their ego and self. A complex of mental tools that serve as protectors of the ego and the self, especially protecting them from impulses and drives, unpleasant emotions, anxieties, threatening and unpleasant memories and experiences. These mechanisms prevent the threatening mental materials from surfacing to the conscious. One of a number of techniques by which the ego diffuses anxiety and other unpleasant feelings such as conflict, fear, and frustration. Unconscious patterns of response a person learns and adapts in order to protect his internal world and structures, such as his ego and self, from threats that cause anxiety, shame, conflicts, flooding, etc. They are acquired in an unconscious way and are also activated in this manner. Defensive behavior is a common normal means of coping with problems, but excessive use of any mechanism is considered pathological. Many defense mechanisms have been identified and defined; the most commonly known are repression, rationalization, and projection.

denial   A defense mechanism which applies to unconscious mental activities that aim at denying external reality, thoughts, feeling, desires, and needs that arouse anxiety and threaten the self. A defense mechanism that protects the self by refusing to cope with unpleasant facts.

developmental tasks   Mental, emotional, cognitive, and behavioral tasks that the developing child needs to do in order to develop and mature at each developmental age/stage. The fundamental physical, social, intellectual, and emotional achievements and abilities that must be acquired at each stage for normal and healthy development: e.g. talking in early childhood or achieving independence during adolescence.

diadic relationship, dyad   The relationship among pairs of persons in an interpersonal situation, especially in the family, such as husband–wife, parent–child, father–mother. The term relates especially to the emotional dependence between these two people due to their roles, such as mother–child. Also used to describe the relationship between therapist and patient.

gender   The wide range of meanings that being a male/female entails. This includes not only the sexual self, but also many other self-perceptions and roles that are derivatives of being masculine or feminine. Gender roles are highly influenced by cultural norms.

instinctual impulse   Response which is automatic and not learnt. This response system is innate and part of the genetic make-up of the infant at birth. Babies and young children have instinctual behaviors, especially in regard to their basic needs and impulses such as hunger, thirst, safety, love, sex, etc. These needs must be fulfilled in order to maintain physical and psychological equilibrium. An inborn behavior pattern which refers to basic biological drives.

intellectualization   A defense mechanism in which the person relates to the external world through intellectual tools/activities, ignoring and repressing emotions and affect responses. A mental mechanism which serves to avoid feelings and emotional conflicts. It utilizes cognitive-rational mental frames of reference to situations, ignoring and denying affect responses. A mental mechanism that helps adolescents control their impulses.

internalization   Acceptance and internalization of beliefs, values, positions, manners of behavior, and making them part of one's own mental self. Incorporation of attitudes, standards, and opinions of others, particularly parents, into one's personality.

intrapsychic   Every response that is evoked in the internal emotional–psychological world. Refers to the interaction of hidden emotional components such as conflict between beliefs, needs, impulses, and desires. Impulses, ideas, conflicts, and other psychological phenomena that occur within the emotional world.

modeling   Giving/taking another person's manner of behavior as a model for imitation. A large part of the child's learning process embraces imitating others who serve as his role models. Most of the child's learning and imitating relates to the role modeling of parents, brothers, peers, and other significant persons. Children also see as their role models figures and characters from television, movies, books, etc.

object, internal object, object consistency   A person and/or feature of a person through which the infant's instinctual needs are gratified. Through continually gratifying experiences the mental representation of the experience becomes part of the internal mental–emotional world of the baby/small child. It becomes part of his or her identity, part of his or her internal object. Object consistency is accomplished when the process of internalizing these features comes to a maturation point and these features become a solid part of the internal world.

omnipotence   The belief that wishes, hopes, and thoughts can influence and change the external facts of the world.

pathology   Abnormal functioning which causes suffering to the person. As a field of human science it explores and tries to find ways to intervene in situations of mental–emotional–psychological abnormal responses and behavior. The scientific study of the structural and functional changes involved in physical and mental diseases and disorders.

personality disorder   Patterns of perceiving, relating to, and thinking about the environment and the self, when these patterns interfere with long-term functioning of the individual. In the past, this term was used to describe a wide range of psychological disorders that involved inadequate relationships with the social environment. Today it commonly refers to behavioral disorders, except neurosis and psychosis, which evolve in a general pathological personality.

projection   A mental process in which the person puts onto the outside world/people what is his own: emotions, traits, experiences, wishes, etc. This mental process is usually accompanied by denial of these components within himself/herself. Projecting them upon others serves as a defense, which relieves anxieties and inner conflicts. Assigning to others the characteristics or motivations that the individual would prefer not to recognize in himself.

repression   Repressing in the sense of stopping, controlling, censuring, avoiding, etc. Selectively forgetting disturbing material such as painful experiences. Repression works at the unconscious level. It is a mental process aimed at protecting the person from ideas, impulses, memories, etc. that might cause anxiety, fear, or guilt had they surfaced to the conscious. The repressed material is not dormant. It exists and "works" at the unconscious level, and appears through "disguised" symbolic reflections such as dreams or acting out. Transferring unpleasant memories and forbidden desires to an unconscious level of the emotional existence. These can include unpleasant and traumatic childhood memories. Repressive mechanisms are usually used only after age 6, with the development of the superego. Till then the young child uses more "primitive" defense mechanisms such as denial, and through these mechanisms he handles the unpleasant anxieties which arise from unpleasant situations.

separation–individuation   The process and state of mind that the child reaches when he realizes that he is a separate and distinct being, apart from his mother. The process in which this realization develops starts after the symbiotic stage; the stage in which the interrelation and bond between mother and child are very strong and dominant. A term used by M.S. Mahler to describe the process in which the infant gradually differentiates himself from the mother and attains the relatively autonomous status of a toddler.

Recommended Reading

Adams, D.W. and Deveau, E.J. (1995) *Beyond the Innocence of Childhood: Helping Children and Adolescents Cope with Death and Bereavement.* Amityville, NY: Baywood.

Altschul, S. (ed) (1988) *Childhood Bereavement and its Aftermath.* Madison, CO: International University Press.

Bloom-Freshbach, J. and Bloom-Freshbach, S. (eds) (1987) *The Psychology of Seperation and Loss.* San Francisco: Jossey-Bass.

Bowlby, J. (1969) *Attachment and Loss. Vol. 1 Attachment.* New York: Basic Books.

Bowlby, J. (1973) *Attachment and Loss. Vol. 2 Separation: Anxiety and Anger.* New York: Basic Books.

Bowlby, J. (1980) *Attachment and Loss. Vol. 3 Loss: Sadness and Depression.* New York: Basic Books.

Cain, A. (ed) (1972) *Survivors of Suicide.* Springfield, IL: Thomas.

Cook, A.S. and Oltjenbrums, K.A. (1989) *Dying and Grieving.* New York: Holt, Rinehart and Winston.

Corr, C. and Balk, D.B. (eds) (1996) *Helping Adolescents Cope with Death and Bereavement.* Philadelphia: Springer.

Corr, C.A. and McNeil, J.N. (1986) *Adolescence and Death.* New York: Springer.

Corr, C.A., Nabe, C.M. and Corr, D.M. (1994) *Death and Dying, Life and Living.* Pacific Grove, CA: Brooks/Cole.

Dunne, E.J., McIntosh, J.L. and Dunne-Maxim, K. (eds) (1987) *Suicide and its Aftermath.* New York: Norton.

Fredman, G. (1997) *Death Talk.* London: Karnac.

Furman, E. (1974) *A Child's Parent Dies.* New York and London: Yale University Press.

Gelcer, E. (1983) *Mourning is a Family Affair.* Vernon, NJ: Family Process.

Goldman, L. (1996) *Breaking the Silence.* London: Taylor and Francis.

Goldman, L. (2000) *Life and Loss.* London: Taylor and Francis.

Grollman, E. (1993) *Straight Talk about Death for Teenagers.* Boston: Beacon Press.

James, J. and Friedman, R. (2001) *When Children Grieve.* London: HarperCollins.

Jewett, C. (1982) *Helping Children Cope with Separation and Loss.* Boston, MA: Harward Common Press.

Klass, D., Silverman, P.R. and Nickman, S.L. (eds) (1996) *Continuing Bonds: New Understanding of Grief.* Bristol, PA: Taylor and Francis.

Marris, P. (1972) *Loss and Change.* London: Routledge and Kegan.

Papadatou, D. and Papadatos, C. (eds) (1991) *Children and Death.* New York: Hemisphere.

Parks, C.M. (1983) *Recovery from Bereavement.* New York: Basic Books.

Russel, S. (2002) *Conquering the Mysteries and Lies of Grief.* Baltimore: Publishamerica.

Schaefer, D. and Lyons, C. (1986) *How Do We Tell the Children?* New York: Newmarket Press.

Smith, S.C. and Pennells, M. (eds) (1995) *Interventions with Bereaved Children.* London: Jessica Kingsley Publishers.

Wallerstein, J.S. and Blackeslee, S. (1989) *Second Chances.* New York: Ticknor and Field.

Wallerstein, J.S. and Kelly, J.B. (1980) *Surviving the Breakup.* New York: Basic Books.

Walsh, F. and McGoldrick, M. (eds) (1991) *Living Beyond Loss: Death in the Family.* New York: Norton.

Wolfelt, A.D. (1996) *Healing the Bereaved Child.* Fort Collins, CO: Companion Press.

Worden, J.W. (1996) Children and Grief. New York and London: The Guilford Press.

Index

abandonment 127–33
  of child by grieving parent
    154
  see also emotional neglect;
    rejection
abnormal behaviour
  by abandoned children 132
  response to loss 56, 217
  see also acting out;
    behavioural problems;
    inappropriate behaviour
abuse 129
acceptance
  in children 44–5
  emotional acceptance
    152–3
  third stage of grieving 40
accusatory position, of child in
  grieving 42
acting out 48, 208, 217, 225
  in adolescence 86–7, 92
  see also abnormal behaviour;
    behavioural problems;
    inappropriate behaviour
activities, focus for meaning in
  adolescence 91
addiction, and rejection 128
additional loss 133–7
adequate behaviour 225
adolescence 77–97
  effect of absence of father
    on boys 139–40
  ego strength 67
  relationship with missing
    parent before loss 83–4
  relationships following loss
    68–9, 79, 139, 140,
    141–2
  separation-individuation 68
adult personality
  effect of loss in childhood
    11, 105, 132–3
  loss of trust 115
  of remaining parent, and
    coping 157–62

adults
  processing grief from
    childhood 47, 189, 193
  response to children 12,
    17–22, 35, 64, 65–6,
    84, 107
    guidelines 209–14
  response to grief *see*
    response, to grief,
    adults
  who experienced
    childhood loss 11, 13,
    15, 22
  see also parents; remaining
    parent
age of child
  and mourning 26–7
  and reconciling spiritual
    concepts with finality
    of death 33
age differential, between
  siblings, and effect of loss
  181
age tasks *see* developmental
  tasks
alcohol abuse 128
alternative parent figure 34,
  73–4
  for child who has
    experienced murder
    122
  of grandparent, loss of 8,
    134
  in place of father 139
  following loss of both
    parents 137
  relationship with new
    spouse 198–9
  and sexual identity in
    adolescence 95, 96
  success of relationship with
    144
  see also substitutes
ambiguity
  for child in period of
    uncertainty 111–13,
    113–14
  in divorce 124
  in loss of parent through
    abandonment 131

anger
  in adolescence, following
    loss 82–3
  of bereaved sibling 185
  of child in grieving 42
  expressed through aberrant
    behaviour 189
  over new spouse 199
  in response to murder 121
  resulting from isolation 51,
    52
  resulting from poor
    relationship with
    missing parent 144
  over suicide 118, 119
anniversaries 169
answers, to children's questions
  18–19
  see also questions
anxieties
  of child suffering loss 35,
    43, 76
  about moving 200
  over future 9
  see also fears
assessment, for psychotherapy
  219–20
attachment theory 64–5
attention needs, of children
  grieving 42
attention seeking, in
  dependent relationships
  104
attenuating factors, of effect of
  loss 107
attitudes
  towards bereaved siblings
    180, 185
  towards children and loss
    14, 112, 208
autonomy, development in
  young children, and loss
  72–3
avoidance 34, 225
awareness of effects of loss
  in adulthood 11
  see also unawareness

babies, response to loss 27, 58,
  63–9
  see also young children

behavioural problems
  in absence of father 139
  in adolescence 86–7
    following loss 81
  assessing need for
    psychotherapy 217–18
  following change 196
  following death of sibling
    189
  discussing with
    professional 208
  in early adulthood 97, 99
  expression of distress 48,
    215–16
  in period of uncertainty
    113–14
  projection of parent's
    difficulties 219
  see also abnormal behaviour;
    acting out;
    inappropriate behaviour
bereavement see grieving;
  mourning
betrayal, feelings of child, over
  new spouse 200
  see also emotional neglect;
    rejection
bewilderment, feelings over
  suicide 118
birth order, of siblings, and
  death 182
blame
  child accepting blame 144
    in abuse 129
    discouraging 115, 207
  for murder 122
  of parents by siblings 188
borderline personality disorder
  225
  in remaining parent 158–9
  see also personality disorder
boundaries
  effect of absence of father
    139
  establishment by child 35
  of families, loss of 176–7
  maintaining for security
    and confidence 205
  during period of
    uncertainty 114
  and secrets 178

Bowlby, John 64–5
boys, absence of father and
  sexual identity 139
burden of responsibility, for
  remaining parent 156

care providers see alternative
  parent figure; parental care;
  remaining parent
catharsis 225
cause of death, clarity for
  children 29–30, 71
cemetery visits 212–13
change
  after bereavement 193
  on divorce 123
  within family 163–4,
    164–5
  informing child 205
  instability in remaining
    parent's life 160
  following loss 194–5
  new schools 200–1
  in period of uncertainty
    113–14
  of roles within family 167
  triggering hidden issues
    199
  triggering response to
    previous loss 62
  avoiding unnecessary
    change for child 207
  to way of life 60–1
  see also flexibility
child abuse 129
  see also emotional neglect
child development see
  development; emotional
  development
childishness, reversion to 34
  see also regression
circumstances
  of death, discussion 31
  of sibling loss 187–8
clinical depression, in children,
  signs 105
closed families 177
cognitive development 226
  and loss 54–5
collective mourning 145

comforters
  gifts 34
  substitutes 59–60, 104
commemoration, of dead child
  at home 192
communication
  between parent and child
    prior to change 199
  within the family 170–1,
    172
  see also explanation;
    information
concealment by adults see
  hiding truth from children;
  secrecy
concept formation 226
concrete roles, within family
  166
confidence
  about the future, helping
    child to have 205
  loss of self-confidence in
    adolescence 86
containing situation 226
continuity, sense of, and loss
  85
coping
  abilities of remaining
    parent 157–62
  and additional loss 134–5
  family coping with loss
    162–79
  giving child tools for 206
  setting example 151–2
couple therapy 221–2
creativity, as search for
  meaning in adolescence 91
cultural background
  and language for concept
    of death 30
  view of death 32–3, 38,
    145
cultural customs 145–6
cumulative loss 133–7
customs, for mourning 145–6,
  164

daughters, and loss of parents
  96, 140–2

death
    adults' reaction to and
        effect on children 21–2
    concept of 28–30
    differing cultural responses
        to 32–3, 145
    discussion of events 31
    foreseeable 116–17
    interest of children in 36
    personification 70
    portrayal in media 37
    sudden 117–22
    understanding
        in older children
            (latency period)
            75–6
        in young children
            (Oedipal stage)
            69–70
    see also loss
defense mechanisms
    in abandonment 132
    activated by emotional
        encounters with child
        18
    in adolescence 79, 92–3
    definition 226
    detachment 43, 106
    imagination 34
    not forming relationships
        59
    displayed by parent 153
    of parent with personality
        disorder 158
    reactivated by later
        separations 68
    in shock stage of grieving
        39
    splitting 93
    see also denial; regression
delayed mourning, in
    adolescence 80–1
denial
    in abandonment 131
    by adults relating to child
        18
    of children in grieving 31,
        41
    definition 226
    in early adulthood 100

dependent relationships 104
    see also emotional
        dependence; emotional
        independence;
        independence
depression, in children, signs
    105
detachment, of children in
    grieving 43, 106
development
    babies, effect of loss 63–9
    revisiting loss during 9–10,
        25–6, 31, 49–50
    see also emotional
        development
developmental stages 55
developmental tasks
    of adolescence 82, 84–5,
        98
    definition 226
    separation 158
diadic relationship 226–7
difficult questions see questions
difficult situations, for children
    in everyday lives 45–6, 47,
        206
disappearance, of parent 128
discussion of events
    surrounding death,
    importance 31
dissociation and separation
    46–7, 60
distancing
    in development 68
    from feelings of loss 9
    within family 175–6
distress, signs of 48, 215–16
divorce 122–6
    abandonment of child
        127–8
    acceptance of irreversibility
        32
    period of uncertainty 110
    reassuring child he is not to
        blame 115
    routine for contact with
        missing parent 167,
        214
domestic murder 121–2
drug abuse 128

dysfunction
    in children 47–8
    in parents 158–60

early adulthood 97–106
early childhood and loss 63–9
    see also babies; young
        children
ego strength 67, 100
emotional acceptance and
    adjustment 152–3
emotional blackmail
    by remaining parent 159,
        162, 169
    of siblings 191
    within families 175
emotional closeness, within
    family 173, 174
emotional dependence
    in adolescence 91
    on family 165–6
    on remaining parent in
        early adulthood 100–1
    see also dependent
        relationships; emotional
        independence;
        independence
emotional development
    effect of delayed mourning
        81
    effect of loss 54–5
emotional expression
    assisting child in 204
    by adolescents 83
    by bereaved sibling 189
    by grieving children 43,
        151–2
    prevented by family
        tradition 165
    see also emotions
emotional independence
    from remaining parent,
        problems 159
    see also dependent
        relationships; emotional
        dependence;
        independence
emotional isolation 51–2
emotional neglect
    by grieving parent 154

emotional neglect *cont.*
  by parent in new
    relationship 200
  and relationship with
    siblings 183–4
  and therapy 221
  see also rejection
emotional pathology relating
  to loss 11, 56
emotional problems, resulting
  from loss 11, 56
emotional roles *see* roles
emotional scars
  of bereaved siblings 185
  caused by separation of
    traumatic loss 57–8
  re-awakened in adults
    17–18
emotional support
  of families 165
  from extended family
    171–2
  see also support
emotions
  between siblings 181
  display and sharing 19–20
  in second stage of grieving
    39
  effect of suppression 52
  see also emotional
    expression; feelings
employment, difficulties in
  early adulthood 102
environment
  need for familiarity 203–4,
    211
  surrounding child, effect on
    development 12
equilibrium, of family *see*
  family equilibrium
ethical development, in
  adolescence, and loss 78–9
example, by adult of how to
  grieve 151–2, 152–3, 203,
  204
explanations
  for adolescents who
    suffered loss when
    younger 90
  for bereaved siblings 184

about changes following
  bereavement 201
for children in Oedipal
  stage 70–1
importance of 31, 50–1,
  204
for older children who
  suffered loss when
  younger 75–6
during period of
  uncertainty 112, 115
in sharing problems with
  child 155
in situation of foreseeable
  death 117
for young children who
  suffered loss as babies
  66
exploitation, of children in
  divorce 125, 128
expression of emotion and
  feelings *see* emotional
  expression; feelings
extended family
  and loss of boundaries 176
  support 171–2
external factors, affecting
  child's response to loss 12,
  55–6
external support
  for family 171–2
  and loss of family
    boundaries 176–7
externalization of feelings 9

familial response, to loss
  169–70
familiarity of surroundings,
  following loss 203–4, 211
family
  change following loss 123,
    194
    new relationships
    196–7
  coping with loss 162–79
  destruction of 121, 135–6
  role of adolescent
    providing support 84
  sibling relationships 183
  effect of suicide 119–20
family climate 183

family equilibrium 168–9
  pathological 176
family mourning 163–4
family myths 177–8
family secrets 178–9
  see also hiding truth from
    children; secrecy
family systems 172–9
family therapy 221, 223
family traditions, in loss 165
family unity 173
fathers, role 96, 138–40,
  140–1
fears
  of child 112, 195
  of parents for remaining
    siblings 191
  of remaining parent and
    child 156–7
  see also anxieties
feelings, lack of expression in
  children 9, 13
  see also emotional
    expression
films, representation of death
  37
finality, of death 29
firstborn children 182
flexibility, in families, need for
  168, 175
  see also change
following in footsteps, of
  missing sibling 186
forgetting, that dead person
  not there 39
framework
  for children during period
    of uncertainty 114
  of routine after
    bereavement 213
freedom of thought,
  importance for child 205
frequency of traumatic loss,
  effect 36
funerals, children attending
  211
future, anxieties over 9

games, use with young
  children 71

gender roles 227
  following loss, and sexual
    identity 95–6, 137–8
  of siblings 182
  see also sexual identity
gifts, as comfort 34
"good" children 13, 48–9,
  129, 170, 185–6
good signs, of child's
  readjustment 214–15
grandparents, loss 8, 134
grief, processing see processing
  grief
grief work 104
grieving
  by abandoned children
    131–2
  in adolescence 80–1
  in adults 50, 80, 150–7,
    154, 160–1, 190–2
    setting example
      151–2, 152–3,
      203, 204
  in ambiguous situations
    131
  in children 40–52, 204
    myths 208
    normal signs 105
  of parent 150–7
  of siblings 180–93
  stages 38–40
    in babies 65
    for family 163
group therapy 222–3
guilt
  in adolescence 82–3, 83–4
  of child in grieving 42, 44,
    49, 150–1
  information reducing 115
  engendered by parent's
    pathological reaction
    169
  and poor relationship with
    missing parent 144
  of siblings 182, 185, 188
  over suicide 118, 119, 188
  towards children suffering
    loss 21
  in young children 71

hallucinations, about dead
  person 39
happiness, forbidden after
  death of sibling 192
hiding truth from children 13,
  50, 112, 179
  see also secrecy
homosexuality, and loss of
  parent 101

idealization, of missing child
  190–1
identification, with missing
  sibling 186
identity loss by bereaved
  siblings 184
  see also ego strength;
    self-image; sexual
    identity
illness
  of parent, and loss to child
    130
  period of uncertainty 110
image
  enduring image, of dead
    person 33
  of missing parent
    in divorce 125
    separation from in
      adolescence 94–5
  of missing person 46–7, 60
    reconstruction and
      completion 66–7,
      74–5
  siblings preserving
    after loss 184
  see also memories
imagination, use by young
  children 70–1
inappropriate behaviour 48,
  113
  in response to failing
    family 166
  of siblings 192
  see also abnormal behaviour;
    acting out; behavioural
    problems
independence
  of child from remaining
    parent, problems 159

in early adulthood, effect
  of earlier loss 99–100
  see also dependent
    relationships; emotional
    dependence; emotional
    independence
individual treatment, in
  therapy 221
infants see babies; early
  childhood; young children
information
  for adolescents who
    suffered loss when
    younger 90
  breaking news of death
    210–11
  in divorce 123
  about foreseeable death
    117, 210
  about impending changes
    after bereavement 195
  importance of 21, 31,
    50–1, 75, 204–5
  informing child's contacts
    212
  following loss 210–11
  for older children who
    suffered loss when
    younger 76–7
  during period of
    uncertainty 112, 115
  in sharing problems with
    child 155
  for young children who
    suffered loss, as babies
    66
inner child 17
insecurity in period of
  uncertainty 113
  see also security
instability
  in remaining parent's life
    160
  within family 167
  see also stability
instinctual impulse 227
intellectualization 227
  in adolescence, and loss 79
intensified response, second
  stage of grieving 39

internal object 227
  effect on formation in
    babies 64, 67
internal representation, of
  missing person 59, 60, 143
internal void 103
internalization 227
  in babies' development 64
  second stage of grieving
    39, 163
interpersonal problems
  in early adulthood 104
  resulting from loss 56
intimate relationships
  problems in early
    adulthood 101–2
  siblings 180–1
intrapsychic experience of loss
  103–7
intrapsychic response 227
irreversibility
  of death 28–9
  of other traumatic events
    32
isolation
  of adolescent 79, 91
  of bereaved siblings 190
  in domestic murder 122
  due to grief of remaining
    parent 103
  due to lack of family unity
    173–4
  from situation of loss 51–2

labelling, of loss, social
  acceptability 146
language for concept of death
  30
  see also terminology
latency period, of development
  and loss 75–7
life history, of remaining
  parent, traumatic loss
  160–1
linking objects, to missing
  person 59
literature, search for meaning
  in adolescence 91
lone parent see remaining
  parent
loneliness, of siblings 184

long-term effects of loss 11,
  56, 105, 126
loss
  effect on adult personality
    11, 105
  attenuating factors 107
  through divorce 123
  and effect on capacity to
    form relationships 58–9
  effect on child 8–9, 54, 56
  circumstances 109, 187–8
  factors affecting child's
    response to 55–6
  intrapsychic experience
    103–7
  labelling and social
    acceptability 146
  meaning of term 36
  other than death 8
  response
    of adolescents 78–89
    of adults see response,
      to grief, adults
    of babies 27, 58, 63–9
    effect on coping ability
      for additional loss
      134
    of family 169–70
    of older children 48,
      58, 69–75, 75–6
    of siblings 180, 184–9
    of young children 28,
      48, 58, 65, 71–2,
      73–4
  through rejection and
    abandonment 127–33
  of two parents 135–7
  void left by 168, 181,
    186–7
  see also death; divorce;
    rejection
loss complex 103
lying, importance of not 206
  see also truth

magical thinking 31, 41–2,
  112
maturity, and loss 135
meaning of life, for adolescents
  who suffered loss when
  younger 90–1

media
  representation of death 37
  see also television
memories
  of dead person, "living on"
    33, 37
  evoked by encounter with
    child 17
  fear of loss on moving 200
  supplied by extended
    family 171
  supplied by parent and
    siblings for younger
    children 164
  see also image
mental health problems
  and fear of rejection by
    child 128–9
  personality disorder in
    remaining parent
    158–9
middle children 182
modeling 227
  see also role models
modern society, mourning 38,
  145–6
moral development, in
  adolescence, and loss 78
mothers, role 96, 140, 141–2
mourning 25–6
  and adolescence 80–2, 83,
    84–5, 89
  adults 150–7
  in children 9, 43–4, 150–1
  collective 145
  in family 163–4
  in modern western society
    145–6
  in case of murder 122
  pathological 154
    see also pathological
      response
movies, representation of death
  37
moving house, after
  bereavement 194, 200
murder, impact of 121–2
myths
  about child's response to
    grief 208
  in families 177–8

natural disasters 38
negative responses to child 206–8
neglect *see* emotional neglect
"no more", understanding concept of 27–8
non-response, of children in grieving 41
non-verbal communication, in family 170
normality
    appearance of in adolescence following loss 79–81
    difficulties of children in returning to 47–8
    resumption of life 43, 44–5, 213–14
normative parenting, and sexual identity in adolescence 95
normative separation, effect of traumatic loss 10
numbness, in grieving 38

object consistency 227
Oedipal fantasy 73–4, 162
Oedipal relationship 88, 101, 139, 141
Oedipal stage, and loss 69–75
Oedipal triangle, in adolescence 88
older children
    effect of death of sibling 185
    help with expression of emotion 151
    inappropriate behaviour, as expression of distress 48
    effect of loss 69–75, 75–6
    resumption of life 45
    search for happiness outside home 192–3
    see also adolescence; latency period
older siblings 181
omnipotence 227
open communication, need for in family 171, 172–3

over-protectiveness, of parents for remaining siblings 191
ownership of grief, by parents 190

parental care
    closest adult as primary caregiver 203
    facilitating processing of grief 49–50, 87
    during period of uncertainty 114
    effect of response 12, 46, 107, 150–7
        on adolescents 84
        on babies 64, 65–6
        on young children 72
    see also alternative parent figure; remaining parent
parental child, role of support for parent 161–2
parental crises, and effect of abandonment 130–1
parental expectations, of bereaved siblings 186–7
parental role
    change following death of child 189–90
    of new spouse 197
    required of older siblings 185
parents
    coping with child's death response to siblings 190–1
        use of couple therapy 222
    disappearance 128
    grieving 150–7, 160–1
    illness 128–9, 130
    imposing changes on children 195
    loss of both parents 135–7
    projection on to child 219
    see also (entries beginning with) parental; remaining parent
pathological equilibrium, in family 176

pathological response 228
    to loss 11, 56, 105, 154, 169
peer group, problems of adolescents following loss 85, 87
personal relationships *see* intimate relationships; relationships; spousal relationships
personal space 174
personality *see* adult personality
personality development 54–5, 64
personality disorder 228
    and loss in early childhood 69
    in remaining parent 158–9
philosophical approach to loss, by adolescents 78
physical abuse 129
physical contact, importance for child 205
physiological response
    in babies 63
    to grieving 42
preparation, for foreseeable death 116–17, 210
processing grief 49–50, 104, 151–2
    bereaved siblings 189, 193
    loss of both parents 136
    opportunities triggered by change 62
    postponement to later life 47, 189, 193
    remaining parent's previous grief 160–1
professionals
    choosing for therapeutic help 220–1
    intrusion of authorities 121
    seeking advice from 146, 208
projection
    by adults onto children 16–17, 161
    avoiding 207
    emerging as behavioural difficulties 219
    definition 228

psychological treatment 146,
   216–23
psychotherapy 146, 216–23

questions
   about death 18–19, 34–5
   about loss, importance of
      allowing 153, 204
   regarding therapy 220

rationalization, by adults
   dealing with affected child
   16–17
readjustment
   of children 44–5, 126,
      152–3
   signs of 214–15
   third stage of grieving 40,
      163–4
reconstruction, of memory of
   missing person 66
regression
   adolescents 82, 84–5
   in babies' development
      following loss 63–4
   defense mechanism 34
   young children 48, 65
rehabilitation, of child with
   murdered parent 122
rejection 127–33
   feelings of following
      suicide 118–19
relationships
   in adolescence, following
      loss 68–9, 79, 139,
      140, 141–2
   of adults abandoned in
      childhood 132–3
   capacity for forming 58
   dependent, from fear of
      separation 104
   diadic 226–7
   with family of missing
      parent 171–2
   loss, and damage to trust in
      babies 27
   effect of loss
      of opposite sex parent
         88, 140–1

of same sex parent
      138–40, 141–2
   with missing parent
      before loss 83–4,
         143–5
      continuance 155, 171
   new relationships of
      remaining parent 88,
      95, 194, 195, 196–7
      use of therapy 221–2
   between parent and
      individual siblings
      183–4
   with person who may die
      111
   with remaining parent 124,
      141, 142, 159
   between siblings 180–3
religion
   solution to meaning in
      adolescence 91
   and view of death 32–3
remaining parent
   effect of attitudes in
      divorce 128
   blame by child for suicide
      of other parent 119
   breaking news of death
      210
   new spousal relationships
      88, 95, 194, 196–7
   effect of personality
      157–62
   response to child 12, 46,
      64, 65–6, 72, 107,
      149, 150–7
   response to loss 46, 50,
      65–6, 80, 84, 150–7,
      160–1
   role in situations of
      abandonment 133
   see also parental care;
      parents
remorse, of siblings 184
repression 131, 228
response
   to child by adults 12, 46,
      64, 65–6, 72, 107,
      149, 150–7
   guidelines 209–14

to death, grieving process
      38–40
   to grief
      adults 46, 50, 65–6,
         80, 84, 150–7,
         160–1, 190–2
      children 40–52, 105,
         204
      myths 208
      setting example
         151–2, 152–3,
         203, 204
      siblings 180–93
   to new spouse 198–9
   resumption of life, in children
      44–5, 213–14
   revisiting loss
      adolescents 89–97
      during development 9–10,
         25–6, 31, 49–50
      when grandparent dies 134
      older children 76–7, 164
      young children 72, 73
   role models
      for emotional acceptance
         and adjustment 152–3
      loss of in adolescence 88
      of remaining parent for
         grief and coping
         151–2, 203
      see also modeling
   role reversal
      children supporting parent
         48, 81, 130–1, 156
      spousal child 161–2
   roles
      of children in family,
         following loss 166–7,
         168–9, 207
      providing a family role for
         bereaved child 206
      adopted by siblings for
         parents 187
      of teachers following
         bereavement 212
      see also parental role;
         remaining parent
   routines, importance following
      loss 213–14

rules
  for contact with divorced
    parent 214
  maintaining for security
    and confidence 205–6

schools
  changing 200–1
  returning to after
    bereavement 213–14
  role of teacher in
    bereavement 212
secrecy
  over abuse 129
  over circumstances
    surrounding death 20,
    112
  family secrets 178–9
  over suicide 120, 188
  see also hiding truth from
    children
security
  development of sense of
    security 64, 85
  from familiar environment
    203–4
  need for 167
  sense of loss in sudden
    death 117
  see also insecurity
self-confidence, effect of
  parental loss in adolescence
  86
self-esteem, low 56
self-image
  damage on loss of sibling
    193
  and loss in adolescence
    85–6, 95
  see also identity
sensitivity
  of adults who experienced
    childhood loss 11, 13
  of older children to
    people's attitudes 45
separation
  in children's grieving 68
  and dissociation, in
    children's grieving
    46–7

in early adulthood,
    confronting earlier loss
    99–100
and emotional memory of
    loss 104
meaning of term 36–7, 60
as normal process of
    development 57, 92–3,
    157–8
as result of loss 57–8
separations allowed within
    family 175
see also divorce
separation anxiety 76
separation-individuation
    process 67–8, 157, 228
  in adolescence 93–5
separations allowed within
    family 175
sexual abuse 129
sexual behaviour, in
    adolescence 88–9, 96–7
sexual identity
  and loss 138–43
    in adolescence 87–9
    in Oedipal stage 73–5
  see also gender roles
sexuality, development in
    adolescence following loss
    89
shame, feelings over suicide
    118
sharing emotions 19–20, 172
sharing problems with child
    155
shock, stage of grieving 38, 41
short-term effects of loss 56
shrines, in home to dead
    siblings 192
siblings
  bereavement 180, 184–93
  death 130
  effect on gender roles
    142–3
  step and half siblings
    197–8
  support in loss of both
    parents 135
signs
  good signs of readjustment
    214

see also warning signs
single parent see remaining
    parent
socio-cultural environment,
    and child's attitude to
    death 37–8
somatic response, to grieving
    42
sons, and loss of parents 96,
    138–40
spiritual world, reconciling
    with finality of death 33
splitting, defense mechanism
    93
spousal child, role of support
    for parent 161–2
spousal relationships
  in early adulthood,
    problems 101
  of remaining parent 88, 95,
    221
stability, need for 167
  see also instability
substance misuse 128
substitutes for missing person
    59–60, 104
  see also alternative parent
    figure
sudden death, effect of
    117–22
suicide 118–20, 127
support
  for child, positive actions
    203–6
  from extended family
    171–2
  for parents by bereaved
    sibling 185
  for remaining parent by
    children 48, 81, 84,
    130–1, 156, 161–2
  see also emotional support
suppression, of emotion,
    effects 52

taboo subjects, child's sense of
    19
teacher, role following
    bereavement 212
teenagers see adolescence; early
    adulthood

television, exposure of children
    to sensationalist portrayal
    20–1, 37
terminal illness, period of
    uncertainty 110
terminology for concept of
    death 33
    see also language
therapy, for bereavement
    216–23
toddlers see babies; early
    childhood; young children
transitions, of children
    between grieving and
    normal routines 43–4
traumatic loss in childhood,
    effects on adulthood
    10–11, 13, 15, 22
traumatic memories, surfacing
    in additional loss 133–4
trust
    of adults 35–6
    development of 64
    loss of
        in babies 27, 68
        during period of
            uncertainty
            114–15
        through secrecy 179
truth
    about cause of death
        29–30
    giving child accurate
        information 21, 31,
        50–1, 75, 204–5
    hiding from children 13,
        112, 179
    importance of not lying
        206
    in reconstruction of image
        of missing person 74–5
    see also explanation;
        information; secrecy

unawareness of child in period
    of uncertainty 111–13
    see also awareness of effects
        of loss
uncertainty
    in divorce 124–5
    prior to loss 110–16

unique relationships, of parents
    with individual children
    183–4
universality, of death 29

verbal expression, of grief in
    young children 71–2
video games, portrayal of
    death 37
void
    in family 168
    left by sibling 181, 186–7
vulnerability
    in additional loss 133–4
    in situation of murder 122

warning signs
    in bereaved siblings 189
    of child's inner distress 48,
        215–16
        ignoring 13–14
    clinical depression in
        children 105
    of detachment defense
        mechanism 106
    of unresolved loss, in older
        children 76
wars 38
western society, mourning 38,
    145–6
worries see anxieties; fears

young adults see adolescence;
    early adulthood
young children
    boys' choice of role models
        138–9
    effect of death of sibling
        185
    expression of emotion 151
    fantasy communication
        with missing parent
        143–4
    effect of loss 28, 58, 65
    need for closeness 173
    postponing tasks of
        grieving 47
    regressive behaviour 48, 65
    response to new spouse
        198

resumption of life 44–5
sexual identity and loss
    73–4, 139
verbal expression of loss
    experienced in earlier
    childhood 72
    see also babies; Oedipal
        stage
younger siblings 181
youngest child in family 182

Lightning Source UK Ltd.
Milton Keynes UK
UKOW08f0744210616

276714UK00001B/28/P